JUSTICE
and *JUDAISM*

JUSTICE

and *JUDAISM*

THE WORK OF SOCIAL ACTION

Albert Vorspan
and
Eugene J. Lipman

Illustrated by
Russell Roman

**UNION OF AMERICAN
HEBREW CONGREGATIONS**
NEW YORK, N. Y.

Revised Fourth Edition, 1959

Fifth Printing, 1961

Dedication

This volume is dedicated to our families—
        totaling two wives and seven children—
without whom this book would have been completed many months earlier. For their patience and understanding while this volume was being written, and for their blessed distractions, we love them.

Authors' Preface

IT WOULD BE ARROGANT FOR ANY TWO HUMAN BEINGS TO PRETEND to be experts in the vast number of complex subjects encompassed by this volume. Of this sin, at any rate, the authors are not guilty. This has been a cooperative venture from beginning to end, and we are deeply grateful to the many persons who have assisted us in this task.

In the chapter on Economic Affairs, we have relied on a group of experts, each of whom contributed working papers on his particular field of interest. They are: Dr. Harry Laidler, executive director of the League for Industrial Democracy and writer on monopoly and other economic problems; Rev. Shirley E. Greene, of Denver, Colorado, assistant to the President of the Farmers Educational and Cooperative Union of America; Messrs. Solie Ringold and Benjamin Asia, of Seattle, Washington, both practicing attorneys in that city and students of conservation and public power; Mr. Gilbert Jonas of New York City, formerly of the firm of Delson, Levin, and Gordon, attorneys at law; Mr. Kalman A. Goldring of Pittsburgh, Pennsylvania, a practicing tax attorney; and Mr. George Silver, formerly of the Jewish Labor Committee, which works closely with the American labor movement in the promotion of better human relations. We are deeply indebted to each of these experts for their working papers which will be published separately as a symposium by the Commission on Social Action. The chapter on Economic Affairs which appears herein constitutes a condensation of their material. Needless to say, we accept full responsibility for this as for every other chapter in the book.

Many persons aided us in the collection of materials for the various chapters. Upon the completion of every chapter, it was read in manuscript by experts in the particular field. Their criticism and comments have been invaluable. They bear, however, no responsibility whatsoever for the final text of this work. We acknowledge our gratitude to:

ARNOLD ARONSON, *National Community Relations Advisory Council*

RABBI STANLEY BRAV, *Temple Sholom,* Cincinnati, Ohio

JULES COHEN, *National Community Relations Advisory Council*

RABBI SOLOMON FREEHOF, *Congregation Rodef Shalom,* Pittsburgh, Pennsylvania

DR. BENJAMIN FINE, *New York Times*
RABBI MORRIS KERTZER, *American Jewish Committee*
FRANCES LEVENSON, *National Committee Against Discrimination in Housing*
DR. WILLIAM LOOS, *Church Peace Union*
WILL MASLOW, *American Jewish Congress*
LEO PFEFFER, *American Jewish Congress*
JUDGE JUSTINE WISE POLIER, *Domestic Relations Court,* New York City
JOSEPH RAUH, JR., *Commission on Social Action of Reform Judaism*
JOSEPH ROBISON, *American Jewish Congress*
SOL RUBIN, *National Parole and Probation Association*
DR. ABRAHAM STONE, *Margaret Sanger Clinic*

In addition, the entire manuscript was read by Rabbi Maurice N. Eisendrath, Mrs. Hugo Dalsheimer, Rabbi Roland Gittelsohn, and Mr. I. Cyrus Gordon, for the Commission on Social Action and by Judge Emil N. Baar of the UAHC Executive Board. For their painstaking efforts and invaluable comments, we express our deep appreciation.

We are grateful to the people who labored so diligently with the manuscript of this book and with its production. Miss Miriam Wolfe, Miss Alfreda Anker, and Mrs. Vivian Mendeles have been most conscientious and tireless in their preparation of the various typescript drafts. Mr. Ralph Davis, production manager of the UAHC, has done his usual brilliant work in designing the volume. The art work by Russell Newton Roman has added greatly to the book.

A special word of appreciation must go to Mr. Harry Freedman of the Kittatinny Country Club, Columbia, N. J., whose genial hospitality made it possible for us to work uninterruptedly and comfortably in order to finish in a few days concentrated editorial work.

We also wish to express appreciation to the following: to Cornell University Press for permission to quote from *Ancient Israel* by Harry Orlinsky; to Hutchinson and Co. Ltd. for permission to quote from *Jewish Ethics* by Israel Mattuck; to Justice William O. Douglas and to the *New York Times Magazine* for permission to quote from the article, "Black Silence of Fear"; to Beacon Press for permission to quote from *Church, State, and Freedom* by Leo Pfeffer and from *The Foot of Pride* by Malcolm Hay; to Philosophical Library for permission to quote from *Hebrew Marriage* by David Mace; to Bloch Publishing Company for permission to quote from *The Ethics of Judaism* by Maxwell Silver, *The Synagogue and Social Welfare* by Sidney E. Goldstein, and *Chronicle* of an American Crusader by Samuel Mayerberg; and to World Publishing Company for permission to quote from 1,000,000 Delinquents by Benjamin Fine.

Finally, we add our gratitude to the late Rabbi Sidney E. Goldstein. In a sense, he was the catalyst for this book. The manuscript of his The Synagogue and Social Welfare brought on a series of conferences, in which the outline of this book was blocked out. We regret deeply the fact that he did not live to join in the actual writing of it, as was contemplated. His memory and inspiration have been very much with us during these months of work, and we hope that this volume will serve to advance the noble cause of Jewish social justice to which his entire life was dedicated.

POSTSCRIPT

Some time ago there appeared in the New York Times Book Review Section a whimsical cartoon, depicting two bemused authors commiserating with each other. Said one, "Everybody liked our book except the darn public."

We have no such complaint. Now, four printings and three years after publication of Justice and Judaism, we continue to be moved and deeply grateful for the warm response the book has received from Jews and Christians alike.

It is our hope that this book has contributed, in a small measure at least, to the recent strengthening of the social action movement in all branches of Judaism. These three short years have been filled with a host of breath-taking challenges which make the task of religious social action even more urgent today. The "space war," the new challenge to American education, the revolutionary tide sweeping Africa and Asia, the mounting racial crisis in America, the world population explosion, the intermittent threats of nuclear extermination, the profound political and social changes in American society—all these, and so many more, face us.

Justice and Judaism is a topical book, affected by daily events. So we have made some revisions in the text, but, knowing there is nothing more dated than even this morning's newspaper, we have no illusions that we have managed to catch up with onrushing events. We maintain our conviction, however, that religion in general, and Judaism in particular, can and must play an active role in shaping these great events of our time.

ALBERT VORSPAN
EUGENE J. LIPMAN

December, 1959

Introduction

by RABBI MAURICE N. EISENDRATH

President, Union of American Hebrew Congregations

ALTHOUGH THAT GENTLE CYNIC, THE AUTHOR OF THE BOOK OF Ecclesiastes, lugubriously insisted that there is nothing new under the sun, a unique phenomenon has occurred, for the first time, in our generation. Nor do I refer here to the myriad of novel inventions and discoveries of modern scientific ingenuity. Rather do I have in mind that concept—altogether new under the sun at least of Jewish experience—whereby many of our contemporary fellow Jews would "crib, cabin, and confine" the whole of our Judaism to the four walls of the synagogue; of the synagogue, however, not generically speaking, but of the synagogue literally interpreted as the actual physical structure to which the whole substance of our faith, according to this novel interpretation of Judaism, is to be restricted.

This is indeed something altogether new under the sun! The historic synagogue of the Jewish past subsumed the whole substance of life. Its Torah, its teachings, its moral mandates, touched every facet of human living. Be it ever so humble, no phase of daily experience was beyond the purview of the synagogue's direct influence. Nor was this influence limited to rites and rituals, diet and dishes. But it had relevance to the "wages of the hireling," the "feeding of the hungry," the "clothing of the naked, the taking of the homeless into one's habitation."

Consequently, those who today would partition the synagogue, Judaism, religion itself, from life; those who would rear a wall of separation, a curtain of fear or expediency, between faith and practice, between worship and the work of justice, are doing violence to a Judaism which epitomized its noblest teaching in that Great Summary of all religion: "To do justly, to love mercy, and to walk humbly before God," which divine injunction the Union of American Hebrew Congregations has inscribed indelibly in stone on the façade of its House of Living Judaism, the national center of Reform Judaism in New York. But be it noted that in this exalted summation, "to do justly" precedes even the command "to walk humbly before God."

This book, so conscientiously written by two most devoted and dedicated members of the staff of the Union, Mr. Albert Vorspan and Rabbi Eugene Lipman, has to do with "doing justly," with the work of righteousness, which alone can bring peace to the individual human soul and to humanity as a whole. It not only unequivocally establishes the inescapable moral mandate of Judaism to carry the message of Israel into the throughways and byways of life, to apply the prophetic precepts to the marketplace, to mine and mill, to street and slum, to factory and farm, but, in addition, offers a concrete guide and tangible aids whereby each synagogue and every member thereof might become a true and living Temple of the Lord.

In this most timely volume we find the timeless truths of Judaism applied cogently and challengingly to the problems of our day. For the first time, we have a basic publication which deals with the major social issues agitating society—civil rights, civil liberties, marriage and the family, international relations, immigration, housing, interreligious relationships, economic justice, farm problems, juvenile delinquency and crime, and a host of other subjects—in their relationship to the eternal ethic of Judaism. I am confident that this volume will prove to be an invaluable aid to rabbis, social action committees, adult education groups, post-confirmation religious school classes, and, even more, to individuals concerned about the application of religion to the contemporary scene.

I am certain, also, that this study will prove useful not only to members of Reform synagogues but, equally, to Conservative and Orthodox Jews and to Christian ministers and laymen of all denominations. One of the rare achievements attained by Rabbi Lipman and Mr. Vorspan in this volume is that they have avoided narrow and parochial emphases while at the same time using Judaism as the focus for their material.

The current religious revival, of which we read much and see considerable evidence these days, if it is valid, if it is to be more than a vain and vapid "peace of mind" anaesthetic, must impel man to reshape his community, his nation, and the world in accordance with the judgment of conscience and God's moral law. This book is at once a rationale, a resource, and a guide to action in this preeminently urgent—and religious—task.

Contents

JUSTICE
and *JUDAISM*

PROLOGUE

IT WAS AFTER 11:00 P.M. and the monthly meeting of the Board of Trustees was apparently over. The long agenda had been disposed of, with no more than the usual amount of pyrotechnics, and some of the members were already rising from their seats, looking at their watches, when the president said, "Just one more item, if you don't mind. It won't take long."

He then read a circular letter which had been sent to the temple and to all the synagogues associated with the Union of American Hebrew Congregations, by the president of the Union. The letter described the work of the Commission on Social Action of Reform Judaism in helping congregations apply "the ethical insights of Judaism to the specific social problems of our generation." The letter concluded with a request to each congregation to establish its own Social Action Committee to study the moral and ethical problems involved in major social issues nationally and in our

3

own communities and "to bring the principles of Judaism to bear upon these problems."

There was a long moment of silence. Then everybody seemed to speak at once.

"I don't get it," said one. "What is this social action?"

"Politics, politics!" exclaimed Mr. Robinson. "They want us to get mixed up in politics!"

"Not so fast," pleaded the president. "I read some of the material the Social Action Commission has put out. I don't know if I go along all the way, but I certainly think that Judaism has something to say about modern-day problems. Take equal rights, for example. Do you mean to say that Judaism has nothing to say about civil rights or—"

"No, it doesn't!" shouted another. "There's no such thing as a Jewish attitude toward civil rights, or peace, or housing. We're for civil rights as *Americans,* not as Jews. There's no such thing as a Jewish vote. We don't live in a ghetto. We're free Americans like everybody else and I resent this kind of minority thinking."

"Who said anything about a Jewish vote or living in a ghetto?" put in the secretary, despairing of taking notes on the discussion. "Let's be more specific. Last week I was in a restaurant—took the kids in for dinner. A Negro couple came in and sat down. The kids and I were waited on, got our food, and finished our meal. Nobody waited on the Negro couple. Finally, they got up and left. I know how I feel about that kind of thing. You mean to say that's not against our religion? Then what's this brotherhood we pray about in the temple?"

"That's a good example," said the president.

"I think it's a terrible example," blurted the man who had warned about the ghetto. "If you didn't like it, you should have done something about it as an American citizen. Talk to the manager. Write your Congressman. Write a letter to the *Times.* What do you want from the temple?"

"Answer my question, please," persisted the secretary. "What about our prayers about social justice, love thy neighbor, and all that? What is that—just talk? What does it mean?"

"Prayer is one thing, social *action* is another. Let the rabbi preach about these things, that's okay with me. But I will apply them for myself as I choose to do as an American citizen."

"That's right," echoed another. "Keep the church and the synagogue out of politics, that's what I always say. I'm for separation of church and state right down the line."

"I think we're going off in all directions at once," said the president. "As I understand this letter, Rabbi Eisendrath is saying that the synagogue has no right to cloister itself and evade responsibility for the problems of the community. I agree with him. We have a terrible slum in this town—isn't that our business?"

"Well, the rabbi is working on that as a member of the Human Rights Committee—"

"I don't mean only the rabbi. How about us?"

"What about us?" demanded his opponent. "Many of us are active in civic causes. That's the American way—as individuals. Not as a synagogue!"

"I have been listening to this discussion," said another, "and I want to ask a question. This Board meets every month. We discuss the budget, the cantor's salary, the plaster falling in the classrooms, membership. Fine. But when do we ever discuss what Judaism has to say about the great issues of our community, our country, and the world? It's just a question."

"I'm warning you," said another. "Start up with these outside issues and you'll split the congregation. I say let's stick to religion."

"Yes, sure," said the secretary, "but what is religion? What is Judaism? Is Judaism concerned with the falling plaster or the Negro couple in the restaurant? It seems to me . . ."

* * * *

At one A.M., the bone-weary Board adjourned. They had agreed on one thing which was—naturally—the appointment of a committee to look into the matter and to examine the questions which had been raised in the discussion.

This book is written for that committee, for all committees, and for individual Jews everywhere—Reform, Conservative, and Orthodox—who, similarly, seek answers to questions about the relationship of Judaism to modern social problems. It is written for Jews and Christians everywhere who feel impelled by their religious heritage to give of themselves for the betterment of their communities so that mankind may move a step closer to the Kingdom of God on earth.

FOUNDATIONS

A PASSIONATE belief in and concern for justice for all men is inherent in Judaism. It stems, not alone from the immortal utterances of the Biblical prophets, but from the fundamental nature of the Jewish faith. It stems first and foremost from the Jewish concepts of God, His universe, and His greatest creation, man.

The watchword of Judaism is: "Hear O Israel, the Lord our God, the Lord is One." This is more than a denial of many gods, more even than an affirmation of monotheism. It is a fundamental insight which, when enunciated 3,000 years ago, revolutionized the thinking of man about the whole universe and his role in it. Were all mankind to take it seriously today, the implications of those eleven short words could still transform human society from a jungle of fear and hate into a literal Kingdom of God on earth.

For the Jewish belief in one God has inevitable corollaries. The creative, creating God of Judaism is the power behind a physical

6

universe characterized by absolute harmony, precision, and unity. Increasingly, as man learns more about the laws governing the natural universe, it becomes apparent that our universe is not a mechanistic, accidental mass of phenomena, but a purposeful oneness, guided by a Divine Power Who is perfection and Who has created perfectly.

It has followed inevitably in the thinking of Jewish sages through the centuries that man as an integral part of God's universe must also be governed by immutable laws. It has followed further that man, created by God, must be good by nature. For how could a good God create evil men? Man, like all God's creatures, is good, was created that way, and has a noble purpose to serve on God's earth.

But man *is* different from all of God's creatures, and the differences between man and the animal, plant, and other organic kingdoms are fundamental. These differences center in the free will granted by God to man alone among His creatures. Only man can, by his own whim or will, disobey God's laws. Man can, if he wishes, trample upon the Divine commands to live justly, to love his fellow, to practice love and not hate, and instead can express in his life evil and not the goodness which is his natural potential. Man has the right to choose. "See," said God, "I have set before thee life and death, the blessing and the curse; therefore choose life, that thou mayest live, thou and thy seed; to love the Lord thy God, to hear His voice, and to cleave unto Him." (*Deut. 30:19–20*)

This power to choose between good and evil is, in Jewish teaching, part of man's nature. As man's creator, God is the ultimate source of moral law and moral power. He is, in Matthew Arnold's words, "the Power not ourselves that makes for righteousness." Man, created in His image, should strive to emulate God: "Ye shall be holy, for I, the Lord your God, am holy." (*Lev. 19:2*) Maxwell Silver, in *The Ethics of Judaism from the Aspect of Duty,* explains: "One's motive, in accordance with this principle, is to strive after holiness in character, in imitation or emulation of God's holiness—the desire of the copy to be like the Pattern." The nerve-center of this striving within man's soul we designate as his conscience. This concept of man as a mirror of the Divine, committed by his nature to strive toward personal holiness, with personal holiness attainable only through social morality and justice, was revolutionary in and of itself. But, in a development unique in the history of human thought, the concept became socialized, became the heritage, the duty, the mission of a whole people: Israel. Israel could fulfill its covenant with God, made at Mt. Sinai, only by living the moral laws of God and by teaching them to all mankind. To quote Dr. Silver:

> "Israel, through its historic Sinaitic covenant, established a special moral relationship to God. Through this covenant, Israel voluntarily covenanted itself, obligated itself, assumed as its unique national duty for all time, to be a 'holy people' unto God, a people just and humane, loving God and following His law, without regard to the conduct of other nations. From this 'peculiar' historic relationship to God, then, flows Israel's chief national duty—to be this holy people unto God, and its supreme motive—to be faithful and loyal 'with all thy heart and all thy soul' to its 'appointment' or its historic role as a holy people."

Thus, and only thus, can the concept of "the chosen people" be understood.

Judaism conceives as its function and its mission the teaching of mankind to obey God's moral law, committing man to a way of life consistent with God's will, impelling him to dedicate his life to the bringing about on earth the kind of perfection in human affairs which is implicit in the universe.

Prophetic Heritage

The noblest expression of this mission is to be found in the writings of the literary prophets of the Bible. Beginning with Amos in the eighth century before the Common Era, these God-driven men attacked every evil of their society, every violation of God's moral law. Because of the visionary greatness of the prophetic minds and spirits, the ethical ideals of which they reminded their people 2,500 years ago have remained the peaks of human insight into man's relationship with man and the ultimate destiny of mankind in its search for God and godliness.

For all time, the ancient prophets proclaimed God as the root of human morality:

> "I am the Lord thy God
> Who teaches thee what is of avail
> Who leads thee the way to follow." (*Isaiah 48:17*)

They then proclaimed in ringing and incontrovertible terms what God taught and where His way led:

"Seek the Lord that ye may live
Seek good and not evil, that ye may live;
And that the Lord, the God of hosts, may be truly with
   you
As ye think he is.
Hate evil and love good
And establish justice in the gates of the land." (*Amos
   5:4, 14–15*)

"If one practices justice and righteousness
If one champions the cause of the poor,
Then it is well with one—
This indeed is to know Me, says God." (*Jeremiah
   22:15–16*)

"He has told thee, O man, what is good;
And what doth the Lord require of thee,
But to do justice and to love mercy
And to walk humbly with thy God." (*Micah 6:8*)

But let it not be thought for a moment that the prophets of Israel
were content with generalizations or dreams of the peaceful world
which would come "in the end of days." Forthrightly and simply,
they reacted to real-life situations as they saw them and demanded
that God's justice reign in the affairs of man. Throughout this
volume, their imperishable words will serve to remind us once
again, not only of God's will, but also of man's moral freedom—
freedom used too frequently to thwart His will and too seldom to
fulfill it. A noted scholar thus described the debt mankind owes
to the prophets:

   "It is to the prophetic tradition more than to any other
   source that Western civilization owes its noblest concept of
   the moral and social obligations of the individual human
   being. Even if the prophets preached only to their fellow
   Israelites and saw justice only in the terms of their covenant
   with their God, their ringing words have carried from age
   to age their belief that justice was for the weak as well as
   for the strong; that its fulfillment was as much the spirit as
   the letter of the law; that one could not serve God at the
   same time that he mistreated his fellow men; that to love
   God was to love justice and that the love of justice placed
   within the conscience of each human being the ultimate
   inescapable obligation to denounce evil where he saw it, to
   defy a ruler who commanded him to break the covenant,

and to live in the law and the love of God no matter what the cost." (*Ancient Israel* by Harry M. Orlinsky)

The *goy kadosh,* the holy people, appointed to try to live and to teach God's will, truly became, as Deutero-Isaiah had prophesied, the suffering servant of the Lord.

With its lofty insights into the nature of universal law and the existence of equally immutable moral laws, it was inevitable that Judaism should develop into a religion based on law. All the principles and practices of Judaism, as they evolved through the centuries, expressed themselves in *mitzvos:* positive and negative religious commandments, Divinely-sanctioned because through their fulfillment man could fulfill his moral purpose in living. Ritual and ethical commandments alike became systematized as *mitzvos.*

Early in the evolution of rabbinic Judaism it became crystal-clear to the great sages of Israel that only through institutions could the noble humanitarian and ethical *mitzvos* of Judaism find fulfillment in the life of the individual Jew and of the Jewish people. Since the synagogue already existed as the core institution in Jewish life after the destruction of the Temple in Jerusalem (70 C.E.), it was natural for Jewish institutional life to center around the synagogue. To the synagogue came the poor to receive, not charity, but *tse'dakah* their righteous due. To the synagogue came the lame and the sick, to be cared for in community hospices. To the synagogue came the sinned-against to cry out against injustice, and to receive justice. From the burial of the dead to the redemption of the captive, a whole network of institutions developed through and around the synagogue in which the individual Jew and the *am segulah,* the holy people with a mission, could obey the will and law of God.

As Rabbi Jacob Schwarz put it: "When the synagogue was at the height of its strength it was coextensive with Jewish life. No avenue of Jewish thought or interest was closed to it and no concern of Jews was beyond its purview. It was the embodiment of the history, doctrines, ideas, and achievements of the Jewish people. The synagogue and Jewish life were inseparable." (*The Synagogue in Modern Jewish Life,* p. 1)

The institution of the synagogue sought to make the Jew ever-aware of the nature of his religion: a way of life which offers no escape from the problems of life. Judaism rejects the device of passing all responsibility for social problems to God. In Jewish tradition man is called the co-worker or partner of God in the creation of a better world. Judaism has always insisted that every Jew must bring the ethical insights of the Jewish heritage to bear on the specific social problems of our generation, just as we do to the personal and individual problems of our lives. Jewish tradition has never constricted Judaism solely to the relation between man and God. The relations between man and man were actually placed on an even higher pedestal than those between man and God. Transgressions committed by man against God are atoned for on the Day of Atonement, but transgressions committed by man against man can be forgiven only when the injustice is rectified. Significant is the declaration attributed to God in the Midrash: "Would that they had forsaken me but kept my Commandments." (*Midrash, Echah Rabati,* Introduction)

Middle Ages

During the Middle Ages, the *mitzvah* of study assumed ever-greater importance in Jewish life. Study for the sake of study became a major preoccupation. To be sure, Jews had ever before them the dictum of the rabbi, who, when asked which was more important, study or action, replied: The most important thing is study which leads to action. Gradually, however, the need for individual and group action to right wrongs, to secure justice and peace for all men, became submerged in a Jewish society understandably preoccupied with the problems of physical survival in a milieu of hate and repression. As Jews became increasingly isolated by this repression from the world about them, the ethical ideals of Judaism tended to turn inward, too. Theoretically they applied to all men; in function, they were applied in the only society most Jews knew, their internal, synagogue-centered society.

By the end of the seventeenth century, the fog of mysticism descended, the worldliness inherent in Judaism was threatened by an other-worldly concern for the *olam ha'ba,* the world to come, with this life becoming increasingly considered only an anteroom leading to the *real* life, life after death. Superstition became rampant, evil spirits were everywhere, mischievously at work to cause man to sin so frequently that eternal damnation would be his post-mortal lot.

Increasingly, *mitzvos* came to mean ceremonial commandments, ritual details, requirements of daily religious routine. The *mitzvos* between man and God dominated completely; the *mitzvos* between man and his fellow man became less and less the conscious preoccupation of the Jew. Even the institutions surrounding the synagogue which had the task of fulfilling communal responsibility in matters of health, social welfare, death and burial, became more concerned with the pin-point details of *how* than they were with the ethical principles of *why* which undergirded their mission.

This uncharacteristic and unhealthy situation could not continue indefinitely, and it did not. As ghetto walls began to crumble under the impact of the ideas and ideals which produced the American and French revolutions, as Jews emerged into the sunlight and grabbed eagerly at freedom, secular education, civil and political rights, new economic opportunities, the ever-present rumblings of discontent with other-worldly Judaism grew quickly into a thunder-clap of revolt from which emerged the beginnings of Reform Judaism.

Possibly the greatest achievement of Reform Judaism was the re-establishment of prophetic ethical idealism as the purpose and goal of Jewish faith and living. In Reform, God's moral law became the absolute good; all other traditional laws, practices, and customs of Judaism became acceptable only insofar as they could be made relevant to the moral law and to its fulfillment. They took seriously the admonition of Isaiah:

> "I am full of the burnt-offerings of ram,
> And the fat of fed beasts;
> And I delight not in the blood
>   of bullocks, or of lambs, or of he-goats.
> When ye come to appear before Me,
> Who had required this at your hand,
> To trample my courts?
> Bring no more vain oblations;
> It is an offering of abomination unto Me;
> New moon and sabbath, the holding of convocations—
> I cannot endure iniquity along with the solemn
>   assembly . . .
> And when ye spread forth your hands,
> I will hide Mine eyes from you;
> Yea, when ye make many prayers, I will not hear;
> Your hands are full of blood.
> Wash you, make you clean,
> Put away the evil of your doings
> From before Mine eyes,
> Cease to do evil;

Learn to do well;
Seek justice, relieve the oppressed,
Judge the fatherless, plead for the widow."

(*Isaiah 1:11 ff*)

At precisely this juncture in the history of Judaism, as the new Reformers were molding their justice-centered faith and Orthodoxy was condemning Reform for its violations of the ritual fabric of Jewish observance, two other related events occurred which were vitally to affect the course of Jewish life.

First, the center of gravity of the Jewish population began to shift from Central and Eastern Europe to the United States. And, second, the synagogue gave up its position of centrality in the Jewish community.

The Synagogue Defaults

As tens of thousands of immigrants made their way from Central Europe to the American continent, the synagogues of America by and large were either unable or unwilling to assume the massive burdens of accepting them, caring for them, helping them to settle. Occasionally, synagogues did undertake the social welfare functions traditionally associated with them. The Spanish and Portugese Synagogue of New York led in the movement to establish Mt. Sinai Hospital, the Hebrew Orphan Asylum, and other agencies now entirely separated from synagogue influences. In 1885, Temple Emanu-El of the City of New York established its Sisterhood of Personal Services to help the Jews beginning to flock into America from pogrom-ridden Russia. But these, and a few similar programs, were exceptions to the general situation, which found the synagogue defaulting to secular leadership. The reasons for this failure are many and complex, and are still the source of disagreement among students of Jewish history. Indisputable, however, is the fact that secular agencies were organized, for the first time in Jewish history, to take over welfare, hospital, and other functions hitherto reserved to the synagogue. It is surprising, perhaps, to note that synagogue leadership, rabbinic and lay alike, apparently made little effort to prevent these incursions into their prerogatives. Gradually, a whole new pattern of institutional relationships developed. The synagogue remained the center of Jewish worship and, to an extent, of Jewish education. All other expressions of Jewish belief, concern, and need found their outlet in specialized, secularly-sponsored Jewish agencies.

For a time, the defense of the civil rights of Jews in the United States and abroad did remain in religious hands. The Board of Delegates of American Israelites was founded in 1859. It became part of the Union of American Hebrew Congregations in 1878. For many years, the Board of Delegates was the only instrumentality in America active in preventing encroachments upon the rights of Jews and in aiding in their relief from unjust discrimination and oppression. By 1925, however, even this field had been so completely taken over by secular agencies that the Board of Delegates was relinquished.

For nearly a century, then, Orthodox, Conservative, and Reform synagogues, as religious institutions, generally did not relate themselves directly to the problems of contemporary society. Their rabbis, however, continued to be active in every field of endeavor.

Individual and collective rabbinic activity in behalf of social justice can be found in every specific area which is the concern of this volume. Many are cited herein. From the early days of organized American Jewish life to the present, Jewish spiritual leaders have fought courageously for justice.

The UAHC, since its formation in 1873, has consistently spoken out for civil rights and world peace. From its inception (1889), the Central Conference of American Rabbis has been in the vanguard of liberal religious thought and action in America. Its Social Justice platforms of 1918 and 1928 were landmarks of social thought, were widely distributed, and played a role in shaping opinion throughout the country. (See Appendices E and F) The annual statements of the Commission on Justice and Peace of the CCAR, and the periodic proclamations of its Institutes on Justice and Peace have set high standards of insight into the processes of democracy.

During the twenties and thirties, the CCAR, in particular, was active not only in the formulation of public statements, but in function as well. A number of incidents are related in this volume in which the Conference as a body became involved in labor situations together with representative Catholic and Protestant leaders. Joint statements and activities of all three faiths were not uncommon. The Conservative rabbinate, too, through the Rabbinical Assembly of America, has interpreted the teachings of Judaism courageously in every area of contemporary life. The Social Action Commission of Conservative Judaism continues this tradition.

Individual Rabbinic Activity

Individual rabbis through the years accepted in their own communities the challenge of their faith. Rabbi David Einhorn, of Baltimore, in 1861, attacked the institution of slavery and its defenders. Such boldness was perilous, and the rabbi was forced to flee to Philadelphia after his life had been threatened.

In 1928, a serious general strike broke out in the coal fields of Pennsylvania. Rabbi Samuel H. Goldenson of Pittsburgh was invited to tour the mining area. Upon his return, despite the presence in his congregation of leading coal producers, he said from his pulpit:

> "If ethics does not enter into the question as to a man's claim to share in the fruits of his own labor, then, where in the world of practical experience do questions of right arise and become controlling and imperative? There are some that may not see the imperativeness of the morals involved because they are inclined to confuse the right to have with the right to share. By sharing I do not mean mere having, irrespective of any claim, but securing a part of the total output that one may rightfully claim as the result of his own labors. That, I submit, is the very essence of ethical thinking.
>
> "Has the clergyman, then, the right to talk about these things? My answer is that no man in the entire world has as much right, and there is no man upon whom the responsibility to speak about such questions is so great as upon the one who raises his voice in the name of ethics and religion.
>
> ". . . If we are really in earnest in our desire to lift the burdens from the backs of those heavily tried, we should be willing to bear some of the burden ourselves. The higher pay for the miners' labors comes in the end from the public, and not from the employers themselves. If the public wishes to have a more righteous world, it must be willing to pay the cost of it." (*Am I My Brother's Keeper?* A sermon by Rabbi Samuel H. Goldenson preached before Congregation Rodef Shalom, Pittsburgh, Pa., Feb. 5, 1928.)

In Toronto, during the "Red scare" of the early 30's, the police denied the right of liberal groups to use Queens Park, the Canadian counterpart of Union Square, New York, or Hyde Park, London. Rabbi Maurice N. Eisendrath, spiritual leader of Holy Blossom Temple, initiated a petition which was signed by sixty-eight religious leaders, resulting in restoration of traditional civil liberties in Toronto.

In 1947, Rabbi Roland B. Gittelsohn served as a member of President Truman's Committee on Civil Rights, which produced the trail-blazing report entitled "To Secure These Rights."

No righteous cause was foreign to the active interest of the American rabbinate. They joined with humanitarians of all faiths in demanding laws limiting child labor and hours required of adult laborers. They helped working men to gain better working conditions and a fair wage for their labor. Rabbis worked for prison reform, for better housing for the poor, for social security, for international peace, for the establishment of the League of Nations and later the United Nations.

The rabbis who devoted themselves to social idealism did not expect their congregations to support them at all times, and sometimes the laymen did not. Not infrequently was there vocal opposition expressed both to the views and actions of the rabbis.

In his second year as leader of Congregation Bene Israel, Cincinnati, Rabbi David Philipson fought against Boss Cox and his political gang, frequently called "a perfect machine even excelling Tammany." He attacked municipal corruption from his pulpit. At a congregational meeting, one of the lay leaders of the congregation, who was also a leader of the Cox group, called for the censuring of the rabbi for daring to discuss controversial subjects in the pulpit. Though, as we shall see, this was not always the case, this congregation supported their rabbi.

THOU ART THE MAN!

Rabbi Sidney E. Goldstein, in his *The Synagogue and Social Welfare,* recounts this incident from his own experience:

"I was in Sinai Temple the Sunday Dr. Hirsch preached one of his most prophetic sermons. That morning the newspapers of Chicago had spread across the front page the words, 'The Packers Are Stealing the Water of the City.' Hirsch arose in the pulpit, stern and grim: 'I have been announced to speak on such and such a theme but I have decided to change my topic to 'Thou Shalt Not Steal.' He not only exposed and denounced the packers of Chicago for robbing the city, but condemned them for the shame they had brought upon the community and upon themselves. Then in the midst of one of his passionate passages, he turned to Nelson Morris, who was then a member of his congregation, and thundered, 'Thou art the man!' The congregation was startled and aghast. Nelson Morris, of course, resigned, and so did a number of his friends. The next Sunday Hirsch arose and said with a wry smile, 'I have this week received notice that a number of our members have resigned. I have always known that the Jews possessed at least one virtue—the virtue of resignation. But let me state that while the members are free to resign, the rabbi is also free to resign.' The resignations stopped."

Rabbi Ephraim Frisch, Rabbi Emeritus of Temple Beth El, San Antonio, Texas, tells of a similar experience (*Hebrew Union College Monthly,* Nov. 1942):

"In 1925 I had a dramatic experience bearing on the freedom of my pulpit. I preached that Friday night on 'The Rising Tide of Illiberalism' in answer to the hostility to immigrants, to the native population of the U. S. colonies, and like sentiments, voiced that week by a forum speaker, and, among other things, criticized strongly our own imperialism in the Philippines and called for their independence. A member of the congregation of exceptional prominence and authority—a former president—rushed up to the pulpit at the end of the service just as I lowered my hand at the close of the benediction and, before a congregation of Jews and non-Jews, pointed his finger at me and exclaimed, 'That man is using the pulpit for political propaganda; what does the rabbi know about the Philippines? I have just come back from a visit to the Philippines as a part of my trip around the world.' I knew that there was a crucial question at stake for me—the question of a free or a subservient pulpit with the almost certain loss of my position as the price of my freedom in this unequal public test of strength between one of the most powerful laymen in the state and myself, a newcomer who had not yet had time to win the abiding confidence of his people. I made my decision on the spot—that I would be a free man; requested the congregation to remain, and announced that I would have a statement to make in a moment but that I desired first to ask my challenger a few leading questions concerning certain bad conditions in the Philippines for which our American imperialism was responsible. I described the evils, and proved to the satisfaction of the congregation that I did know what I was talking about in my sermon, and received unexpected support from a Christian gentleman in the audience who was personally well acquainted with conditions in the Philippines. I then did something for effect that I have never resorted to before or since: I pounded the pulpit and declared: 'This pulpit must be free or else I will not serve as your rabbi. If the congregation by a vote should declare that it is not free, I'll resign immediately.' To my gratification the audience broke forth in wild applause, happy to see their appointed religious leader stand up for his independence."

Pressure on Rabbis

A number of rabbis have been ousted from or have resigned under pressure from their congregations because of their advocacy of unpopular social causes. In 1919, Rabbi Abraham Cronbach, who later became Professor of Social Studies at the Hebrew Union College, resigned as the leader of Temple Israel, Akron, Ohio, after his pulpit utterances had been strongly challenged, and his right to speak freely officially questioned by his Board of Trustees.

Rabbi Cronbach was not alone in this kind of decision. On June 4, 1932, Congregation Sherith Israel of San Francisco heard a farewell address from Rabbi Jacob J. Weinstein, in the course of which he said:

". . . in the face of such conditions as we have had in the last three years, this prophetic tradition, this wild insistence on true justice, this demand that sinning by syndicate can be remedied only by social action seems to be so perfectly geared to the crying needs of our time that a rabbi who failed to preach them was simply derelict in his duty. In failing to win you over to this belief in the saving power of the prophetic teachings of Judaism, I suffered the keenest failure in my ministry among you."

Rabbi Weinstein proceeded to analyze the reasons for this "failure": his youth, the conflict between materialist leadership of the temple and the changes demanded by the rabbi, and concluded:

"Had I been content to point out the evils of our present social system and assume a sort of academic unwillingness to cast judgment as to the responsibility for them, my pathway would have been much smoother, but I insisted on giving concrete suggestions and pointing out definite ways in which the people of this very congregation could do their share in putting an end to the savage conditions about us. This definiteness was most unwelcome to many of you."

The rabbi told his congregants that he was reminded of the minister who visited a small, rural church and preached on the commandment, "Thou Shalt Not Steal." The congregation was so impressed by his sermon that they urged him to preach again the next Sunday. The preacher on that occasion announced to the congregation that he was so pleased with their reaction to his previous sermon that he was going to preach on the same commandment, "Thou Shalt Not Steal," only this time he was going to add specifically, "Thou Shalt Not Steal Chickens." Whereupon, "the congregation escorted the preacher to the town limits and bade him a hasty farewell."

Religion and Society

What should be the proper relationship between religion and social issues? This is an old debate, and one which flares up everywhere. A typical incident took place in March, 1954, when Congressman A. L. Miller (Rep., Nebraska) took the floor of the House to condemn Washington clergymen who, he complained, "took off their ecclesiastical robes and put on their political robes" when they criticized Congress for failing to clean up slums and crime in the nation's capital. Retorted Dr. Albert P. Shirkey of the Mount Vernon Place Methodist Church of Washington:

> "Christianity is not here to lull the minds and souls of men to sleep, but rather is the bugle call to action against every wrong to any life anywhere. God pity America when the pulpits no longer speak out against such ingrained wrongs."

Dr. Edward Hughes Pruden, pastor of Washington's famed First Baptist Church, said that the congressman's "antiquated conception of the area of religious concern is almost as deplorable as the existence of the slums themselves . . ."

In 1955, when Roman Catholic Archbishop Rommel of Louisiana, urged the state legislature to defeat a "right to work" bill, sixty-six Catholic businessmen in New Orleans published an ad in the newspaper taking issue with the prelate.

It would be false, however, to give the impression that laymen have always opposed social justice crusades. The record is replete with the activities of many laymen, Jews and Christians alike, who have given of themselves in good causes in America's evolution toward full democracy. But we are primarily concerned in this volume with the synagogue as such. Has the synagogue as the organized expression of Judaism played a direct and active role in social action? Or has activity perforce been limited to individuals, rabbis and laymen?

Synagogue Social Action

These questions have been asked frequently in the councils of all the national Jewish religious institutions. One of the most heated and stirring of such debates took place at the Biennial Assembly of the Union of American Hebrew Congregations in February, 1929, at San Francisco. It was touched off by a prominent Reform layman, Mr. Roscoe Nelson, who said:

">. . . the truth is that this Union has never conceded that any subject is more vitally Jewish than that of Social Justice. . . . *Our privilege and our duty in this behalf is not discharged by the most gracious of permits to the Central Conference of American Rabbis to adopt a program of Social Justice. It would be a strange voice in Israel which suggested that gropings for Social Justice must be vicariously conducted through a Hierarchy of Rabbis or a House of Bishops. I have grossly misinterpreted the history, philosophy, and tradition of our people, if passivity and impersonality in connection with the most profound interests of humanity suffices for spiritual identification with the sources of Jewish inspiration.*"

In a real sense, Mr. Nelson's remarks and the discussions which followed them can be called the beginning of the *synagogue* social action movement in twentieth century America. He insisted that rabbis have no monopoly on social justice—that the laymen must discharge their responsibility. It took many years before the call was heeded. Resolutions were passed, speeches were made, debates provided clarification and heat—but there was still no organized social action movement in the synagogue. After a strong call for action by Rabbi Maurice Eisendrath at the 1946 Biennial Assembly of the Union of American Hebrew Congregations, a Joint Commission on Social Action was finally organized in 1949. Its charter was approved both by the UAHC and the Central Conference of American Rabbis. (See Appendix C) The Commission met three times, sponsored an institute on Judaism and Public Health, drafted ambitious plans, then became quiescent for more than three years. In 1953, the Joint Commission on Social Action was reorganized, and undertook a simple-sounding task: the organization of Social Action or Community Affairs committees in every Reform temple in America. By early 1955, a virtual ground-swell of opinion had developed in Reform temples; so had some opposition. The issue came to a climax at the Forty-Third Biennial Assembly of the UAHC in Los Angeles in February, 1955. Rabbi Eisendrath led off the controversy in his presidential address:

> "A guide for Reform Judaism do we desire? Indeed we do. But not for ritual and rites alone—but for righteous conduct and decent behavior between man and man; not merely for the forms of services but for the service of God in the affairs of men; not merely a minimum code for liturgical worship but a minimal code of moral conduct incumbent upon anyone who calls himself a Reform Jew presuming to be the heir of Hebrew prophet and sage. Even the prophet prefaced his command to 'walk humbly' with the demand to do justly and to love mercy.' The resemblance between the noble name we bear and our bearing toward our neighbor must be more than coincidental. It must be fundamental. It must translate our preachment into practice, our dogmas and doctrines into deed, our creed into conduct, our prayers into programs of moral righteousness and social justice, our invoking of God's name—too frequently in vain—into the establishment of His Kingdom on earth."

Rabbi Eisendrath called for nation-wide support of the program of the Commission on Social Action, which had enlarged its scope to include the National Federation of Temple Brotherhoods, National Federation of Temple Sisterhoods, and National Federation of Temple Youth. He appealed to every temple to develop a social justice program to apply realistically the ideals of Judaism in solving the problems of contemporary society.

After a spirited, frequently moving, debate, the Assembly overwhelmingly approved the program of the Commission on Social Action. This approval, coupled with positive action on a number of specific topics of major concern, touched off a ferment of activity in temples throughout the country.

A large number of Reform synagogues have set up Social Action or Community Affairs Committees. The typical committee is a standing committee of the congregation, similar to the Education or Building Committee. Usually, it includes representatives of the various affiliated groups of the synagogue, including the men's club, the sisterhood, and the youth group. It works in close co-operation with the rabbi who serves as informal adviser to the group.

THE LOCAL COMMITTEE

The initial task of the committee is to analyze its own community and to select those social problems locally, as well as one or two of national or international character, which require study and action. Many committees, as the subsequent chapters will indicate, have turned their attention to problems of discrimination and segregation. Others have looked into local housing problems and slum conditions. A number have been concerned with problems of religion in the public schools and their effect upon the principle of separation of church and state. Securing recreational facilities, stimulating mental hygiene programs for the community, protect-ing civil liberties from groups bent on censorship, building support for the United Nations—these, and many similar issues, have won the attention of synagogue social action groups. The whole gamut of national issues—from American immigration policy to imple-mentation of the United States Supreme Court desegregation order —has come under study by these committees. The role of the na-tional commission is to make materials and guidance available to local committees. It functions in an advisory capacity and issues no "directives" to local groups.

Having selected those issues which require attention, the syna-gogue committee makes its own study of these problems from the standpoint of the moral principles of Judaism. When its study is completed, the committee then undertakes its basic task: educat-ing and sensitizing the members of the congregation to the moral implications of the issue. This is done in many ways, including dis-tribution of literature, use of the congregational bulletin, special forums after services, the rabbi's sermon, and similar media. At this point, the committee will decide, depending upon the au-thority given it by the Board, whether to proceed from the task of education to needed community action in concert with like-minded community groups. Some committees are limited by their boards to the program of education, leaving it to the members of the con-gregation to take such action as individuals as they may feel im-pelled to take. Other committees are empowered to take public ac-tion upon approval of the Board. (See Appendix A, nos. 9, 17) Usually such action is taken in concert with local Jewish Commu-nity Councils where they exist.

Fortunately, the growth of local synagogue social action has not been limited to the Reform movement. In October, 1954, a Joint Commission on Social Action was organized by the institutions of Conservative Judaism in America: the Rabbinical Assembly and the United Synagogue of America. This commission, too, has set itself the task of organizing local study and action groups. The Union of Orthodox Jewish Congregations has a Communal Affairs Committee, and there is growing interest in this activity within the Orthodox community.

All three national congregational groups are now affiliated with the National Community Relations Advisory Council (usually referred to as NCRAC), coordinating body for national and local Jewish organizations engaged in community relations or social action. They play their full role in the councils of the NCRAC and have particular responsibility for that facet of the community relations program known as interreligious activities, which involves continuing communication and cooperation with Christian religious groups, local and national. That the synagogue should be recognized as the opposite number of the church on the local scene, and that national Jewish religious organizations should serve as the counterpart of the national Christian institutions, may seem axiomatic to most readers, but this principle was established in the American Jewish community only recently and as a result of bitter struggle. Nor is it acknowledged even now by all Jewish organizations.

Without doubt, Christian denominations have set the pace in the direction of organized programs of social action for many years. The Roman Catholic Church and virtually all Protestant denominations have social action programs functioning nationally and in many local parishes. The Social Action Department of the National Catholic Welfare Conference, and the Division of Christian Life and Work of the National Council of the Churches of Christ serve as the coordinating bodies of the major Christian branches. The denominations, such as the Congregationalists, Methodists, Baptists, and Friends, maintain wide-ranging programs, with substantial budgets and staffs, to educate their laymen to the social responsibilities of their faith.

The Essence of Judaism

Social action is not politics or sociology or economics, though it involves all of them. It is of the essence of religion, certainly of the

Jewish religion. It involves not only stirring sermons from the rabbis but effective grassroots action by the men and women who make up the congregation. Far from being an extraneous area of synagogue life, social action is an integral and essential part of synagogue activity. A synagogue which isolates itself from the fundamental issues of social justice confronting the community and the nation is false to the deepest traditions and values of the Jewish heritage. By working through synagogues for the advancement of social justice, we bridge the gap between confessional and commitment, between word and deed; we bring a sense of greater reality to our faith; and we fulfill ourselves as Jews. In this way we put living flesh on the words of our prayerbook: "O may all created in Thine image recognize that they are brethren, so that, one in spirit and one in fellowship, they may be forever united before Thee. Then shall Thy Kingdom be established on earth and the word of Thine ancient seer be fulfilled: The Lord will reign forever and ever."

BIBLIOGRAPHY

ARONSON, DAVID. *The Jewish Way of Life*. Binghamton, New York: Vail-Ballou Press, 1944.

COHON, SAMUEL S. *Judaism, A Way of Life*. New York: Union of American Hebrew Congregations, 1948.

CRONBACH, ABRAHAM. *The Bible and Our Social Outlook*. New York: Union of American Hebrew Congregations, 1941.

CRONBACH, ABRAHAM. *Religion and Its Social Setting*. Cincinnati: The Social Press, 1933.

CRONIN, JOHN FRANCIS. *Social Principles and Economic Life*. Milwaukee, Wisconsin: Bruce Publishing Company, 1959.

FREEHOF, SOLOMON B. *Reform Jewish Practice*. Cincinnati: Hebrew Union College Press, 1944. Vol. II, 1952.

GITTELSOHN, ROLAND. *Little Lower Than the Angels*. New York: Union of American Hebrew Congregations, 1955.

GOLDSTEIN, SIDNEY E. *The Synagogue and Social Welfare*. New York: Bloch Publishing Company, 1955.

MEYEROWITZ, ARTHUR. *Social Ethics of the Jews*. New York: Bloch Publishing Company, 1935.

ORLINSKY, HARRY. *Ancient Israel*. Ithaca, N. Y.: Cornell University Press, 1954.

RAUSCHENBUSH, WALTER. *A Theology for the Social Gospel*. New York: Macmillan Company, 1917.

SCHWARZ, JACOB D. "The Synagogue in the Present Crisis." A pamphlet. New York: Union of American Hebrew Congregations, 1940.

SILVER, MAXWELL. *The Ethics of Judaism from the Aspects of Duty*. New York: Bloch Publishing Company, 1938.

STEINBERG, MILTON. *Basic Judaism*. New York: Harcourt, Brace and Company, 1947.

THOMAS, GEORGE. *Christian Ethics and Moral Philosophy*. New York: Scribner Bros., 1955.

WAXMAN, MEYER. *Judaism, Religion and Ethics*. New York: Thomas Yoseloff, 1958.

HOUSING

"Look, ye blind, that ye may see.
Here are people robbed and
 spoiled,
They are snared in hovels,
And hid in slums.
They have become a prey, and
 none to rescue,
A spoil, with none to say restore."
                    (Isaiah 42:18 ff)

IN 1937, in his Second Inaugural Address, President Roosevelt declared: "I see one third of a nation ill-housed, ill-fed, ill-clothed."

By 1960, after the kaleidoscopic passage of more than two

decades, the picture was drastically improved. Americans were much better fed and much better clothed. But their housing was still a national disgrace.

There were many reasons for this situation. The depression and World War II left a vast backlog of unmet housing needs. Our population has been mushrooming since the end of the war, creating new housing needs. The population is expected to reach 175 million by 1960 and 200 million by 1970. Despite the fact that the volume of private building has reached unprecedented heights throughout the country in the post-war years, we are failing miserably to meet the challenge of providing a decent home and living environment for every family in the rapidly expanding American population. We have been building at the rate of more than a million housing units a year, but experts tell us that we must have two million new units a year if we are to eliminate the accumulated housing backlog and meet the expanding needs of our people.

The high volume of building in recent years has primarily served the upper and middle income groups in our society. It has hardly begun to solve the tragic problem of slums which comprise from one-fifth to one-third of all the dwellings in most American cities. The 1950 census revealed that 15 million American homes were sub-standard. The number has increased since then. Perhaps one-third of them can be rehabilitated; the other two-thirds must be razed and replaced.

A forward-looking National Housing Act was adopted in 1949; a much less adequate housing program was enacted in 1954 and another in 1959. The latter provided for an expenditure of $1,050,000,000, including $650,000,000 for slum clearance, $50,000,000 for housing for the elderly, and 37,000 new public housing units.

As a nation, we have not yet come to grips with the fact that our slums are increasing faster than we are replacing them. Only twelve communities in the United States have developed Citizens' Housing Associations to deal with the evil of slums. Contrasting this with the six-hundred communities which have a Humane Society or a Society for the Prevention of Cruelty to Animals, one housing leader commented that the nation is fifty times better organized to protect cats and dogs than to insure decent shelter for human beings! The growth of slums poses a serious threat to democracy. It represents a challenge which must be met by conscientious citizens in every community—and one which the synagogue and the church, custodians of the conscience of society, ignore at their peril.

For slums are destructive of the values which underlie both democracy and religion. No community can regard itself as healthy so long as one part of it is an unhealthy blight. The cost we pay for our slums is staggering, even in simple financial terms. Slums breed illness, delinquency, crime. Fires and accidents are much more frequent there. The entire population must assume the heavy financial burden required for augmented municipal services—police, fire, sanitation, hospital—in these blighted areas. We pay an infinitely heavier price in the squandering of human and social resources, impairing the dignity which is the birthright of every human being, thwarting the development of young people into decent citizens.

As the Committee on the Hygiene of Housing has pointed out, "more damage is done to the children of the U. S. by a sense of chronic inferiority due to the consciousness of living in a substandard dwelling than by all the defective plumbing which these dwellings may contain." The dank and dreary slum can and does poison the spirit, shatter sound family relations, and stunt psychological and moral growth. It exacts a toll which we as a nation cannot afford to pay.

Negroes and members of other minority groups are the chief victims of slums. For, even if their economic lot changes for the better, there is little likelihood that they can move to the suburbs, as their white neighbors can, or find other housing anywhere but in the least desirable sections of town. The 1950 Census showed that the Negro population within the city limits of many Northern cities increased much more rapidly than did the white population. Negroes are being hemmed into densely populated areas in the heart of the city, while whites increasingly flee to the restricted residential suburbs. It becomes inevitable that most racially-segregated housing is slum housing. The 1950 Census revealed that 54% of all non-whites live in dwellings that are dilapidated or lack a private bath, toilet or running water, as contrasted with only 18% for all urban families combined.

Slums are serious evils. But racial slums—confining millions of Americans within ghettoes—strike at the integrity of our democratic principles and constitute one of our most serious and conspicuous moral failures as a nation.

"Equality of opportunity to rent or buy a home should exist for every American," said the President's Committee on Civil Rights in its splendid report, "To Secure These Rights" (1948). The Committee recognized the gap between this worthy ideal and the reality of American life. "Many of our citizens face a double barrier when they try to satisfy their housing needs. They first encounter a general housing shortage which makes it difficult for any family without a home to find one. They then encounter prejudice and discrimination based upon race, color, religion or national origin, which places them at a disadvantage in competing for the limited housing that is available."

At a time when the barriers of discrimination and segregation are falling rapidly in education, employment and use of public accommodations, discrimination in housing continues virtually undiminished. Synagogues and Jewish community organizations, dedicated to equality of opportunity for all, have particular reasons for concern and interest in this continuing problem.

The Jewish Stake

Jews are peculiarly sensitive to the dangers to democracy arising from racial or religious segregation in housing. Jewish experience under European tyranny gave rise to the word "ghetto." The rise of that institution in American cities must arouse serious concern. Moreover, Judaism is fundamentally opposed to such desecration of man's God-given dignity and equality.

While Negroes, Puerto Ricans, Mexican-Americans and Orientals are the primary victims of housing discrimination in America, Jews are far from being immune from such maltreatment.

It has been estimated by the American Jewish Committee that more than a score of U. S. cities with populations over 250,000 still have residential neighborhoods which are restricted against Jews. Despite all the strong civil rights laws in New York State and New York City, it is acknowledged that a sizable section of New York City's fashionable East Side north of Fifty-Seventh Street maintains a virtually unbroken "restricted" policy against Jews. Many of the new cooperatively owned apartment buildings in various parts of the country are being set up on a basis which makes it easy to restrict them against unwelcome groups, including Jews. There seems to be no question of the legality of this procedure since ownership agreements forbid resale of an apartment without agreement of the other co-owners.

Another device to by-pass the Supreme Court's decision that restrictive covenants are not enforceable is to link home ownership to club membership. The American Jewish Committee *Reporter* for January, 1956, cited the following example of such a method: "In New Jersey, for example, the large Smoke Rise development advertises itself as just such a 'club plan' community. Recreational facilities and certain services, including a private commuter bus, are available only to club members. The net result has been that no Jews have entered this development, although it is within commuting distance of New York City." A similar tactic has been utilized in Florida by the sponsors of Fort Lauderdale's Galt Miracle Mile.

In Seattle's Sands Point suburb a few years ago, a Jewish family bought a home. Members of the local improvement association suggested they were "making a mistake" and indicated that the association would withhold access to garbage space, garbage disposal facilities, and other vital services. This undemocratic policy was challenged by the Seattle Civic Unity Committee, which brought the issue before the public, but, by the time the policy had been changed, the Jewish purchaser had become fed up and moved away.

The most important technique for keeping Jews out of a neighborhood is the development of a town's reputation for being unfriendly to Jews. Real estate agents are aware of how sensitive Jews are to such mild hints as "You wouldn't be happy here." Sometimes the community's bad reputation is undeserved. In many communities, always assumed to be inhospitable to Jews, the actual entry of Jewish home-owners was received with full acceptance.

Actually, the American people as a whole are becoming increasingly receptive to the idea of having Jewish neighbors. A few years ago a national poll was taken which asked the question: "Suppose a Jewish family were going to move next door to you, what difference would it make?" Seven out of ten white Christians answered: "It would make no difference." Three years later, eight out of ten gave this response, and, in 1954, the figure rose to nine out of ten. Only 3% of those replying to the 1954 query stated categorically that they would not like to have Jews as their next-door neighbors.

The denial of the right to buy or rent a home solely because of race, religion, or national origin demands action from those who take democracy and religious values seriously.

Jews have been in the forefront of the struggle for civil rights in the United States. Together with other Americans, they have rejoiced in the exciting gains of recent years, many of which are described in the chapter dealing with civil rights. (See pages 98 ff)

We cannot fail to appreciate that the continuation of discrimination in housing will, in effect, nullify much of the progress achieved in other areas. Where a person lives shapes, to a great extent, his social experience. Since most children attend schools near their homes, segregated housing results in segregated schools. Segregated neighborhoods lead to segregated community institutions and public accommodations. Thus, the elimination of segregation and discrimination in housing is basic to the achievement of true equality of opportunity in all areas of American life.

Not only the victims of discrimination in housing but also the discriminators and society-at-large are seriously hurt by the evil of housing segregation. Recently, six hundred social scientists were asked: "Does enforced segregation have detrimental effects upon those segregated and/or upon those who do the segregating?" Over 90% of the replies said "yes" with respect to the victims of segregation, and 83% said "yes" with respect to those who do the segregating.

Segregation causes over-crowding. In 1950, according to the U. S. Bureau of the Census, overcrowding in non-white homes was nearly four times greater than in white homes. Unthinking observers like to explain such facts in terms of racial factors, but the explanation lies elsewhere. Since Negroes and other racial groups are penned into specific neighborhoods and denied the opportunity to move into other areas including the residential suburbs, the demand for housing within these ghetto neighborhoods builds up increasingly. It is not surprising that discrimination in housing is a most potent source of riots and other violence.

Our racial slums constitute a grave handicap in our efforts to persuade the peoples of the world of the validity of democracy. The Communists know full well how to use such sure-fire anti-American propaganda as pictures of slum housing in Harlem or Chicago's "Black Belt." The State Department has pointed out that: "The United States has been embarrassed in the conduct of foreign relations by acts of discrimination taking place in this country." This restrained observation is a manifest under-statement. The fact of the matter is that screaming headlines from Bombay to Bonn keep our racial practices—and especially our misdeeds—under the harsh glare of world attention. Many Americans may have already forgotten, but the two-thirds of the peoples of the world who are non-white have long memories for such events as took place in Levittown, Pennsylvania, in 1957, when a howling mob demonstrated to try to prevent Mr. and Mrs. William Meyers from becoming the first Negroes to move into this previously all-white community; or the events of 1958 when the home of a Negro war veteran was bombed in Louisville, Kentucky; or the protracted racial conflict in Trumbull Park, Chicago, where heavy police protection was required month after month to prevent violence against Negroes who sought to live in housing built at public expense.

Interracial Housing

Those who seek to justify segregated housing usually resort to the bromide that various racial and ethnic groups "prefer to live with their own kind." Besides, they say, mixing members of different racial or religious groups creates tensions which may very well erupt into violence. That these arguments are specious is demonstrated by the fact that for many decades, before patterns of segregation became fixed, people of different races, religions, and national origins lived alongside one another without difficulty in every part of the United States. Even more striking are the dozens of current examples of interracial housing, both public and private, in which are refuted anew the myths and the dire warnings of the apologists for segregation. These experiences are summarized in an excellent pamphlet entitled "Equality of Opportunity in Housing," published by the National Community Relations Advisory Council (NCRAC):

> "Interracial public housing developed slowly and gradually. It has included low-rent unsubsidized public and war housing. And the conclusions that may be drawn from ten years of integrated living are very clear.
>
> "Experience has demonstrated time and again that where Negro tenants are integrated with white; where the occupants have daily contact with their neighbors of different races; where all families enjoy the same privileges and share the same responsibilities; initial tensions, if any, soon subside and a cooperative spirit develops. Almost invariably, an harmonious interracial environment is the result. Children play with each other with no self-consciousness about their racial or religious differences. Community responsibilities are accepted by the tenants without favoritism or regard for creed or race. The entire public benefits from the daily example of democracy in action.
>
> "The foregoing conclusions have been demonstrated in public housing developments in New York City, Pittsburgh, Los Angeles, Chicago and numerous other cities.

"Nor is successful, democratic housing limited to public housing. Integrated housing exists and succeeds in private housing also. In Minneapolis and St. Paul, Minnesota, there are a number of residential areas where Negroes live in predominantly white neighborhoods. A survey by the Governor's Interracial Commission of Minnesota in 1947 found that the white neighbors are invariably friendly and exhibit little or no prejudice. In New York City, the manager of the New York Amalgamated Houses, an interracial private development, reported: 'Not one of the tenants, old or prospective, has ever objected to mixed occupancy.' In city after city, throughout the United States, the feasibility of non-segregated housing has been proved."

Of course the question of housing for minority-group families is seldom considered on the basis of facts or experience but rather on the basis of prejudice and stereotype. The most common stereotype holds that the entrance of a minority group into a neighborhood will result in the depreciation of property values. The truth is that it is not race or religion which affects real estate values but a combination of factors which vary from city to city and from case to case. Nonetheless, there have been situations where the entrance of certain racial or religious groups into a neighborhood has resulted in the immediate depreciation of property values. This was not due to the persons coming in, but to the foolish hysteria and panic of the property owners running away. It is the panic which induces old residents to sell, and not the introduction of a few Negroes or Jews which brings down the selling price. Property owners who have avoided hysteria in such situations learned that, when the initial anxiety subsided, their property regained its original value and frequently even increased in value because of the enlarged market.

Jewish religious groups have maintained a deep interest in the problem of housing. The Central Conference of American Rabbis in 1918 called for "proper housing for working people secured through government regulation when necessary." In 1948 it said: "We again call attention to the grievous need for low-cost housing throughout the country, especially among people in low income categories and war veterans. We deeply regret that Congress failed to take action to correct the situation and we strongly urge it to enact legislation for federal subsidies for the remedy of the national disgrace."

The Union of American Hebrew Congregations has indicated a

growing interest in this area of social concern. It endorsed the report of the President's Committee on Civil Rights.

In 1957, at its biennial General Assembly in Toronto, the UAHC adopted the following statement of principle:

"We recognize that racial segregation is not a problem which applies to one section of the country only, but that it presents a moral challenge to every community in America with varying forms and intensity. One of its serious and widespread expressions is in residential housing. In the North, as well as in the South, the continuing pattern of segregation in private housing threatens to invalidate much of the progress which has been made in civil rights in recent years and, also, to impair the spiritual values of religion and democracy alike. We therefore commend those Christian denominations which have recently met this challenge. . . .

"In this spirit, the Union of American Hebrew Congregations herewith pledges its support to the principle of equal housing opportunities for all and urges the members of its constituent congregations to follow non-segregated practices in the selling, buying, and leasing of residential housing. By such action, we will contribute significantly to the strengthening of democracy, and to the health of our communities. . . ."

Much progress has been made in eliminating discrimination and segregation in public housing. The progress made in ending segregation in such housing through law and administrative regulation is commendable. A small amount of progress can be recorded in connection with publicly assisted housing, by which is meant housing that receives direct and indirect government financial assistance with tax waivers or abatements, land clearance and assembly, the right of eminent domain, subsidies, mortgage insurance and such. But it is tragic that frequently homes erected with such public assistance have been and are being sold or rented on a discriminatory basis. Still virtually untouched is the vast field of private housing.

Changing Neighborhoods *

The American people are on the move. Between April 1952 and April 1953, one person in five in the United States changed his

_____
* Much of the material in this section is drawn from data developed by the NCRAC Committee on Discrimination in Housing and published as "A Guide to Changing Neighborhoods."

place of residence. Thirty-one million people moved to different homes; sixteen million moved across state lines. In the decade 1940–1950, the 168 metropolitan areas of the United States increased in population by 22%. While most of the migrants are native white Americans, minority groups have moved in numbers which have drastically changed previous balances. The total Negro population between 1940 and 1950 increased a little more than 10% but the number of Negroes outside the South increased by over 40%. Jews, too, are moving. The Jewish population of Los Angeles increased by more than 150%; Miami by 500%. And in many of our large cities, the exodus of Jewish families to the suburbs has been so rapid as to lead to the development of whole new Jewish communities. Sections of Long Island provide dramatic illustrations of such growth.

Jews often are confronted with discrimination when they seek to move into new areas. To some extent, this problem has been lessened by the United States Supreme Court decision of 1948 that restrictive covenants in housing are not enforceable by the courts. However, this decision does not in itself solve the problem of equality of opportunity in housing, not only for Jews but for all Americans. An additional aspect is of special concern to the synagogue. As Jews move into new areas, they want to construct new community institutions such as synagogues. The older residents may invoke zoning ordinances and other technical regulations to prevent the erection of such institutions. (See pp. 142–3) Difficult situations have resulted in several communities, notably Port Washington, Long Island, and Cleveland, Ohio.

The most severe changing neighborhood problem emerges when the incoming group is one that is seeking to escape from intolerable conditions. Usually this means the Negro, who is trying to break new ground in order to find the decent home that is denied to him in the established ghetto. He has no other choice; he cannot find decent housing without upsetting the established patterns in some area.

An interesting and significant feature of this kind of change is that it often takes place in existing Jewish neighborhoods. Discrimination against other groups is usually less severe in the areas where Jews live. In addition, especially in older cities, the homogeneous Jewish neighborhood is itself likely to be the result of an earlier "invasion" by Jews. For these and other reasons, it is frequently the case that Negro in-migration is taking place in Jewish neighborhoods in large cities throughout the United States. What the synagogue can do to cope with the difficult problems involved in such neighborhood changes is outlined at the conclusion of this chapter. Suffice it to say at this point that the fundamental principle upon which Jews must proceed is that which is compatible with democratic tradition and our religious heritage: the right of a person, regardless of race or ancestry, to live where he wishes. This was the principle which led a Catholic priest, confronted by sharp protests against the invasion of Negroes into the community, to publish the following in his church bulletin:

"Christian principles of Justice and Charity have been seriously defied by participants in a neighborhood racial disturbance within the boundaries of our parish. It is well to remember that: the very First Law of Christianity is to love our neighbor as ourself, regardless of language or color. That it is a serious sin to deny a colored family an opportunity to live in decent quarters. That to encourage prejudice; to help foster hatred; to deny another race the same opportunities we enjoy is not 'just politics,' it is acting against the primary laws of God."

"Would you like to have a Negro move next door to you?" is almost as common a shibboleth as the query: "Would you like your sister to marry a Negro?" But the movement of a Negro family into an all-white block confronts every family in the block with an acid test of its principles, including those grounded in religious faith. The reactions of each individual become crucial in determining whether a panic or a mature acceptance of change results. A Jew named Sam Marcus, who owned a 16-room brick mansion in St. Louis, recently demonstrated the power of an individual to affect such a situation. The Marcus family lived on a residential street that had been restricted to one-family homes. A zoning change relaxed the restriction to permit two-family occupancy. As a result, two Negro families moved into the neighborhood. Trouble brewed. Neighbors agitated. "For Sale" signs blossomed on lawns along the street. An incipient stampede threatened.

Mr. Marcus looked at his neighbors' signs, decided to put up one of his own. It said: "THIS HOUSE IS NOT FOR SALE. WE LIKE OUR FINE NEIGHBORS. YOUR RACE, RELIGION AND POLITICS ARE NOT OUR CONCERN. ALL WHO TAKE PRIDE IN THEIR HOMES ARE WELCOME ON THIS STREET." Mr. Marcus' neighbors paused in front of his sign. Quietly, "For Sale" signs were taken down. The tide had turned. The panic had died a-borning. One neighborhood, its good sense and decency prodded by one forthright man, had passed a major test of democracy.

But not every block has a Sam Marcus and, unfortunately, there have been a number of ugly and hysterical incidents in American cities when Negro or other non-white families moved into previously all-white sections. In such emergencies, the synagogue social action group can cooperate with other religious and racial groups in the area to achieve the following aims: (1) stop false rumors which sweep such blocks like uncontrolled fires; (2) allay the fears of those who feel the neighborhood will now "deteriorate"; (3) slow down the flight of residents to a point where only those persons sell who do so for rational and natural reasons rather than hysteria; (4) prevent the area from becoming a new Negro ghetto.

Above all, the synagogue must affirm the right of individuals to own and live in homes of their own choosing, regardless of race or ancestry. If this right is threatened by vigilantes, emergency action must be taken. Adequate police protection must be demanded. Through visits by the rabbi, the minister, and the priest to their own congregants living in the affected area, hot-heads may be somewhat restrained and the latent sense of decency in the residents may be aroused. Unscrupulous real estate operators must not be allowed to aggravate the hysteria in order to stimulate "panic" selling. Through such methods and others which the Social Action Committee can devise to meet the particular local conditions, it is frequently possible to stabilize a situation which would otherwise cause untold damage to the community.

The only real solution to the problem of discrimination in housing is more housing—much more housing. We need a drastic increase in the housing supply. Public housing is one part of the answer, but public housing is useless, and even harmful, if it proceeds without careful attention to site location and to the urgent problem of tenant relocation. Slum clearance must not be allowed to become minority clearance. Here again, pious and well-intentioned pleas for public housing by church and synagogue groups are no substitute for informed understanding of the complex problems involved in making public housing really effective. And, beyond public housing, is the need for federal and state action greatly to expand the private housing supply for all economic groups so that, in truth, we may realize the goal of a decent home for every American family.

How can the individual synagogue, through its Social Action or Community Affairs Committee, assist in the achievement of better housing for all regardless of race, religion, or national origin? There is much that can be done.

In this particular issue—perhaps more than any other—educating the congregational membership is of paramount importance. The Social Action Committee must develop a program through which to sensitize the congregants to the ethical implications of discrimination in housing. This will not be as easy as it seems. The overwhelming majority of Jews, it is true, are in principle opposed to discrimination of all kinds. But frequently they display the same irrational reactions when they and the principle are put to the test—when a Negro, for example, moves into their all-white block. A meaningful social action program in a congregation must develop in the members of the congregation something more than a verbal, passive acceptance of the principle of equal rights. It must instill a conviction, grounded in religious faith, that equality of opportunity is not something remote having to do with somebody else (probably in that "decadent South") but something painfully immediate and personal, having to do with us, our neighborhood, our community, our city. A genuine social action program is not intended to make us feel noble by playing God—but to be worthy of God by acting like men.

It can be done. It has been done in many congregations, notable among which is K.A.M. Temple of Chicago. K.A.M. is located on the South Side of Chicago, not far from the "Black Ghetto, Bronzeville." When Rabbi Jacob Weinstein came to K.A.M. in 1939, he found that the Negro slum "was bursting at the seams and spilling its problems of disease, delinquency, crime into the white community and especially the neighborhood of K.A.M., which was adjacent to the Black Belt." Perhaps the easiest thing would have been to ignore the problem, to build a psychological wall between the synagogue and the community, for the rabbi to have devoted himself exclusively to the internal needs and problems of his synagogue. But Rabbi Weinstein was not built that way. He did not believe that Judaism can be lived in a vacuum, that a rabbi can retreat into an ivory tower, or that the synagogue can be healthy in a sick neighborhood.

Rabbi Weinstein sought out the individuals and couples in his congregation who were alert and concerned with the application of their faith to the problems of the community. Starting with a small nucleus, he organized the Community Affairs Committee of the Sisterhood which served as the liaison between the congregation and the community and whose task it was to "put our profession of faith to the living test of the deed." At the same time, in order to reach more of the men in the congregation, he organized a Discussion Group which met every Wednesday at a downtown hotel to grapple with the religious implications of better public schools, housing, cleaner politics and other issues agitating the community.

This investment in education paid rich dividends, not only in terms of sparking community action on the problem of the Negro slum, but also in terms of the broadened social sympathies of the congregation itself.

"I shall never forget a crucial board meeting," Rabbi Weinstein recalled years later in an address at the Hebrew Union College–Jewish Institute of Religion, "when final decision was to be made as to the building of our Community House. There had been a serious split depriving the congregation of much-needed resources, Negroes were beginning to move into the neighborhood, some of our most prosperous members were moving to the North suburbs. It seemed like a ten-year-old dream was vanishing, when a member with whom I had spent many hours arose and said: 'Gentlemen, I would feel as though I had betrayed my religion to acknowledge that the presence of Negroes in this neighborhood would keep me from worshipping here or sending my children to the Community House. Perhaps the Community House will serve as an agency to bring about better understanding between the races.' This expression evoked the latent decency in the majority of the board and they decided to build. It may not prove to be a good property investment, but it is a wonderful investment in human understanding. It is the kind of work which best proclaims the faith."

The Community Affairs Committee made an important contribution to the community in its work on a number of issues, including the Negro housing problem. Synagogue social action committees in other communities, depending on their resources, can undertake many of the same kinds of activities. The K.A.M. Committee made its own investigation of the housing situation in "Bronzeville" through visits, study of city reports and census information. It undertook a study of community resources to determine what agencies and organizations were doing and not doing to meet the situation. On the basis of these investigations and studies, the committee saw the need for a community-wide approach to the problem and sparked the creation of an inter-sectarian instrumentality known as the Kenwood–Hyde Park Council of Churches and Synagogues. Continuing and friendly relationships were established with the Negro community. Conferences were held to educate the community-at-large to the need for community action. Discussions were had with civic officials and legislators in order to place into motion slum clearance projects and needed new housing developments. Programs were developed to maintain strict enforcement of fire and housing regulations. In short, the power of an informed and aroused citizenry was tapped and applied to the amelioration of one of the community's gravest civic problems.

K.A.M. Temple is far from being unique in being faced with the problem of changing neighborhoods. Of approximately eighty-seven communities which have Jewish populations of 4,000 or over, virtually every community has already experienced, or will experience, these problems. In fifteen of these eighty-seven communities the non-white population more than doubled between 1940 and 1950. In another twenty-one of these communities, each having more than 50,000 whites, the non-white population increased at least 13% in the decade between 1940 and 1950; in 13 of the 21 it increased by over 33%. There is no doubt that the question of changing neighborhoods, and specifically the emergence of Negro and other racial groups into formerly Jewish neighborhoods, represents a major challenge for Jewish communities. Millions of dollars worth of Jewish community investments in Jewish institutions— and specifically synagogues—are affected by such neighborhood changes. These structures represent years of planning and fund-raising. To the extent that such structures are located unreasonably far from the constituency they are designed to serve, their functioning is impaired and, frequently, new funds must be expended for facilities elsewhere.

New York City is only the most extreme example of a community in which many Jewish community institutions and synagogues find themselves surrounded by the in-migration of Negroes or Puerto Ricans, while, at the same time, the local Jewish population gravitates toward Long Island or Westchester or other sections of New York City. What should a synagogue do in such a situation? The problems are baffling and delicate. A synagogue confronting such a problem should waste no time on idle discussion of its need for a Social Action Committee. Whether it acknowledges it or not, it has a social action problem. The only question is whether it will simply try to muddle through or will entrust to a committee of devoted persons the task of analyzing the situation and planning an intelligent, sensible program designed to meet the needs of the congregation and the community.

A first requirement in such a situation is to make perfectly clear to all concerned that, so far as the congregation is concerned, the right of a person to live where he pleases is inviolate. Regardless of the difficult problems which may arise for the congregation, its position in support of the fundamental principle of equality of opportunity must be affirmed. How this can best be done should be determined by the Social Action Committee. In some cases, a statement of policy, along the lines of the NCRAC statement quoted earlier, might be formulated for the guidance of the community as well as for each member of the congregation.

As a corollary to this first requirement, the Social Action Committee should use its influence to make certain that the right of the new neighbor—be he Mexican, Negro, Puerto Rican, or whatever —to live where he pleases is not nullified by threats or coercion. If threats of violence take place, the police should be called in immediately. In some situations, a friendly and sympathetic visit to the new neighbors by a representative of the Social Action Committee will be extremely helpful in easing tension.

With the help of the rabbi, the Social Action Committee should develop techniques and programs intended to prevent the development of an atmosphere of panic or hysteria within the Jewish group in the neighborhood. When panic can be averted, it is often possible to stabilize the neighborhood and forestall the mass exodus of the old residents. In many communities it has been found helpful to have the rabbi visit the Jewish families who live in the block or neighborhood "broken" by a Negro or Puerto Rican family to discuss the situation calmly and frankly, in order to dispel emotional thinking and prevent hasty, impulsive decisions. The entrance of one or two Negro families need not portend a "black belt" unless the existing residents, succumbing to fear and rumor, throw their homes on the market and run. Those who flee because they think the neighborhood will become black or brown or yellow help to create the very condition they fear. Preserving the stability of the neighborhood serves the best interests of all—the congregation, the congregants, the community. Negro leadership is not interested in seeing the creation of new "black belts." Like other decent Americans, they want to live with their neighbors of all races and religions in dignity and harmony, without segregation.

Sometimes, despite all efforts, so many of the members move to other sections of the city that the existing synagogue structure becomes a useless shell. In such cases, a new synagogue building in a new section becomes necessary. Here, too, the activities of an effective Social Action Committee can be invaluable in initiating sound relationships with the churches and community agencies functioning in the new neighborhood.

Usually, however, despite neighborhood changes, the synagogue is likely to stay where it is for a long time to come. Despite some inconvenience to members no longer near their temple and religious school, the synagogue continues to serve the congregation. The synagogue has both an opportunity and a responsibility to help maintain the moral and social health of the neighborhood. The Stephen Wise Free Synagogue of New York City, a pioneer in the field of the synagogue and social service, stands in a neighborhood experiencing many of the difficulties of fast-flowing population changes. This synagogue has developed, through its Social Action Committee, an effective program of service to the community. This program includes financial grants to overburdened social welfare institutions in the community; free legal aid to needy residents regardless of race or ancestry; cooperation with other church and civic bodies in the achievement of better housing, recreation, and education and an harmonious integration of new residents into the community.

The synagogue should join with other community groups in helping to increase the supply of housing available to all people. This includes slum clearance and public housing. Great care must be exercised in site selection and to assure in advance that plans are made for tenant relocation. It also includes support of state and federal legislation greatly to expand the housing supply for all Americans. Only when the housing supply is tremendously increased can we hope to begin to resolve fully the acute problems of discrimination in housing.

Many resources are available to the synagogue. Guidance and information on current practices can be secured from the National Committee Against Discrimination in Housing. Of particular value are materials which demonstrate that the entry of minority groups into a neighborhood need have no negative effect on property values. Among such materials available from the committee are: "The New Gresham's Law of Neighborhood" by Charles Abrams; "Effects of Non-White Purchase on Market Prices of Residences" by Luigi M. Laurenti; and "Values in Transition Areas, Some New

Concepts" by Belden Morgan. The UAHC has additional materials.

One of the most hopeful signs is the growing awareness on the part of some builders of their responsibility to foster democratic housing. Outstanding among these has been Morris Milgram, a young Jewish builder, who has pioneered in fully-integrated private housing developments in Pennsylvania and New Jersey. Concord Park, Greenbelt Knolls, and similar projects have been so successful—both financially and idealistically—that Milgram has now organized a national corporation, called Modern Community Developers, to assist communities and builders interested in integrated housing.

BIBLIOGRAPHY

ABRAHAMSON, JULIA H. *A Neighborhood Finds Itself:* How an Urban Community Integrated Its Forces to Keep from Becoming a Slum. New York: Harper and Brothers, 1959.

ABRAMS, CHARLES. "A Housing Program for America." League for Industrial Democracy pamphlet, 1947.

ABRAMS, CHARLES. *Forbidden Neighbors. A Study of Race Prejudice in Housing.* New York: Harper and Brothers, 1955.

BANFIELD, EDWARD C. and MORTON M. GRODZINS. *Government and Housing in Metropolitan Areas.* New York: McGraw-Hill, 1958.

Community Council of Greater New York. "Our Changing Community," 1957. A pamphlet.

DEUTSCH, MORTON and MARY EVANS COLLINS. *Interracial Housing, A Psychological Evaluation of a Social Experiment.* Minneapolis: University of Minnesota Press, 1951.

MEYERSON, MARTIN and EDWARD C. BANFIELD. *Politics, Planning and the Public Interest:* The Case of Public Housing in Chicago. Glencoe, Illinois: Free Press, 1955.

National Community Relations Advisory Council. "Equality of Opportunity in Housing." A pamphlet.

National Community Relations Advisory Council. "A Guide to Changing Neighborhoods." A pamphlet.

President's Committee on Civil Rights. "To Secure These Rights." New York: Simon and Schuster, 1948.

STRAUS, NATHAN. *The Seven Myths of Housing.* New York: A. A. Knopf, 1944.

STRAUS, NATHAN. *Two Thirds of a Nation, A Housing Program.* New York: A. A. Knopf, 1952.

WEAVER, ROBERT. *The Negro Ghetto.* New York: Harcourt, Brace and Co., 1948.

WENDT, PAUL F. "The Role of the Federal Government in Housing." Washington, D. C.: American Enterprise Assoc., Inc., 1956. A pamphlet.

EDUCATION

"Thou shalt teach them diligently
unto thy children."
(*Deuteronomy 6:7*)

SINCE THE DAY the Jewish people, assembled at the foot of
Mount Sinai, pledged themselves to accept the Law and its
teachings, the love of learning has been an outstanding Jewish
characteristic. The prophets and the sages glorified education.
Moses, making his dearest wish to God, asked only to know more.
Solomon chose wisdom above all other things. Rabbi Jochanan
ben Zakkai, summoned before Vespasian, commander of the
Roman troops besieging Jerusalem, begged him for only one con-
cession: a school. Wherever Judaism found expression—in the
Bible, the Talmud, rabbinic sayings—we are met with re-affirma-
tions of the Jewish love of learning, such as: "Let your house be
a meeting-place for the wise"; "secure for yourself a teacher";

"an ignorant man cannot be pious"; "the study of Torah surpasses all other *mitzvos.*"

It is not without reason that the Jewish people became known as the People of the Book. As the Levingers point out in *The Story of the Jew:* ". . . the people without a land became the People of the Book, a keeper of the holy Torah. In the little village of Jabneh, and later in the prison-house of Rabbi Akiba, the rabbis carried on the work of the priests, who had served in the Temple, and of the prophets, who had defied the ungodly kings of Israel and Judah. First in Palestine, later amid the dim, rich glories of Babylon, the rabbis compiled their Talmud; exiled and persecuted, the scholars of Judah forged a chain of learning which was to bind the Jew forever to his glorious past. The People had created the Book; now the Book re-created the People . . . A man with dreamy eyes bending over an open Book is our picture of Israel in exile."

Throughout their history, Jews have maintained this thirst for learning. In the Middle Ages, when illiteracy was virtually universal, the shabby Jewish ghetto was an island of learning in a sea of ignorance. There, Jewish youngsters not only learned to read and write but could—and did—master the complexities of the Talmud. It was the learned man, not the wealthy, who was accorded status by his fellows.

In modern times, as well, the Jew has distinguished himself by the tenacity with which he has fought for an education against all the barriers of ostracism, prejudice, and discrimination. The contributions which individual Jewish scholars and scientists have made to society is testimony to the way in which Jews continue to exalt knowledge and education. Education of children remains one of the highest values in the Jewish home.

Judaism and the Public Schools

It is not surprising that American Jews have, from the beginning, given full and unremitting support to the system of free public schools. The modern American educational system is only about one-hundred years old. Prior to that time, American schools were church-controlled. It took from 1647, when the first common school was established, until the 1840's to establish the principle of tax-supported secular education.

In July, 1892, the Central Conference of American Rabbis met in New York City for its third annual convention. A highlight of the program was an address by Rabbi Edward N. Calisch on "Judaism and the Public School System of America":

"Judaism most unequivocally encourages, most emphatically indorses, most stoutly supports it [public education].

"Judaism earnestly upholds the public school system of America, because it believes that the strength and the glory of the country lie therein. The public schools are the cornerstone of the nation, on which and by means of which, she has reared the superstructure of her unparalleled achievements. They are the great beating heart of the land whence is pulsed forth year after year the throbbing life-current of character and knowledge, whose benign influence vivifies each minutest capillary of the tremendous body politic. It was a military foreigner, who when looking over the land, asked, 'Where are your fortresses and ramparts?' The answer given was an oak in an acorn: 'There,' replied his guide pointing to the little log school house, 'there are our forts.' And stronger ones, more formidable and more invulnerable, never existed. Europe may tremble beneath the tread of her weaponed warriors. The great standing armies may eat the bread out of the mouth of the peasant of Austria, Russia, Germany and France. The strength of England may lie within the 'wooden walls' of her navy. America has her public schools and needs no more.

"The public schools are essentially the children of the State. It is their parent and support. In them lie cradled the future destinies of the republic, the fledglings that shall soon put on the broad pinions of citizenship. As such they must remain under influence and authority that are purely secular. They must be kept aloof from every sectarian tendency. Judaism as an institution is certainly not an irreligious one. Its adherents cannot be classed among those opposed to religious instruction. None more earnestly than they desire the widest diffusion and the universal possession of religious knowledge. Yet Judaism believes that religious instruction of any kind or character has no place in the public schools. Religious teaching shall have its sway in the church, in the Sunday school, in the home, but not in the public schools.

"Happily our country is one where Church and State are divided . . . The introduction of even the simplest kind of religious exercise in an institution of a public nature, that is designed for all the people and supported by all the people, jars at once upon the harmony of our national independence. It, of a necessity from which there is no escape, must favor some to the exclusion of others . . .

"In the vast heterogeneous mass which makes up the American people today, with the many different elements of civilization and varying degrees of religious training, who can determine on a creed that shall satisfy the heart and conscience of all the people? And there is none whose right to satisfaction shall not be recognized.

"It is this right of the individual to be recognized that made our nation what it is today. The attempt at the denial of this right sent the Mayflower of the Puritans to battle with unknown seas, till its keel grounded on the ledge of Plymouth Rock. The assertion of this right roused our revolutionary sires, took them from their plows, and made Boston Harbor and Lexington and Concord watchwords of the people. The consciousness of the possession of this right makes every American citizen today prouder than a king, nobler than a throned monarch. Therefore not to disturb this right, not to cross the line that lies between the parallel paths of Church and State, Judaism declares that the public schools shall be purely and completely secular. Its sentiment is voiced by its own philosopher, Mendelssohn, who (in his book *Jerusalem*) has said, 'The State has no right to appoint men to teach and enforce certain special religious principles.' Says Judaism, let the public schools be public schools, dedicated by the State to innocence and education. Let the children of the Republic furrow the broad and limitless fields of secular knowledge, under secular guidance, all equal—all free—all alike, unhampered by aught that shall divide or separate."

THE PICTURE TODAY

Jews are no less committed to the American system of public education today than they were when Rabbi Calisch spoke and before. Precisely the same basic principles which impelled him are enunciated, to take a recent example, in the testimony presented on June 4, 1954, by the agencies of the National Community Relations Advisory Council before the Senate Committee on Labor and Public Welfare:

"Our constituent bodies have as their main purposes the protection of Jewish rights through the preservation and extension of the American democratic way of life, for only in a democratic society can equality of opportunity for Jews and all others be truly secured.

"Our concern in the field of educational opportunities is long-standing and well-known. Education being the foundation upon which true democracy rests, we could not fulfill our obligation to preserve and maintain democracy without expending our energies towards the extension of educational opportunities. We have therefore been vigilant and active in the struggle to achieve for all equality of educational opportunity in accordance with the traditions of American democracy. We have opposed racial and religious discrimination and segregation in education and have striven in the legislatures, courts and before administrative bodies to eliminate such discrimination."

Because of this commitment to the American public school system, Jews cannot afford to be indifferent to serious threats confronting this system. Among these threats are some which are of special interest to synagogue groups: (1) the inability of the school system to meet growing responsibilities without federal assistance; (2) attacks on the secularity of the public school; (3) attacks on the modern approach to public education.

Federal Aid to Education

"Tomorrow is today in public education. The children whose education is being cramped and starved today will be less able to shoulder the burden of responsibility for community and national welfare tomorrow. Our schools are NOW inadequate to serve the needs either of the pupils or of the nation, and every day this inadequacy becomes more pronounced and takes a greater toll. This trend toward breakdown of the institution of which America has justly been most proud must be stopped and reversed. Not only must schools be built and manned to serve many more pupils, and to serve them for a longer span of years, but also the schools must be equipped to serve their pupils better than the system can serve them now. 'Must' is a strong word, but behind it is the imperative of personal and national success or failure in meeting the demands of a responsible twentieth-century American society." *

In American tradition, public education is a matter of local responsibility. But the federal government has the right and should assume the responsibility of assuring that there shall be available the physical facilities for a basic public school education throughout the country. Substantial federal aid to conserve the nation's educational health has become a prime necessity.

Effective federal aid is needed because of the inequality in edu-

* *Christian Century*, March 9, 1955.

cational opportunity among various sections of the country. Because of the accident of geography, a child born in New Jersey or New York can anticipate a much better public education than can a child born in Mississippi or Alabama. In the year 1953–54, New York spent $356 and New Jersey spent $338 for the education of every pupil. In contrast, Mississippi spent $103 and Alabama, $112. These sharp differences stem solely from differences in financial resources and not from higher or lower valuations placed on the importance of education. Indeed, such states as Mississippi and Alabama spend a higher percentage of their income for public education than do richer states like New York and New Jersey. Only through effective federal aid can the glaring geographical inequalities be rectified, and equality of opportunity in education be made a reality.

The shortage of teachers is the worst in history. At least 75,000 teachers leave the profession annually, many of them because they cannot live on their low salaries. (In 1954, the national average for teacher's salary was $3,605.) Even more potential teachers are deterred by the salary limitations from entering the profession. More than 50,000 new teachers a year are needed to meet enrollment increases and overcrowding, but our colleges are graduating only 35,000 persons annually who are qualified to teach in the elementary schools. Thus we are not even meeting minimum needs, much less replacing the large number of defections from teaching ranks.

The number of pupils in our schools continues to zoom skyward. Comparison of the number of children in public and private schools from 1930 to 1950 reveals a net gain of 1 million children in the public schools. In 1930, approximately half of the seventeen-year-olds stayed in school; in 1950, the percentage had risen to 65%. The combination of a higher birth-rate and greater holding power of the schools has virtually swamped school facilities, despite the record number of new facilities in recent years—47,000 new classrooms in 1951, 50,000 in '52, and still more in following years. To catch up with accumulated need, we would have to build 340,000 classrooms and then continue building 117,000 new classrooms every year. Until we do, our children will continue to be the victims of double and triple sessions, obsolete and even dangerous buildings, and overworked and harried teachers.

In addition, there are many, probably some hundreds of thousands, of children who now receive little or no education at all because their parents are migrant laborers. These wandering, poverty-stricken families do not remain long enough in any community to be able to utilize the educational resources available. The President's Commission on Migratory Labor has emphasized the plight of these children in its reports. Who but the federal government can assume responsibility for their education?

That educational deficiencies are causing us serious harm as a nation, is all too clear. We are deprived of many potentially vigorous, informed citizens. In World War II fully 12% of the men found unfit for military service were rejected solely for educational deficiencies. Later, in the Korean War, 16% of the men who sought to enlist between July 1950 and June 1951 were rejected for inability to meet the minimum educational standard imposed by the Armed Forces Qualification Test. Approximately 10-million adults have less than five years of schooling. The toll we pay for neglecting our educational system is beyond calculation in terms of the political, economic and social health of a vital democracy.

If federal aid to education is so demonstrably necessary, why hasn't the Congress adopted far-reaching legislation to meet this need? There are several apparent reasons. In recent years, Congress has been preoccupied with balancing budgets and cutting costs and has had little stomach for expensive social programs. Another factor is the belief, held by some, including some educators, that federal aid will ultimately mean federal control of education and the breakdown of local autonomy. Not the least of the factors, however, is the continuing conflict as to whether or not federal funds for education should also be made available to parochial schools. This was the controversy which erupted publicly in 1948 when Francis Cardinal Spellman denounced Mrs. Eleanor Roosevelt as "an anti-Catholic bigot" because she expressed the opinion that public funds under our system of church-state separation should be used for the support of public schools only. Since leaders of the Roman Catholic Church have made it obvious that they will regard as hostile any federal aid-to-education bill which fails to provide for non-public schools, such legislation is now regarded on Capitol Hill as a "religious issue," a particular kind of hot potato which acute politicians like to avoid.

Delegates to the White House Conference on Education, which was held in November, 1955, voted overwhelmingly to recommend a program of federal aid to education. This demonstration of public opinion, together with increasing evidence that our educational problems cannot be solved without bold federal action, seems to have made some form of federal aid to education inevitable.

Religionizing the Public School

Current attempts to breach the wall of separation of church and state are dealt with in detail in another chapter. (See pp. 146 ff) But it must be noted here, in considering the problems facing public education in America, that the mounting attack being waged by religious groups against the so-called "secularism" of the public school has provided ammunition and respectable allies to other forces which seek for ulterior purposes to discredit our public schools.

It must be recalled that we had sectarian domination of our common schools in America until about 1840. It was the embittered conflicts between Catholics and Protestants and among the Protestants themselves as to which should receive the greatest share of the school monies which led, in large measure, to the establishment of free, secular public schools, based on respect for freedom of religion and the rights of individual conscience for all citizens. Because of secular education, we have been spared, for the most part, the religious conflicts and recriminations which accompanied sectarian domination of the common schools.

In reality, the public schools, while avoiding religious instruction, have always fostered the ethical and moral values inherent in the subject matter of democratic education. As Professor L. P. Jack, writing in *Living Universe* said about the role of the schools in inculcating such values:

> "We teach it in arithmetic, by accuracy.
> We teach it in language, by learning to say what we mean
> —'yea, yea, and nay, nay.'
> We teach it in geography, by breadth of mind.
> We teach it in handicraft, by thoroughness.
> We teach it in astronomy, by reverence.
> We teach it in the playground, by fair play.
> We teach it by kindness to animals, kindness to servants,
> by good manners to one another, and by truthfulness
> in all things."

But today various religious leaders are foremost among the critics of our public schools. Some churchmen rival one another in assaulting the public school as "Godless," "secular," "atheist," and influential religious groups seem determined to re-establish religious orthodoxy and authoritarianism in education and to make education an adjunct of religion. Groups which insist upon the freedom of public education from religious control are denounced as "totalitarian" and the concept of secular education has come to be regarded in some circles as blasphemous. Why?

One reason for this pressure on the public schools is widespread dissatisfaction among church groups with the state of their own programs of religious education. When, after the First World War, the U. S. Office of Education published a report which found that "only a small proportion of the children throughout the country have even brief contact with church influence," many Protestant clergymen reacted by demanding released time in the public schools. Instead of examining and rectifying the failures of their own religious training, they sought a solution which would let the public schools do much of the job for them. Why teaching that was not effective in the church should be any more effective in the still more attenuated form it could be given in the public school is still not explained. Roman Catholic groups, on the other hand, made it a religious duty for every Catholic child to attend a parochial school rather than a public school. Still, almost half the Catholic children in the country do attend public schools, and the Roman Catholic Church has in recent years become perhaps the most outspoken opponent of "Godless" public education.

The campaign to put God and religion back into public education is usually justified as indispensable to the fight against the rising tide of juvenile delinquency. Actually, our public schools have done much to combat juvenile delinquency, and there is much more they can do in utilizing the modern insights of social science. But it is highly questionable whether more religious programs in the public schools will reduce juvenile delinquency. Our entire society must be considered delinquent. We cannot place the onus on our public schools which only reflect the home and the culture of which they are a part. Moreover, there is no evidence whatsoever that juvenile delinquency has declined in communities which have adopted released time, Bible reading, and other religious practices in the public schools.

School authorities are understandably loath to engage in public controversies with reputable church leaders. The result is that many educators have been put on the defensive and seek either to demonstrate that the public school is already teaching "moral and spiritual values" or to invent new formulas for getting small doses of religion into the public schools. Thus, the distinguished American Council on Education, through its Committee on Religion and Education, has completed elaborate studies designed to demonstrate the need for the inclusion of factual study of religion in the public school curriculum. It might possibly be desirable to have factual study about religion in the schools if that were practicable. But is it practicable? Do the churches really want a critical reading of the Bible? Do they want an objective study of their theological tenets? Are public school teachers equipped to teach such subjects objectively and without intruding their own religious bias? Are non-religious teachers not to be allowed to teach? The dangers of religious intrusion into public education are no less real when they are fashioned by well-meaning educators than when they are imposed on the schools by religious bodies. The drive for religious education in the schools must be resisted even at the risk of unpopularity lest our schools become arenas for religious conflict and tension. The place for religious education is still the home, the church, and the synagogue—and not the public school.

The Crisis of Education

The launching of the Russian Sputnik threw the American people into a panic. The first scapegoat was our public school system. How did the Russians beat us? Why were Russian scientists able to do what ours were apparently not? Ignoring the many complex factors which contributed to this debacle—not excluding the simple truth that our Government had not been willing to spend the money which winning the missile race required—the finger of blame was pointed at the schools.

While the American public was still reeling from the shock of the Sputnik, the U.S. Office of Education issued a report on the current status of Russian education. It revealed that the USSR is producing three times as many engineers as the U.S.; that Soviet students are receiving a much more intensive scientific and technological training; and that the gifted Russian child is given special attention to take advantage of his excellence. Immediately, there was a great outcry for the production of more scientists in America. In the hysteria which engulfed the nation, few paused to wonder whether it was not to be expected that Marxist Communists would exalt science and whether it was wise for a democratic nation to worship at the same shrine. Must American cultural, social, and spiritual values be subordinated to technology because a Russian Sputnik has split the heavens?

Only a few short weeks before Sputnik, a comprehensive $1.5

billion bill, to aid school construction, had been passed in the Senate but was beaten in the House by a mere five votes. But, in the wake of Sputnik, a new approach and a new bill were formulated to be sold, not as education, but as national defense. Shelving the idea of federal aid to school construction—the most urgently needed kind of assistance—the Administration put forward a bill which became known as the Hill-Elliot bill and which was adopted in 1959. Chief among its many grab-bag provisions were these:

(1) Federal funds for student loans, starting at $47.5 million and increasing to $90 million by 1962. "Special consideration" will be granted to students preparing for science, mathematics, engineering, foreign language, or those planning to be public school teachers.

(2) $246 million is authorized for new equipment in science, mathematics, and language classes, the sum to be matched by the states. In addition, $295 million is made available for student fellowships and additional funds for the establishment of some guidance and counseling programs, for visual aids, and for Area Vocational Education programs.

The new law, which has apparently set a pattern for federal aid for years to come, leaves much to be desired. Not the least among the objectionable features is the completely gratuitous inclusion of loyalty oaths required for students receiving loans under the act. Protests from many universities and embarrassed legislators offer reason to hope that this particular evil may be rectified. But the basic spirit of the new law raises other far-reaching and deeply troublesome questions about the directions of American education under the impact of emergency pressures.

For example, the premise of the law is that we must proceed, in a crash program, to strengthen the teaching of physics and math in American schools. But Professor James B. Conant, after a comprehensive study and nation-wide survey, offered no criticism with regard to the way these courses are being taught in American high schools. Indeed, he expressed concern that too many of our best students are flocking to these subjects, at the expense of the liberal arts. Notwithstanding the challenge of the Russians, the educational goals of American democracy cannot be calculus and physics for everyone—but, rather, the fullest possible realization of the potentialities of the whole person, to prepare American youth for mature and thoughtful citizenship in the twentieth century. It is one thing for the U.S. to compete with the Russians; it is quite another for us to abandon our own deepest democratic values in the process.

The Challenge of the Future

With or without the Communist competition, the United States faces vast challenges in the second half of the 20th century.

In September, 1959, only four out of every 10 Americans aged 15 and over were high school graduates. Only 7.3% of the population aged 20 years and over were college graduates. The average education of Americans amounted to only 10.8 years. According to a study of "educational attainment" by the U.S. Bureau of Census, projecting current educational levels, there will be 70 million high school graduates in the U.S. in 1970 and 11 million college graduates. This will be progress compared to the figures of 1950; but it will not be adequate for the changing scene in 1970 when the nation will need fewer unskilled workers and farmers and will require millions of additional professionals and skilled craftsmen.

Implicit in the above figures is a hard economic problem which the nation as yet has hardly dented: thousands and thousands of young Americans simply cannot afford to go on to college. In a period of rapidly spiraling costs, the fitful governmental steps toward financing education have thus far been too little, too late.

An additional problem, which institutions of higher learning have not yet overcome, is that of discrimination on the grounds of race, religion, or national origin. Considerable progress has been made as a result of persistent Supreme Court decisions which have opened the door to Negroes in many Southern Universities. Similarly, in Northern states, fair educational laws have reduced the patterns of discrimination in many colleges. Yet, through subtle devices of "personality," "geography," and other elusive criteria, special difficulties continue to confront many Jewish applicants—and frequently Catholics as well—in seeking admission to medical schools and some other departments of private universities and colleges.

Still another problem, increasing in intensity, is related to the rapid population movements of the past decade. Increasingly, American public schools are becoming one-group schools—predominantly one race, one economic class. Such homogeneity, stemming from housing patterns, defeats a central goal of public education: learning to live with one's neighbors in all the richness and variety of democratic life. How can a student learn to respect differences and grow to inter-cultural understanding if he is educated in the hot-house setting of a gilded or ungilded ghetto where sameness is the rule and difference the exception?

The synagogue, through its Social Action or Community Affairs Committee, can do much. It can inform itself on the problems confronting the local school system. Where a bond issue becomes necessary to meet the growing needs of the schools, the committee can see to it that the members of the congregation as individual citizens know the facts and extend their support. Representatives of the Social Action Committee, either directly or through the local Jewish Community Council, should establish and maintain a friendly and continuing relationship with school officials so that school problems of particular Jewish interest—such as religious practices in the schools, school activities on the Sabbath—can always be discussed in a frank manner and, if possible, resolved without conflict or unnecessary difficulty. Conversely, the cooperation of the membership of the synagogue as citizens of the community can be secured in support of worth-while projects of the schools.

Members of the congregation should be urged to play active parts in supporting the public schools as members of PTA and of Citizens Committees for the Public Schools.

The Social Action Committee can work with the school authorities in developing intercultural education programs in the public schools or in strengthening existing programs designed to promote intergroup understanding and maintain good intergroup relationships. Most school systems welcome such constructive suggestions and ideas from community groups, and are eager to utilize the resources of the schools to promote better relationships among all the children. Before approaching the school authorities, however, the Social Action Committee should familiarize itself with all aspects of intercultural education. Excellent resources include the Anti-Defamation League of B'nai B'rith, the American Jewish Committee, the National Community Relations Advisory Council, the National Conference of Christians and Jews, and the National Education Association.

Without violating the principle of separation of church and state, some congregations have undertaken to arrange Institutes on Judaism for community leaders including local public school teachers and education officials. These institutes, sponsored by the Union of American Hebrew Congregations, have been generally regarded by the teachers themselves as helpful to them in better understanding the nature of Jews and Judaism and, not incidentally, their Jewish pupils.

Synagogue Social Action Committees must be ready to defend the public schools against irresponsible attack as distinguished from legitimate, reasonable criticism, which is the continuing responsibility of alert citizens. In order to be helpful when an emergency develops in the community, the Social Action Committee must have already armed itself with a body of facts. It should know of the important developments in other parts of the country and be informed on both the foes and the allies in the fight to safeguard public education. It should be in touch with the National Commission for the Defense of Democracy through Education and the National Citizens Committee for the Public Schools. It should help establish and maintain local Citizens Committees. And it should stimulate in its congregants a healthy and abiding interest in their children's schools and their own PTA organizations. Wherever decent citizens have been as vigilant and as well organized as the crackpots and the know-nothings, attacks on the public schools have been beaten back soundly.

As Dr. James Bryant Conant has said:

> "We must face the realities of the 1950's. The tide of reaction is flowing strong; there are sincere opponents of all forms of non-denominational schools and colleges; there are others far from sincere who, as in every age, like to exert power by causing trouble, by urging the posse to lynch the victim, the mob to burn the dissenter's house or the school board to fire the 'progressive' administrator . . . A debate on school issues is a healthy sign and informed criticism is to be welcomed even by the most devoted friends of the public schools. But . . . against intimidation all believers in democracy must be ready to stand, whatever their personal views about education."

BIBLIOGRAPHY

American Jewish Congress. *Crisis in the Classroom*. A Guide for Study Groups on Attacks Against Public Education. 1955.
BRAMELD, THEODORE. *Minority Problems in the Public Schools*. New York: Harper and Bros. 1946.

CONANT, JAMES BRYANT. "The American High School Today; A First Report to Interested Citizens." N. Y.: McGraw-Hill, 1959. Paperback.

CONANT, JAMES BRYANT. *Education in a Divided World.* Cambridge, Mass.: Harvard University Press, 1948.

CONANT, JAMES BRYANT. *Education and Liberty: The Role of Schools in a Modern Democracy.* Cambridge, Mass.: Harvard University Press, 1953.

CREMIN, LAWRENCE A. and MERLE L. BORROWMAN. *Public Schools in Our Democracy.* New York: Macmillan, 1956.

FINE, BENJAMIN. *Democratic Education.* New York: Thomas Y. Crowell Co., 1945.

FREEMAN, ROGER A. "Federal Aid to Education—Boon or Bane?" Washington D. C.: Enterprise Association Inc., 1955. A pamphlet.

GRISWOLD, A. WHITENEY. "Liberal Education and the Democratic Ideal." New Haven, Conn.: Yale University Press. Paperback.

GROSS, NEAL. *Who Runs Our Schools?* N. Y.: Wiley, 1958.

HULBURD, DAVID. *This Happened in Pasadena.* New York: Macmillan Co., 1951.

KILPATRICK, WILLIAM H. and WILLIAM VAN TILL. *Intercultural Attitudes in the Making.* New York: Harper and Bros., 1947.

KNIGHT, EDGAR WALLACE. *Education in the U. S.* Boston: Ginn and Co., 1929.

MELBY, ERNEST O. "American Education Under Fire: The Story of the Phony 3-R Fight." Anti-Defamation League Freedom Pamphlet.

MELBY, ERNEST O. and MORTON PUNER. *Freedom and Public Education.* New York: Praeger, 1953.

PERKINS, JOHN A. *Plain Talk from a Campus.* New York: University Publishers, 1959.

SMITH, MORTIMER, Ed. *The Public Schools in Crisis:* Some Critical Essays. Chicago: H. Regnery Co., 1956.

THAYER, VIVIAN TROW. *Public Education and Its Critics.* New York: Macmillan Co., 1954.

MARRIAGE AND
THE FAMILY

". . . and thou shalt rejoice, thou
and thy household." (*Deuteronomy*
14:26)

THERE ARE MANY scholars who believe that one of the
greatest contributions that the Jew has made to civilization,
second only to the idea of ethical monotheism, has been his concept and organization of the family. Still others are convinced, with
David R. Mace, in his book *Hebrew Marriage,* that "the miracle by
which the Jewish community, though stateless and constantly suffering the impact of alien social patterns, has survived and maintained its specific nature and culture, is explained by the fact that
religion and tradition have been rooted in and transmitted through
the life of the family."

What are the principles and values upon which the Jewish family traditionally has rested?

First, marriage is an exalted state in the view of the Jew. The concept that marriage is more than a biological union or an arrangement for perpetuating the race, but is a holy communion of two souls is expressed in the Hebrew term for marriage, *Kiddushin* —"sanctification." Marriage was not regarded by the Jewish people as a compromise with the weakness of the flesh. Judaism has a positive, not an ascetic, attitude toward sex. Not only is the satisfaction of legitimate drives not wrong; it is a duty, so long as it is not misused. Through marriage, man becomes complete, creates children, and grows in character. Celibacy was regarded as unnatural and therefore bad. Kaufmann Kohler has pointed out that, in contrast to other religions which regard the celibacy of priests and saints as measures of sanctity, Jewish law specifically required that the high priest was not allowed to observe the rites of the Day of Atonement unless he was married. Only if he himself had founded a family could he intercede for the household of Israel.

Marriage was regarded as a God-given blessing which stressed, as Dr. Felix Levy put it, ". . . the spiritual elements, the communion and community of soul, the development of character and personality, the purity of the individual and the family life, the institution of the home, the sacrifice, the friendship and the comradeship that it demands and fosters—these are the gifts of the very highest order among life's choicest values."

Marriage in Jewish tradition is a religious experience. David Mace has pointed out the sharp contrast between the traditional Jewish and Christian attitudes toward marriage:

". . . Finally, I wish to draw attention to the profoundly religious significance of marriage in Old Testament times. No other society than that of the Hebrews can have woven religion so inextricably into the daily life of the family. There is a marked contrast between the Hebrew idea that the sexual union of husband and wife was not only blessed of God, but given by Him as a good thing to be enjoyed; and the shadow which, in Christian tradition, has too often been thrown upon the sex life of married people. To cast suspicion upon the wholesomeness of the basic foundation of the married state, and of the normal means of human procreation, would for the Hebrew mind have implied dishonouring the Creator. It is a pity that we cannot recover that valuation today. No attempt to speak of marriage as sacramental, or to extol the sanctity of family life, can really ring true unless it is accompanied by the unequivocal assertion that the bodily union of husband and wife is, or is capable of becoming, an experience of religious significance and of spiritual enrichment." (*Op. cit.*, p. 264)

The begetting of children was regarded as the overriding purpose of marriage. Jewish law went so far as to provide that a couple who had been married ten years and had no children should be divorced. Emphasis was placed in choosing a mate on similarity of background as essential to marital happiness, and intermarriages were rigorously discouraged. To some extent the ancient Jews anticipated the science of eugenics by evolving a complex body of law designed to produce healthy children. Dr. Felix Levy, in his pamphlet on "Judaism and Marriage," writes:

". . . A considerable body of statute and lore is discoverable in Jewish literature which attempts to protect the group against physical or moral taint by insisting on sexual purity for man and woman before and after marriage; by discountenancing any union except in marriage; by advising early matings; by asserting rightly or wrongly that disparity of ages, character, and temperaments make for unhappiness and perhaps even weak offspring; by emphasis upon seeking quality in the family of one's partner; by regulation of intercourse to safeguard the woman and the possible child; by the high esteem in which parenthood, especially motherhood, is held; by prenatal care of the child and its mother; by the prohibition of marriage with a person in whose family or in whom epilepsy, leprosy, or other diseases are present; by insistence on caring for bodily health even to the extent of regulation of diet, and so on."

Divorce was recognized in Jewish tradition and Jewish law. While the Bible indicates that the husband could send away the wife at will, there is little evidence that this right to easy divorce was abused. Rabbinic legislation also acknowledged the right of divorce but hemmed it in with an increasing number of restrictions to prevent arbitrary abuse of divorce. Jewish tradition has come to regard divorce as a sometimes necessary evil, a remedy of last resort, a tragedy for which the "altar of God sheds tears." Judaism holds that the way to avoid this tragedy is to invest the holy union of matrimony with sacredness and religious dedication.

The Jewish attitude toward children was unique among the nations of antiquity, even the most enlightened. In Greece, the practice was to leave weak children on a mountain to die. The Romans allowed a man to put his son, even a grown son, to death. In his condemnation of the people of Judea, the Roman historian, Tacitus, includes the criticism that "it is a crime among them to kill any child." While other civilizations denied the child any rights or status, the rabbis elevated the child as the highest of human treasures, the Messiahs of mankind, God's instrumentality for giving humanity another chance. The children in turn were enjoined to honor their parents as set forth in the Fifth Commandment. To the parents fell the responsibility of educating the children in religious and ethical matters. Not the individual, but the family was the unit in Jewish society.

Despite the commandment to "be fruitful and multiply," birth control was not flatly condemned in Jewish tradition as it has been by Catholicism. Jacob Z. Lauterbach, the late distinguished scholar, concluded from his studies of rabbinic law that "it is not forbidden to use contraceptives when conception would bring harm to the mother or the child born or unborn." Dr. Israel Mattuck in his *Jewish Ethics* declares:

> "Without such a limitation (planned parenthood), most parents cannot fulfill their responsibility toward their children. Judaism puts that responsibility very high. It is a social, and moral duty, that goes with marriage to have children; but it is the duty of parents, constantly emphasized in Judaism, to give children a proper education and general upbringing. That duty can be fulfilled only by considering the economic factors and social conditions which are involved. They justify the regulation of births for the sake of the child.
>
> "Another factor in Jewish thought which may give ground for the view that it should recognize the legitimacy of responsible birth control is its conception of marriage as a relation valuable in itself, as well as for the propagation of children. The objection that birth control allows coition without a purpose beyond itself can receive no support from Jewish thought. Marriage is not a mere concession to human weakness; it enlarges and enriches life. Sexual intercourse is an integral part of it . . ."

Modern Jewish thought approves the practice of birth control. The Central Conference of American Rabbis in 1929 and the Rabbinical Assembly (Conservative) in 1935 adopted formal positions supporting birth control. The Orthodox Rabbinate is far from unanimous in this regard, even if contraception is practiced by the woman. (The man is specifically prohibited in traditional Jewish law from the practice of birth control in any form.) There is no question, however, that the overwhelming majority of American Jews accept birth control in principle and in practice.

Contemporary Marriage

It is clear that many of the ideals of family life to which Jews aspire in the mid-twentieth century were anticipated at the very beginnings of Jewish history. But, in twentieth-century America, the gulf between religious ideals of family life and the American reality is deep and disturbing.

The institutions of marriage and the family are in a seriously disintegrated state. The number of estrangements, separations, desertions and divorces in American life has reached shocking proportions. In 1867, about 10,000 divorces were granted in the United States. Since 1870, the population of the United States has increased 300%; marriages have increased 400%; and by the peak year of 1946 divorces had increased 2000%. There has been considerable levelling off in the last decade. The very bases upon which marriages have rested are changing under the impact of multiple economic and cultural forces. Dr. Abraham Stone, eminent expert on marriage, has pointed out that "we are witnessing a major transformation in the structure and function of marriage and the family from the former patriarchal and authoritative type to the modern companionate and democratic form." It is imperative that we understand clearly the many and complex aspects of these changes if we are to be able to proceed intelligently to maintain marriage and the family as basic human institutions.

Among these factors are:

(1) Many human relationships find it difficult to flourish in a society like our own with its frenetic tempo of living, its neuroticism, its fear of impending atomic destruction, its frantic search for pleasure and escapes from reality. Marriage, by nature a sensitive adjustment, is susceptible to these forces.

(2) The pressures of our society, and particularly of urban society, have changed basically the nature and role of the home. Contemporary homes are wryly, but too-aptly, referred to as "filling stations," where only the physical functions of sleeping, eating, and clothes-changing are performed. While this may be an overstatement, particularly as it applies in new surburban communities,

too many American homes today are not the centers of living experiences which can make for stable marriage and integrated families.

(3) The American lower and middle economic groups are under financial pressure. Worried husbands and wives, harassed by installment payments, children's medical bills, and a high cost of living never quite balanced by a salary, are in no position to give each other and their children the relaxed affection which successful family living requires. It is ironic that such economic anxiety continues despite national prosperity. Apparently the American's concept of a proper standard of living continues to be pushed upward by advertising ballyhoo, keeping up with the Joneses and other factors.

(4) Millions of American wives have moved into the job market. The working wife is no longer impelled only by the desperation of poverty or by career ambitions. In addition to these still-present causes, many middle-class wives who would prefer to concentrate on their homes and children feel themselves forced into the job market to supplement the earnings of their husbands in order to provide the expanded "necessities" of the family. For such families, regardless of specific individual cause, cohesiveness and the security of the children are the frequent victims.

(5) Since the beginning of World War II, Americans have been marrying at increasingly earlier ages. Many of these young brides and grooms have shown remarkable maturity and have built fine family relationships. But too many young Americans were not prepared by their own homes, their schools, and their churches and synagogues, for the realities of marital relationships and family living. Realistic, intelligent education for marriage is still an incompletely-filled gap in the educational process.

(6) Instead of a sound and scientific preparation for marriage, American youth is dosed with misinformation about the nature of marriage, the role of sex and of family relationships. Fed by Hollywood's "romantic" fantasies, both on the screen and in the over-publicized "private" lives of its stars, torrents of literature, fact and fiction, have inundated millions of young Americans with the notions that love means sex alone. They seem to say that sex is an end in itself, not an integral and enriching part of the fabric of marriage, and that pre-marital sexual chastity is a silly anachronism. The late Dr. Kinsey had contributed materially to the perpetuation of this attitude both with the publicity fanfare given what were supposed to be serious scientific studies, and his

gratuitous generalizations and moral judgments which tended to say that what is, is right. Sexual incompatibility continues to be the largest single cause of divorce.

(7) The influences of religious idealism, moral suasion and home observance do not permeate the lives of most American families. The relationships between millions of American families and our religious institutions are tenuous, even where existent. If it is true that "the family which prays together stays together," then the absence of family worship, in public and at home, must take its place as a factor in the breakdown of family life. The purposefulness and direction which religion can impart have been brought to too few American families.

(8) There has been a marked change in society's attitude toward divorce and divorced people. The stigma previously attached to both the process and the persons involved no longer is applied. Too many socially-acceptable people have been divorced—some of them many times. Easy acceptance of divorce must tend to increase its frequency since so many other disrupting factors are weakening the structure of contemporary marriages and families.

These same pressures and factors are at work upon the Jewish population as upon the population in general. While the proportion of Jewish divorces is still much lower than that of the general population, the number of such divorces is steadily rising and already poses a real and unavoidable problem for the Jewish community.

Closely related to the breakdown of the family is the disturbing spread of juvenile delinquency. For a full discussion of this problem see pp. 79 ff.

Problems of the Aged

A problem affecting the family in an increasing number of American homes is that of the aged members of the family. The United States is rapidly becoming a nation of older people. Thanks to incredible medical strides, the average life span has leaped from thirty-five in 1800 to forty-five in 1900, to almost seventy in 1955. A life span of 100, experts assure us, is practically in sight. Exciting as is the prospect of an ever-increasing American life span, it also poses grave problems. More than 10-million Americans are now over sixty-five, 16 million, over sixty. Where should they live? Should they be supported, if indigent, by their children, by private agencies, by government? How do they relate emotionally to their children, children-in-law, grand-children? How can they be provided with the opportunity for some vocational activity consistent both with their experienced skills and their physical limitations? What should they do with their extensive—usually full-time—leisure? Society has only begun to come to grips with this major social concern. The aged are usually given good physical care, but their equally urgent social and psychological needs are too frequently ignored. Community institutions owe a responsibility to the older members of the community to provide vocational, recreational, and activity programs which will dispel loneliness and feelings of rejection and give a feeling of usefulness and acceptance.

Day Centers and Golden Age Clubs have been developed in many communities to help meet the needs of the older members of the community. Many synagogues as well as local sections of the National Council of Jewish Women have helped develop such clubs in many cities. Similar programs have been developed by Jewish Centers and other agencies. Programs in such clubs are premised on the idea that constructive activity is as necessary for an older man or woman as food and drink, and that lack of such activity contributes to physical and personality deterioration. The human resources which are salvaged enrich both society and the individuals themselves whose last years are made warm and purposeful. Synagogues can contribute significantly to the welfare of the community by encouraging and augmenting such beneficial programs.

Despite the many perplexing problems confronting the institutions of marriage and the family, there are solid grounds both in Jewish tradition and in the contemporary scene for a measure of optimism. In the words of Dr. Abraham Stone: "We are witnessing a strengthening of family life. Marriage and the family are in confusion because today we expect much more out of marriage and family living than formerly. The family can no longer be held together by the external forces of law and religion and social pressures. It requires an inner cohesive force of affection and companionship and tolerance. The synagogue can be immeasurably helpful in fostering these ideas and ideals."

THE ROLE OF THE SYNAGOGUE

What can the synagogue do? It can, at the very outset, make its own congregants of all ages aware of the uniquely Jewish conception of marriage and the family. This can be done through the rabbi's sermon, through occasional lectures by students of Jewish family life, through adult education courses, through the religious school, in a course on "Preparation for Jewish Marriage" and especially in an active, vital youth program.

In addition, current information, including the results of research, on marriage and the family should be made available to members of the congregation. Such information should include such materials as may be distributed by the Committee on Marriage and the Family of the CCAR, Rabbinical Assembly, and other religious and civic agencies. Particularly useful is the growing body of educational films which deal, in dramatic and moving fashion, with problems confronting marriage and the family. The synagogue library should include a section on Marriage and the Family, containing basic works along with current pamphlets for the members to keep.

The Social Action or Community Affairs Committee should undertake to determine what resources are available in the community for members of the congregation needing guidance on marriage and family problems. If no such resources are available at reasonable cost in the form of a Jewish Family Service, Community Consultation Center or a similar service, the committee should address itself to ways of meeting this need. The Social Action Committee of Temple Emanuel in Grand Rapids, Michigan, following its thoroughgoing survey of existing facilities in the community, started a successful community drive for a Mental Hygiene Clinic in the community. Other congregations have found it necessary or desirable to create a consultation program of their own to serve the needs of their own congregants. Usually, the rabbi himself serves as the point of contact with the congregant. If he is trained in pastoral counseling, he is able to guide and assist the congregant in coping with many of the anxieties and disturbances which, if unchecked, can undermine a marital or parental relationship. Where the psychological problems involved are deep-seated, the rabbi will refer the person or couple to qualified experts. Through such a service, the synagogue accepts its responsibility to perpetuate the ideal of family relations which has always been sacred to Jewish thought.

In applying itself to the strengthening and improvement of the family, the synagogue may find it necessary occasionally to take a position of principle which may place it in opposition to other groups in the community. Controversy may arise over the propriety of sex education in the public schools, or the right of a Planned Parenthood Society to function in the community, or the need to amend immoral state divorce legislation. In attacking each problem, the synagogue's committee must lead the membership intelligently on the basis of demonstrable fact. Once the best knowledge of our society is combined with the religious insights of Judaism, however, neither pressure nor fear of controversy must deter the synagogue from proceeding with vigor, courage, and effectiveness to take its position—and live it.

BIBLIOGRAPHY

BRAV, STANLEY. *Marriage and the Jewish Tradition*. New York: Philosophical Library, 1951.

CHRISTENSON, HAROLD T. *Marriage Analysis*. New York: Ronald Press, 1950.

DYER, DOROTHY T. *The Family Today*. Minneapolis: University of Minnesota Press, 1950.

ERNST, MORRIS. *For Better or Worse*. New York: Harper and Bros., 1952.

FOLKMAN, JEROME D. *Design for Jewish Living*. New York: Union of American Hebrew Congregations, 1955.

GITTELSOHN, ROLAND B. *Modern Jewish Problems*. New York: Union of American Hebrew Congregations, 1943.

GOLDSTEIN, SIDNEY. *Marriage and Family Counseling*. New York: McGraw-Hill Co., 1945.

GOLDSTEIN, SIDNEY. *The Meaning of Marriage and the Foundations of the Family*. New York: Bloch Publishing Co., 1940.

LANDIS, JUDSON T. *Building a Successful Marriage*. New York: Prentice-Hall, 1953.

LANDIS, PAUL H. *Your Marriage and Family Living*. New York: McGraw-Hill Co., 1954.

LEVY, FELIX. "Judaism and Marriage." A pamphlet. New York: Union of American Hebrew Congregations.

MACE, DAVID R. *Hebrew Marriage*. New York: Philosophical Library, 1953.

MARK, MARGARET B. and BERNARD J. STARKOFF. "The Jewish Family in the World Today." A pamphlet.

MATTUCK, ISRAEL. *Jewish Ethics.* New York: Hutchinson's University Library, 1953.
National Council of Jewish Women. "American Jewish Family Life." A pamphlet, 1955.
SHOULSON, ABRAHAM B. Editor, *Marriage and Family Life:* A Jewish View. N. Y.: Tayne Publishers, 1959.
STONE, HANNAH and ABRAHAM. *A Marriage Manual.* New York: Simon and Schuster, 1952.

CRIME, PUNISHMENT, AND JUVENILE DELINQUENCY

"The right of society to protect itself against those who constitute social menaces implies also the solemn obligation to do everything possible to remove the causes which tend to make men criminals and to make punishment corrective in spirit rather than retributional." (*Central Conference of American Rabbis, 1935*)

IN NOVEMBER, 1955, Governor Raymond Gary of Oklahoma stirred up a first-class storm by invoking the Bible in support of legislation which would legalize whipping some boys and girls in the state's training schools. The governor cited Proverbs 23:13–

14: "Withhold not correction from the child; for if thou beatest him with the rod, he shall not die. Thou shalt beat him with the rod, and shalt deliver his soul from hell." (King James translation.)

What this proves, presumably, is that governors, too, can quote Scripture for their purposes. As Oklahoma churchmen were quick to point out, the governor may have read this text accurately but he had mis-read the Bible in its essential spirit and meaning. His use of the Bible in this way did violence to Christianity as well as to Judaism.

That Judaism developed as a religious way of life expressing itself in law is well known. It is not nearly so well known, however, that Jewish law underwent thoroughgoing changes over the centuries, both within the Biblical period and thereafter. It was always a creating, evolving attempt on the part of the greatest minds in Jewry to express, in terms of the specific requirements of each era, each environment in which Jews lived, the legal principles through which the Jew could fulfill his eternal covenant with his God. But this creative legal evolution had to proceed in a peculiar framework: the long-held traditional Jewish belief that the totality of law, unto all eternity, was given to Moses at Mt. Sinai.

In the earliest Biblical documents, Hebrew society was primitive and so were its laws. Capital punishment was frequent for crimes considered trivial by later generations. But those later generations could not blandly repeal the ancient law. It was divine in origin; it was eternal. They could, however, and did arrange for the law to be so hedged in, so fenced about, that its enforcement was impossible. For example, the law with regard to punishment for assault is quite clear: "eye for eye, tooth for tooth, hand for hand, foot for foot, burning for burning, wound for wound, stripe for stripe." (*Ex. 21:24*) Yet we know that early in the evolution of Jewish law, money fines were substituted for these corporal punishments, and the law as written was never enforced. According to Deuteronomy (*21:18–20*), a "stubborn and rebellious son" could be turned over to the elders of the city who could order him stoned to death. The law was clear. But it was never enforced. In all of rabbinic literature, there is not one case cited of a rebellious son being executed. That law, like all laws pertaining to capital punishment, apparently remained purely theoretical and was not applied in practice.

For the death penalty prescribed in Deuteronomy, the restrictions in Mishnah Sanhedrin VIII are so numerous that the effect has been virtually to abrogate the death penalty. In Mishnah Makkot I: 10, a court is branded as "murderous" if it imposes the death penalty as often as once in seven years; according to Rabbi Eleazar ben Azariah, once in 70 years. Rabbi Tarphon and Rabbi Akiba opposed the death penalty altogether 1900 years ago!

There is ample evidence in the Talmud and in Jewish legal literature through the centuries that these were not alone in their stand. It was impossible for the rabbis to abrogate capital punishment altogether; God had ordained it in His word. But they certainly did their best to make it impossible of accomplishment!

Only deliberate murder was punishable by death. Previous hatred, treacherous lying in wait, the use of a deadly weapon had to be proved. The murderer had to know the nature of the act and the severity of punishment—before he committed it. And most important, *two* competent witnesses were necessary to establish the commission of the murder.

Legal restrictions like these made Judaism's concept of justice deeply humanitarian and forward-looking. Increasingly, punishment for a variety of crimes was transferred from the jurisdiction of man to that of God alone. Of course, this shift was brought about not alone by the mercifulness of Judaism and Jews. Discussion in the area of criminal law has been theoretical for twenty centuries, since the Jewish people has been subject to the civil law of nations in which they have lived. Nevertheless, while understandably retaining the concept of punishment for crime, rabbinic authority has always remembered that Judaism is not the harsh legalistic system alleged by the ignorant or the malicious, but the living faith of "merciful sons of merciful ones."

In our day, liberal Jews have not hesitated to continue the Jewish process of testing ageless principles in the crucible of contemporary knowledge. Many Jews have been in the vanguard of the movement against capital punishment, for prison reform, for liberalization and modernization of our concepts of justice, rehabilitation of criminals, and related concerns.

There is nothing in either Christian or Jewish teaching which militates against effective cooperation by modern-day churches and synagogues in tackling contemporary problems involved in crime, punishment, and juvenile delinquency. Indeed, the basic values of both Judaism and Christianity require a much more serious grappling with these problems which have grown to constitute a major moral crisis in American life.

With the mushrooming of organized rackets, crime has become

big business in the United States. Attorney General Herbert Brownell has estimated the total cost of crime in the United States at $20 billion a year, most of which is paid by the taxpayer. F. B. I. reports show 1,763,290 serious crimes—one every six seconds—known to the police in 1954. There were approximately 200,000 inmates in state and fereral prisons in 1955 and many more than that in local jails and workhouses. Crime is a major national problem. The financial cost is insignificant compared to the exorbitant moral price we pay as a nation for our failure to meet this problem with intelligence and humanity. Despite the magnitude of the problem, the public appears to be woefully ill-informed of the important moral issues involved in crime and crime prevention. The American public in 1952 revelled in the spectacular televised revelations of the Kefauver crime hearings, and it is now obviously concerned about juvenile delinquency. Yet there has been little public attention to the basic questions of what causes a criminal, what we do with the criminal, and whether what we are doing is right.

The stark truth is that we have not yet cast off the medieval concept that society's responsibility toward the criminal is to punish him. We have talked much of the need not only to isolate the criminal to protect society, but also to rehabilitate him if possible. Some improvements in this direction have been made in our prison systems, but essentially, they still represent, more than anything else, institutions of social vengeance. Incarcerated for years in a fortress-like, forbidding institution, surrounded by a high massive wall; subjected to the deadly, demoralizing routine of prison regimen; placed in contact with hardened criminals and sex perverts; deprived of normal sexual and affectional needs—this is not the way to reclaim the law-breaker. It is the way to stifle hope, to break the spirit, to warp already disturbed personalities, to deepen hostility and aggression against society, to prepare a person for a life dedicated to crime.

Students of American criminology have long been aware that our prison system is a demonstrated failure. The American prison system was developed one hundred and fifty years ago, through the leadership of the Quakers (Society of Friends) who conceived it as a humane alternative to widespread corporal and capital punishment. Over the years, American prisons have improved in some respects but it is doubtful that even the modern prison is really much better than the system of corporal punishment. Five or ten years of gradual rotting behind prison walls are at least as demoralizing as fifty lashes. Prison routine is more cruel than any form of corporal punishment. But, unpleasant as it is, does not the modern prison accomplish its purpose? Apparently not. If the purpose is to deter the criminal from committing another crime, statistics prove that our prisons are failing badly. In one Massachusetts state prison, 70% of the inmates had previously been in prison. In the Eastern Penitentiary of Pennsylvania, 67% of the prisoners had been in prison before. In New York, as many as 80% of the men sent to prison had previous prison experience. More than half the convicts in all our prisons have previously been convicted of one or more crimes. If punishment prevented crime, there might be some justification for our present prison system. But it doesn't. On the contrary, we could not devise a system better calculated to transform troubled youngsters into confirmed, chronic criminals. In his book, *The Psychology of the Criminal Act and Punishment,* the distinguished psychiatrist Gregory Zilboorg summarizes the views of most students of this subject:

> "We must bear in mind also that punishment, despite the traditional belief to the contrary, has apparently no deterrent effects on crime. Since punishment does not precede but follows the antisocial act and, in addition, does not seem to exercise any deterrent effect on crime, it would be a gross error indeed to consider the traditional penal system as a system of social defense."

But, it may be said, don't our prisons try to rehabilitate the prisoners? On paper, yes. Penologists have repudiated, as incompatible with our scientific insights, the idea that the prison exists for punishment. They speak of the need for curative treatment and rehabilitation, psychiatric and psychological attention for every prisoner. Rare is the American prison which actually has a program of this kind. Some progress has been made in some federal prisons and the more enlightened system developed in California under the leadership of former Governor Earl Warren. On the whole, however, our prisons are still primarily instruments of punishment. Why?

Some students of criminology contend that this is what the public wants, that the American public accepts the premise that persons who have transgressed against society must be punished. If this were not the premise of our thinking, they argue, we would have, long ago, demanded that our present prison system be completely overhauled. Harry E. Barnes and Negley K. Teeters, in their authoritative *New Horizons in Criminology,* attribute our failure to dislodge the present prison system to a "convict bogey," an exaggerated fear of men who have been convicted of a crime. They insist that we want the criminal punished because we project onto him the burden of our own sins and by punishing him we expiate our sense of guilt. This attitude results in what they call a "jail psychosis" in the American people which makes impossible a realistic appraisal of our prison system and necessary citizen action to bring the system into line with logic, modern scientific knowledge, and the religious principles of compassion and mercy.

There seems to be a public insistence that prisons punish and not "coddle" prisoners and this attitude tends to dissuade even the most progressive wardens and prison officials from putting modern theories of penology fully into practice. A genuine rehabilitation program requires flexibility and experimentation but, inevitably, it also increases the risk of escape. The public will not stand for escapes, and the result is that even the best systems are constantly afraid of public criticism of their daring. If religious groups are indeed the conscience of America, they have a vast task to perform in developing public awareness and sensitivity to the imperative need for drastic prison reform.

That the public has these attitudes toward the criminal and his treatment should not be surprising. Freudian theories aside, the root of the problem seems to be that citizens generally are woefully ignorant of the purpose, the methods, the effectiveness, and the ethical implications of our penal system. Far from gaining knowledge of these matters, we are confused and misinformed by the press, television, and motion pictures, which, for the most part, prefer to shock and titillate us with lurid crime stories than to inform and enlighten us on the facts of our penal system. Public officials also make little effort to get such knowledge across to the community-at-large. The result of public ignorance is indifference.

Few Americans are aware of what goes on behind prison walls. Corporal punishment is officially frowned upon, but illegal beatings and whippings are still common. Our prisons are old and housing conditions are bad. The Federal Prison Bureau recently listed only nine of the nation's prisons as good in terms of physical equipment, administration, feeding, medical attention and parole practices. We do not have a fraction of the psychiatric facilities we need in our prisons. Guards and other prison personnel from cooks to chaplains are so poorly paid that men of high calibre can rarely be attracted. Food is usually inferior and the way of serving it is even worse. Minimum requirements of privacy and of normal human regimen are seldom respected. Sexual disturbances, homosexuality, and sexual warfare are rife and, even worse, inevitable under present prison arrangements.

Recently, we have witnessed a virtual epidemic of riots in American prisons. A European penologist, after a careful study of American prison riots, reported that in virtually every case conditions in the prison were intolerable and that the riots were the only effective weapons the prisoners had to remedy their legitimate grievances; the concessions granted the rioters did, in every case, help to rectify the inexcusable failures of the prison. The significance of these riots, however, goes deeper than bad prison conditions and physical equipment. Prison inmates feel that the only way in which they can win the interest of the public in improving the prison situation is by rioting. Unfortunately, experience tends to confirm their judgment. Non-violent protests and demands by prisoners are ignored. Riots usually result in improvements. While this does not justify the horror and violence of prison riots, it helps us to understand them. And, above all, it places a blazing spotlight on public apathy about the treatment of prisoners.

What can be done to improve our penal system? Not minor tinkering, but a major overhaul is indicated. It is true that we need new and progressive institutions with more humane concepts of treatment. But there is something more fundamental. One authority contends that our prisons are overcrowded in large part because almost half the inmates should not be in prison at all. Dr. Garrett Heyns, warden of Michigan State Reformatory at Iona and a leading penologist, has stated that one-third of the country's prison inmates ought to be released immediately; these persons were confined for minor infractions and, says Dr. Heyns, do not belong in prison. Many penologists believe that an even higher percentage of our prison population does not belong in prison, and that many of the rest should not be subjected to such long sentences. But, if not prison, what?

The answer lies in a greatly expanded use of the modern practice of probation. Probation does not mean that a person committing a crime is absolved of his crime and sent home scot free. It is a method of supervising, assisting, and treating offenders as individuals in an effort to restore them to normal and productive living. Under the guidance of a trained probation officer, the individual can be helped and treated where prison can only incarcerate.

Probation—in which a person has been convicted of an offense is released on suspended sentence under the direction of a probation officer—and parole—in which a prison inmate is released before the end of his sentence on the authority of a parole board—emphasize the rebuilding of the individual rather than public vindictiveness. The expense of community treatment in probation is one-tenth the cost of institutionalization. But, far more important, it reflects a faith in the individual and in our ability to redeem him. It costs us more in many ways to merely cast him into prison and forget him.

No religious group which takes its values seriously should rest content until the American people demand and get a system which will correct and not punish, which will rehabilitate and not debilitate, which will treat prisoners and not merely stigmatize them, which will regard them as human beings whom we must strive to restore to usefulness and not as open targets for societal vengeance. Religious groups in Belgium, England, France, and Sweden are active in campaigns for prison reform which are based on newer concepts and which hope to achieve the "spiritualization of public policy toward the criminal."

Religion has a responsibility in the field of crime prevention, but this responsibility must go far beyond recitation of the well-worn clichés about religion as a magical cure-all. There is in fact little scientific evidence that religion has played a major role in crime prevention. A host of studies show that the proportion of religious affiliates may even be higher among convicts than among the public at large. Religion's role must become a dynamic and positive one in this area.

Obviously, the problem of crime prevention is a highly complex one and is closely interrelated with other major problem areas ranging from the status of the family to economic security, among others. It must be a conscious factor in the consideration of all of these problems. But, in addition, religious people, dedicated as Jews are to a belief in the rule of law in the world, must make the achievement of good laws, respect for them, and obedience to these by all citizens, a primary goal in social action.

Capital Punishment

Many countries and nine states (Alaska, Delaware, Hawaii, Maine, Michigan, Minnesota, North Dakota, Rhode Island, and Wisconsin) have abolished capital punishment. In its origin, capital punishment was conceived as revenge. Modern apologists for this practice rationalize the need for it as a deterrent to other murderers and capital offenders. The ludicrousness of this contention is illustrated in a speech made in 1923 by Dr. George W. Hirchwey, a renowned penologist:

> "On June 21, 1877, 10 men were hanged in Pennsylvania for murderous conspiracy. The New York Herald predicted the wholesome effect of the terrible lesson. 'We may be certain,' it said, editorially, 'that the pitiless severity of the law will deter the most wicked from anything like the imitation of these crimes.' Yet, the night after this large scale execution, two of the witnesses at the trial of these men had been murdered and, within 2 weeks, five of the prosecutors had met the same fate."

Capital punishment by hanging was practiced in England in the eighteenth century, with hangings as gala public spectacles. There was no evidence that the crime rate lessened. As a matter of fact, pocket-picking became so prevalent in the audiences gathered to watch the public hangings of pick-pockets, it was eventually decided that hangings had to be made private.

Despite arguments to the contrary, there is no correlation between the severity of the punishment and frequency of crime. Warden Lewis E. Lawes of Sing Sing, who opposed capital punishment, noted that the murder rate does not rise when capital punishment is abolished. Minnesota and Michigan are just as safe as Iowa and Illinois even though the former two states have outlawed capital punishment.

In addition, the possibility of judicial error cannot be overlooked. Our system of justice is fallible because human beings are fallible. In 1955, in New York State, Louis Hoffner, who had been convicted of murder and had already served twelve years of a life sentence, was pardoned on the basis of new evidence which had become available. Such grievous errors occur. But what if Hoffner had been given death instead of life imprisonment? We must not make it impossible for such tragic errors to be corrected.

Capital punishment is an inhumane anachronism. It is frequently argued that gas and electrocution have made death painless, but even this has been seriously questioned. Aside from physical pain, the mental torture preceding such a "painless death" is beyond calculation. In addition, the torment and stigma inflicted upon relatives, who have committed no crime, is savagely cruel. Perhaps worst of all is what such barbarity does to society itself. Not only is capital punishment illogical and futile; from the standpoint of religion, it is a brutalization of the human spirit and an arrogation to vindictive man of the life-taking power which inheres only in God.

Juvenile Delinquency

One has only to scan today's newspaper headlines or talk to Americans to sense concern, verging on alarm, about the growth of juvenile delinquency in the U. S. Cold statistics show the picture: juvenile crime has jumped 42% in the past six years. A million children in 1956, according to the Attorney General of the U. S., will commit juvenile crimes serious enough for them to be picked up by the police. "Serious crimes," declared the Senate Sub-Committee on Juvenile Delinquency in 1954, "are being committed by twelve- to fifteen-year-olds in alarming number." F. B. I. statistics show that assaults by children in 1953 jumped 100% above the previous year, and the number of teen-age murderers and rapists is on the rise.

The Senate Sub-Committee was not being unduly melodramatic when it said:

> "In the fight against juvenile delinquency this nation can be said to be fiddling while Rome burns. We devote much attention, energy, and resources—and rightly so—to the fight against communism, both at home and abroad. We are waging that fight to keep this nation free. To what avail is that fight if the moral fiber of more and more of our children is being undermined? These are the children who will one day become our nation's leaders. It is for them that we are fighting to keep America free.
>
> "We devote untold millions to the protection of our national resources through reforestation, prevention of soil erosion, and the like. But we are neglecting our biggest national resource—our children and youth."

What is causing the spreading blight of juvenile delinquency? Narrow "explanations" are not helpful in coming to grips with the roots of this problem. The newspapers frequently quote leading churchmen as contending that the lack of religion is the cause of juvenile delinquency. That there is a moral breakdown involved in the problem of juvenile delinquency is unquestioned, but if we have learned anything about juvenile delinquency, it is that we can no longer rely on any one of the old over-simple "explanations." The White House Conference on Juvenile Delinquency, which was held in 1954, stressed the correct approach that juvenile crime has multiple causes. It results from the interaction of complex psychological, sociological and economic pressures, and solutions must be found in a coordinated approach which combines contributions from several disciplines. Every study underlines the crucial importance of the broken home and rejecting parents in both poor and well-to-do families, in contributing to delinquency. But the delinquency of society is equally responsible. Delinquency is related to the pressures and patterns of society. For example, juvenile delinquency rose during World War II, decreased at war's end, and then mounted steadily with the intensification of the cold war. Bertram Beck, director of the Special Juvenile Delinquency Project, associated with the United States Children's Bureau, has stressed the relationship between the tensions of society and juvenile delinquency:

> "The positive correlation between the rate of delinquency and war and cold war cannot be ignored. It is hard to instill those built-in controls of hostile behavior when children are being reared in a world that reeks of hostility and in which the whole economy is geared to the ultimate in expression of hostility—death and destruction."

There are many other factors which may contribute to the ominous increase in juvenile delinquency, including slums, lack of parental affection, racial discrimination, sadistic crime books, violence on television, and a host of other influences. This is not the place for a detailed study and analysis of juvenile delinquency. It is enough to know that it is a serious threat in virtually every community in the U. S., and thus confronts the synagogues and churches with a major challenge.

The synagogue cannot neglect the general problem of juvenile delinquency in the community. There are two aspects of the problem of perhaps particular interest to the Jewish community. One of these is the small number of Jewish juvenile delinquents, far below their proportion in the population. N. Goldberg in his study of Los Angeles police records of 1933–1947 found this strikingly borne out. Why? This question was put to Justice Justine Wise Polier, an experienced judge in the New York Domestic Relations Court and a distinguished Jewish communal leader. She pointed to the following factors:

(1) Jewish homes are usually characterized by strong cohesive bonds. Alcoholism and desertion are rare in Jewish homes as compared to the general population. The Jewish family usually reflects strong concern by both parents, not just the mother, for the welfare of the child.

(2) The Jewish community in cities throughout the U. S. has pioneered and excelled in providing psychiatric and social work facilities to serve troubled children and to provide family service counselling. These services frequently nip emotional problems before they bloom into anti-social activity.

(3) Jewish parents tend to be less repressive and more accepting of their children than most parents. While it may be true that Jewish parents frequently have exaggerated expectations in regard to their children's achievements, few seem to rely on corporal punishment or other harsh methods of discipline. In addition, in general, Jews appear to hold and to teach their children a more accepting attitude toward sex and also toward divorce where the marital relationship is intolerable.

(4) Jews have made a successful adjustment to American life. In the early years of the twentieth century, when Jewish immigration from Eastern Europe was at flood tide, the number of Jewish delinquents and criminals was not inconsiderable. Similar maladjustments attended most waves of immigration, such as the movement into New York City of the Irish in the nineteenth century, the Italians in the early twentieth, or the Negroes after World War I and the Puerto Ricans in recent decades. It is reasonable to assume that one factor in the low crime rate among Jews today is the successful integration which Jews have made into the pattern of American life.

More studies should be made of the reasons for the low crime rate within the Jewish group as well as within such groups as the Chinese. Perhaps these studies would reveal some insights which might be utilized by the general community in its attack on the problem of juvenile delinquency.

Another important aspect of the problem of juvenile delinquency is that behavior which takes the form of anti-minority violence— that is, anti-social behavior directed against Jews, Negroes, Puerto Ricans, or other minorities. An American Jewish Committee bulletin recently listed the following incidents illustrating such behavior:

Boston: Three teen-agers stop a ten-year-old boy in Franklin Park and ask him if he is Jewish. He replies: "Yes." They beat him savagely. Other hoodlums climax their assaults upon Jewish children by murdering a young rabbi.

Chicago: Five white youngsters chase a lone Negro boy on the South Side. They corner him in an alley, knife him so badly that he is hospitalized.

New Orleans: Teen-agers choose the swastika for their club emblem, attack and severely injure two Negroes.

Philadelphia: High school students organize a Hitler youth gang and stage demonstrations. Other gangs beat up Jewish students. Still others desecrate synagogues.

New York: Gangs of Irish and Puerto Rican youths battle each other with baseball bats, knives and "zip" guns.

Sometimes, analysis reveals, naked bigotry is at the bottom of such incidents. In some Southern communities, segregationalist demagogues have deliberately incited demonstrations by white school children against the integration of Negroes into the public schools. But not all outbursts, which appear on the surface to involve bigotry, actually stem from this cause. A study of conflict between rival groups of Italian, Jewish and Negro boys in New York City showed that it was not prejudice but a clash for use of inadequate community facilities such as parks and playgrounds that sparked the conflict. Premature and hasty explanations of such incidents can work harm. Careful study is indispensable in isolating the real causal factors and planning counteractive and preventive programs. Such programs should include close cooperation between the police, social workers, juvenile courts, and community groups like churches and synagogues.

We are not yet as a nation coming to grips effectively with the basic causes of delinquency in a concerted and intensive manner. The lurid newspaper treatment of juvenile delinquency stirs violent emotions but what is needed is cool thinking and planning by citizens. Too many Americans subscribe to the idea that the way to solve this problem is to beat sense into these "hoodlums" and even to apply the death sentence to fifteen- and sixteen-year-old children convicted of capital offenses. The work of the Gluecks and other social scientists demonstrate that most delinquents had been raised on a fare of severe punishment and that the effect was anything but salutary. The late Msgr. Edward J. Flanagan, founder of Boys Town, Omaha, Nebraska, said the hairbrush is "grossly oversold" as an instrument of character development. Speaking from long and successful experience in dealing with delinquent boys, he contended that such punishment "warps the boy's social outlook, causes him to look upon society as his enemy, hardens and embitters him." Bertram Beck has indicated that there are better methods available than the "nightstick approach":

> "New ways of dealing with delinquents do not advocate a mushy sentimentality or a coddling of these youths. They do advocate both an art and a science of both firmness and kindness, meeting the needs of the youth as they can be perceived through the application of what we know of human development. To carry out these new ways there is demanded, for example, that our juvenile courts have a staff of trained probation officers.
> "Only 11 per cent of all the juvenile officers doing probation work in the United States have the necessary professional training. In half of the juvenile courts in the United States, there are no probation services. To remedy conditions like this, to give new ways a chance, their first chance, is the hard answer to the problem and the answer that most people do not want to hear."

We have, however, made more progress in dealing with the juvenile criminal than we have with adult criminals. For example, there is widespread acceptance of the need for juvenile courts. They are not miniature criminal courts but places where a child's problems may be handled by a special judge in an informal way in his private chambers. This is a significant advance in concept, but our actual practice is disappointing. Of the 3,000 counties in the U. S., the juvenile courts of only a few approximate the standards set twenty-five years ago by the U. S. Children's Bureau and the National Probation Association. Too many such courts are juvenile in name only and actually follow the lines of criminal procedure. Many juvenile court judges are political hacks, hostile to the very philosophy of the court, and swamped by an impossible case load. The number of probation and parole officers is grossly inadequate. The 7,500 such officers we now have are only 30% of those needed on the basis of a maximum case load. These workers are usually poorly trained, underpaid, and so overburdened that often their investigations and supervision are superficial and unsatisfactory. Our detention facilities for delinquent children are disgraceful. Sherwood Norman, director of detention services of the National Probation and Parole Association, has reported that "100,000 children from 7 to 17 are detained each year in jails and jail-like places of detention throughout the country. Most of these county jails have been classified as unfit for federal adult prisoners." With all this, the principle of the juvenile court is constructive and necessary. Aroused citizens can make sure that the high purposes of the program are not defeated by false economy and careless practice.

If juvenile delinquency is so multi-faceted a problem, can we really do something about it? Or can we only wait, as we do with a hurricane, for it to blow itself out? We can do a good deal to cut down juvenile delinquency if we make better use of the tools and the knowledge we already have. We can strengthen and raise the standards of our juvenile courts. We can attack the problem of slum housing which breeds delinquency. We can make sure that we provide adequate recreational facilities, including trained workers supervising attractive programs. We can strongly augment the psychiatric and social work facilities available to the children in our community. We can greatly improve our schools, train teachers better, have smaller classes. We can insist that our public schools do a better job of "screening" potential delinquents; this will require a substantial but urgent increase in the number of psychologists and psychiatric social workers serving the schools. We can, through our churches and synagogues and other institutions, better equip parents for the difficult task of understanding their children's needs and raising them as responsible citizens. We can train special groups of policemen to work with juvenile offenders. We can improve the calibre of our training schools for delinquent children. We can insist upon better coordination among public and private social agencies, police, and community organizations in meeting the community-wide problem of juvenile delinquency. We can, in short, really try to prevent juvenile delinquency and, when a child becomes delinquent, we can try and try hard, to treat him and restore him to decent citizenship.

Would it work? Herman Rikelman, director of Community and Personal Services of the Jewish Board of Guardians of New York, has estimated that we can reduce juvenile delinquency by 75% through intelligent application of present knowledge. This is being done today in several cities. Passaic, New Jersey, for example, has developed a community program which has brought the rate of juvenile delinquency down each year at the same time that the national figures have been skyrocketing. Such programs cost money. They require a drastic change in the philosophy which, for example, leads Washington, D. C. to spend more money for the care of monkeys in the zoo than for children in Washington detention homes. But neglect of this problem costs us much more, not only in terms of dollars but, even more, in the squandering of our human resources.

An enlightened program does not require the substitution of sentimentality for sense. What is needed is a combination of firmness and understanding. An example of what can be done when these qualities are combined is described by Howard Whitman in *Terror in the Streets*. When John Dierke became principal of Everett Junior High School in San Francisco a few years ago, he found a school which was a virtual battle-ground for juvenile delinquents. Many were zoot-suiters armed with blackjacks and knives which they had no reluctance to use. They also enjoyed such less violent pursuits as ringing fire alarms and flooding the school washrooms. Dierke, a former basketball player and coach, worked out an approach which was simple but new to the school: "Boys," he said to the kids, "here's the pitch. You play on our team and I'll do everything I can for you. But you try to bust up the team and, brother—watch out."

The boys soon recognized Dierke as a square shooter—firm but fair. Dierke persuaded them to give up their weapons, stop wearing black shirts, cut their long hair—and they actually seemed relieved. He didn't preach and he didn't "make examples" of anybody. Whitman described the results:

> "After a while, Everett Junior High became a show-school of San Francisco—a place where the city proudly sent visitors, instead of a production mill for hoodlums. Dierke, whether or not he was able to tag on the sociological labels, was actually practising the theory of responsibility: the golden mean between the punishers and the coddlers. He loved his boys without being mushy. He was firm with them without being cruel. For what he handed his boys on a silver platter, he asked just one thing—responsibility—in return."

THE ROLE OF THE SYNAGOGUE

The first responsibility of the synagogue is really to know the community of which it is a part. In relation to the particular problems dealt with in this chapter, the Social Action or Community Affairs Committee should conduct an informal survey and analysis of such questions as these: What is the extent of adult crime in the community? Of juvenile delinquency? Are the figures rising? What are the social agencies doing in this connection? How about the Jewish agencies? Are there sufficient facilities for the mentally ill? Do the public schools have enough psychologists and psychiatric social workers to "screen" troubled youngsters before they become delinquent? Do the schools have remedial reading and other preventive programs? Is there a juvenile court and, if so, does it operate effectively? Are juvenile judges selected on the basis of qualification or political favors? What are the facilities for detention of juveniles who have committed crimes? Are the public and private training schools doing a job of rehabilitating or merely of custody of juveniles? Are juvenile offenders who are sent to institutions being helped to function in society or do most become repeaters? Are probation and parole fully and effectively utilized? Are the prisons which serve the community doing an effective job of treating prisoners through psychiatric and vocational therapy? Is capital punishment still legal in the state? What community agencies and groups are working on these problems in the community?

It is, of course, impossible to indicate on which facet of this picture a particular synagogue should focus its attention; the local circumstances, as revealed by a study, will determine that. Because citizens by and large are ignorant of these problems and how their own community meets or fails to meet them, the synagogue committee can make a significant contribution to public understanding once it has informed itself of the local situation. The process of self-education might well include visits to one or more of the social agencies, juvenile courts, private and public training schools, detention houses, and state prisons. In addition, much information can be secured by mail from the National Probation and Parole Association, and the U. S. Children's Bureau, Washington, D. C.

Having developed a picture of the local scene, the committee should then draw up a report, including its own recommendations of what needs to be done by the committee, by interested individuals of the congregation as citizens, or perhaps by the congregation itself as a body. Ways can be found to bring these problems dramatically to the attention of the congregants. A forum on "Juvenile Delinquency in Our Community—Our Responsibility," a debate on the ethics of capital punishment, an address by a local penologist on the moral issues underlying the prison system—

these and many other techniques can be used to break through the barrier of passivity which seems to isolate citizens from the needs and problems of their own community.

In many communities, where recreational facilities, public and private, are inadequate, the synagogue may well consider making available its facilities to the general community. Recreation programs in synagogues and churches can do much to curb juvenile delinquency and to promote constructive intergroup and interracial relationships among children and adults alike. Not the least of the values to be derived from such a program would be the enhanced status of the synagogue as an institution which has taken its responsibilities to the larger community seriously. One of the synagogues which so opens its facilities is the Stephen Wise Free Synagogue. In a letter written shortly before his death, Rabbi Sidney Goldstein, rabbi emeritus of the Free Synagogue, deplored the "sinful waste of space and accommodations of which almost every synagogue is guilty." He added: "If I had the power, I should commandeer the rooms and equipment of churches and synagogues everywhere, rooms and equipment which are at present in use only a few hours a week, when we so desperately need every facility every day and every evening throughout the year."

In his extremely useful study of juvenile delinquency, Dr. Benjamin Fine stressed the role of religion as one of the important forces needed in developing a rounded program of action. He said in part:

> "On the community front, the church can take a dynamic role in helping to eliminate those conditions within the community that lead toward juvenile delinquency. Young people should be encouraged more by religious institutions to participate in service activities such as helping the sick, aiding the handicapped, promoting citizenship, inspecting their own localities, making reports on health, housing, playgrounds, and assuming some responsibility in promoting the welfare of those younger than themselves.
>
> "A primary factor in juvenile delinquency is the broken home, whether physically broken or emotionally so, and religious institutions must seek ways of trying to lower the rate of this breakage, or ways to meet the resulting needs of the child.
>
> "The churches and temples must find more ways to enhance the moral tone of the adult community, must increase or create in the child a respect for spiritual standards that will be accepted and that will be lasting.

"There should be greater cooperation between the churches and synagogues and all other social institutions that are working against delinquency. Directly coordinated with this is the need for religious institutions to make a greater effort to attract persons released from penal institutions or training schools, to show a sincere interest in making the individual feel wanted, and to encourage them in developing and maintaining a participating interest in the church's valuable activities."

BIBLIOGRAPHY

ABRAHAMSEN, DAVID. "Who Are the Guilty? A Study of Education and Crime," New York: Grove Press, 1958. Paperback.

ALEXANDER, FRANZ and WILLIAM HEALY. The Roots of Crime. New York: A. A. Knopf, 1935.

BARNES, HARRY E. and NEGLEY K. TEETERS. New Horizons in Criminology. New York: Prentice-Hall, 1951.

BARRON, MILTON. The Juvenile in a Delinquent Society. New York: Alfred A. Knopf, 1954.

BLOCK, HERBERT A. and ARTHUR NIEDERHOFFER. The Gang: A Study of Adolescent Behavior. N. Y.: Philosophical Library, 1958.

DEUTSCH, ALBERT. Our Rejected Children. Boston: Little, Brown Co., 1950.

FINE, BENJAMIN. 1,000,000 Delinquents. New York: World Publishing Co., 1955.

FLANAGAN, FATHER EDWARD J. Understand Your Boy. New York: Rinehart and Co., 1950.

Friends Committee on Legislation. "This Life We Take: The Case Against Capital Punishment." 1959. A pamphlet

GLUECK, SHELDON and ELEANOR. Predicting Delinquency and Crime. Cambridge, Mass.: Harvard University Press, 1959.

GLUECK, SHELDON and ELEANOR. Unraveling Juvenile Delinquency. Cambridge, Mass.: Harvard University Press, 1950.

LEIGH, RUTH. Man's Right to Life. New York: UAHC Commission on Social Action, 1959. Issue of Conscience Pamphlet.

LEVY, ANNA. Other People's Children. N. Y.: Ronald Press Company, 1956.

POLIER, JUSTINE WISE. "Parental Rights: The Need for Law and Social Action." N. Y.: Child Welfare League of America, 1958. A pamphlet.

SLAVSON, S. R. Re-Educating the Delinquent. New York: Harper and Brothers, 1954.

WINEMAN, DAVID. Children Who Hate. Glencoe, Ill.: Free Press, 1952.

ZILBOORG, GREGORY. The Psychology of the Criminal Act and Punishment. New York: Harcourt, Brace Co., 1954.

CIVIC REFORM

". . . How mighty are your sins;
Ye that afflict the just, that take a
ransom,
And that turn aside the needy in
the gate." (*Amos 5:12*)

THE PROPHETS poured their wrath upon those public officials who practiced corruption. Condemning the corruption he saw all about him, Amos concluded ironically: "Therefore, the prudent doth keep silent in such a time, for it is an evil time."

The prudent were silent then. And they have been too frequently silent in modern times. At the end of the nineteenth century, virtually every American city was tainted by official corruption. Like the federal government which was rocked by scandals, state and municipal government had fallen to a low estate. When Lincoln Steffens turned his journalistic floodlight upon municipal government, he found city after city run by political machines, presided over by a "boss" who was openly allied with the underworld and with unscrupulous public utilities. The objectives of these machines were massing power and fleecing the gullible citizenry; the task of running an efficient government was scarcely on their agendas. Only when conditions became intolerable did citizens organize drives for reform and "throw the rascals out."

The shocking exposures of municipal corruption by Lincoln Steffens and other "muckrakers" revealed the "shame of the cities" and aroused citizens, at least temporarily, to the plight of their local government. During the past fifty years, the state of our civic health has undoubtedly improved. Many American cities today are models of clean and efficient municipal government. There is no Al Capone casting his fearful shadow over the city of Chicago; the streets of New York are no longer bloodied by the handiwork of Murder, Incorporated; St. Louis is not the private plum of a Boss Tweed, and Kansas City has broken the steely grip of the Pendergast machine.

But civic corruption has not been completely eliminated from the American scene. For every American city that has broken through the barrier of public inertia and insured itself of decent municipal government, there are other cities which continue to be victimized by subtle, usually subterranean, forms of corruption. The Kefauver investigations of 1952 painted an ugly portrait of political corruption in many of our cities, a portrait of cynicism which cuts across political parties.

Unlike the situation of 50 years ago when corruption usually meant an omnipotent and undisguised boss alternately manipulating and intimidating public officials, the situation today is more complex and, like an iceberg, mostly beneath the surface. The stigmata of civic corruption in contemporary American cities include well-concealed connections between city officials and the underworld; political power exerted by racketeers parading as respectable businessmen; widespread graft and extortion; political deals and payoffs; and judicious distribution of fat municipal contracts.

Just as the prophets could not be silent in the face of social and political degradation, neither can those in our time who take their religious convictions seriously, who feel impelled by them to brave the risks of imprudence. The American rabbinate has produced a number of such men who proudly bear the scars of battles gained in honorable and courageous struggle against civic corruption.

A leading figure in this regard has been Rabbi Samuel Mayerberg of Kansas City who was so wanting in prudence that, in 1932, he chose to do battle with the Pendergast machine, one of the most tightly-controlled and vicious political gangs in American history. The full story of Rabbi Mayerberg's campaign is recited in his fascinating book *Chronicle of an American Crusader.*

"While I hold the firm conviction that ministers should never engage in partisan political activities," the rabbi writes, "I also cherish the unwavering belief that, where iniquity runs rampant, where depraved and selfish men prey upon a community, it is not only the right but also the compelling duty of the minister to lead in the movement to eradicate such evil powers from his community. If one holds the fearless, God-intoxicated prophets of Israel as his human ideal as I do, one is impelled by his conscience to enter the fray with all the courage and strength he can summon."

But what has religion to do with civic virtue and political corruption? "A shriveled and pitiful thing," says Rabbi Mayerberg, "is that religion which is an affair of synagogue or church only, of special times and occasions, and nothing else. What is the value of that man's religion, whose fellow-man is not the better for it; whom it does not impel to do something for the common weal; in whom it does not kindle a zealous spirit to diffuse, according to his opportunities, light and joy in the lives of others? Do not, therefore, grow indifferent to the conduct of public affairs. Watch them jealously and zealously with an eye to justice and truth. Keep your indignation warm for genuine abuses. Do not say, they concern me not, not until they touch me will I stir. For as James Russell Lowell has written,

> 'They are slaves most base
> Whose love of right is for themselves, and not
> For all their race.' "

On May 21, 1932, Rabbi Mayerberg entered the fray by exploding a massive bombshell before the Government Study Club of Kansas City in the form of an address entitled "A Non-Partisan and Non-Political Administration for Kansas City." In that address the rabbi proved, with full documentation, that there was an alliance between the city administration and the underworld; and that the city manager was violating the City Charter in countless ways, including the misuse of public funds. He demanded that the City

Council remove the City Manager from office and clean up the mess. In a matter of days, community organizations, ministers, and individual citizens flocked around Rabbi Mayerberg, eager for direction in the campaign to clean up Kansas City. The influential *Kansas City Star* backed the rabbi. The fight was on.

The Reform movement snowballed and a non-partisan political agency, called the Charter League, was created. Rabbi Mayerberg was the president, and other distinguished citizens of Kansas City gave it their full support. The League rocked Kansas City by starting a drive to recall the City Council for its refusal to clean up the corruption, and the *Kansas City Star* carried the story of corrupt bossism to the average citizen. Realizing that the reformers were striking close to the nerve center, the racketeers decided to get tough.

"They tapped my telephones in my temple study," Rabbi Mayerberg recalls, "and in the Charter League offices. They ransacked the files in my study and stole the records from the League office. They threatened me and they attempted to bribe me . . . Constant threats came from the underworld . . . As I drove to a North Side meeting one night, my car was forced to the curb and a shot was fired. Fortunately, friends had equipped my car with bullet-proof glass. After this incident the governor, upon the insistence of friends, assigned to me two men, deputized as deputy coroners." The bodyguards accompanied him everywhere, attended all temple services, and guarded homes at which the rabbi officiated at weddings and funerals. For months, the rabbi kept a loaded pistol on the floor beside his bed. Citizens continued to be so concerned for his safety that the Sanford Brown Post of the American Legion sent word to the leader of the hoodlums that if anything happened to Rabbi Mayerberg they would clean out the North End.

One underworld character went to bat for the rabbi. Apparently disgruntled and hostile to the then-leader of the racketeers, this man, who identified himself only as Pal, took to phoning Rabbi Mayerberg at 3:00 A.M. to pass on leads and bits of useful information about the gangsters. Pal fed information on narcotics, slot machines, illegal liquor, and the rabbi passed on the tips to the United States Attorney and federal agents who would then make the necessary raids. Pal's information was unfailingly precise.

It took ten arduous years to beat the machine. With the help of the federal courts, crooked election officials were sent to jail, and Tom Pendergast himself was consigned to Leavenworth for income tax evasion. In 1940, under the leadership of the Clean-Up Committee, using a broom as a symbol, the people of Kansas City swept out the machine and, by a vast majority, voted in a reform mayor and seven of the eight councilmen endorsed by the Clean-Up Committee. Rabbi Mayerberg described the results of the bitter but successful campaign: "The spirit of our citizenry has changed completely. The pall of fear has disappeared. Heads are held erect and civic pride has replaced cringing shame . . . Our community has learned the full significance of the saying of the Book of Proverbs, 'Righteousness exalteth a nation, but sin is a reproach to any people.' " (*Prov. 14:34.*)

And what about Rabbi Mayerberg's congregation? How was it affected by the agonizing struggle in which its rabbi was engaged? Rabbi Mayerberg doesn't minimize the difficulties of the ordeal: "My congregation suffered severely during these first months of our civic battle. Many members resigned under Pendergast pressure. Some visited me privately (under cover of night) to tell me that they believed in the cause, but that they must withdraw because they were victims of reprisals. Almost every business required some sort of city permit; their owners were certain the threats to cancel permits would be carried out and they would be driven from business. Others informed me their taxes had been raised exorbitantly. One real estate owner told me that a building, assessed at $25,000 had been raised to $150,000 . . ."

Like the rabbi, the congregation survived:

> "While the campaign was in progress, the machine was especially vicious toward me. It persuaded several of my members to denounce me on radio and in the press. It circulated rumors that I was to be dismissed immediately after the campaign. Members were forced to send in resignations. I believed many of the rumors to be false, but I was resolved to fight hard to justify my participation in a righteous and non-partisan cause and to save my cherished career. The regular Board meeting of the congregation fell on the night after election. I attended it as usual. A number of resignations were read. Promptly a Board member moved that they be accepted without regret, explaining that he felt that men who resigned because of my civic activities didn't deserve membership in B'nai Jehudah. One after another the Board members voiced their commendation. A resolution was unanimously adopted commending my activities and thanking me for contributing to the welfare of our city. I had come to that meeting prepared to defend the right of ministers everywhere to translate

their spiritual affirmations into realities of civic righteousness. The generosity of the Board members so overwhelmed me that I could not speak my gratitude; they received it by the smile through my tears."

A majority of the members of the Temple backed the Board's stand, many of them as active members of the Charter League.

Other Jewish religious leaders in America have distinguished themselves in struggles to cleanse their communities of civic pollution. The late Dr. Sidney E. Goldstein, in his *The Synagogue and Social Welfare,* reported on two successful crusades against civic corruption in New York City. The first involved his own congregation:

"In 1907 I served a congregation in one of the suburbs of Brooklyn to supplement my income from the Free Synagogue, which in the early years had a very small budget. There I once preached against the political corruption that was then the shame of our city. Immediately after the sermon the president of the congregation protested, and so did a number of his friends. I discovered, however, what I did not know when I accepted the post—that the president was involved in questionable practices in the community, so unethical that they seemed to me to disqualify him to serve as president. I went to him, told him what I had discovered, and asked that he resign. To my disappointment and chagrin he refused, demanding, "Why don't you resign?" To strengthen his position he called a meeting of the Board of Trustees, but before the meeting appointed an additional number of trustees from among his friends, which was contrary to the Religious Corporation Law of the state. A number of members sympathized with my position, and when the meeting of the Board was called a brilliant young lawyer arose and said, "This meeting is called in violation of the Religious Corporation Law of the State of New York and is therefore invalid." The president looked at him in anger. "To what law do you refer?" The lawyer then read from the law, which clearly stated that the Board of Trustees could consist of only a limited number and that the president therefore had exceeded his powers. The president, becoming more irate, stated with all the vehemence of which he was capable, "I declare that law out of order!" A good part of the congregation resented his action and seceded. We then formed a new congregation, dedicated to a new religious and ethical program in the community."

After Dr. Goldstein had become associate rabbi of the Free Synagogue (now the Stephen Wise Free Synagogue), he and Rabbi Wise became deeply involved in the major effort to rid New York of Mayor James Walker and his corrupt machine.

> "In 1929 I accepted the chairmanship of the Citizens' Committee for the election of Norman Thomas, because I saw in Thomas not only a protest against the incompetence, corruption, and crime in the city government of New York, but also because I believed in the validity of the social program he advocated. Some members of the congregation did not like this action on my part. They gave all the customary reasons for disapproval. But I discovered the real truth that they were all members of the Democratic Party, allied with Tammany Hall. The vote for Norman Thomas in 1929, to the surprise of all of us, totaled 250,000 and more. We looked upon this as a protest vote, and those of us who had been active in the campaign decided it would be an act of betrayal on our part against 250,000 citizens if we did nothing but protest. We met in the home of Norman Thomas shortly after the election, to organize what we called the City Affairs Committee and to adopt a program of action."

What Rabbis Mayerberg, Wise and Goldstein achieved in Kansas City and New York, many Christian clergymen and lay religious leaders have accomplished in their communities. In 1914, in Cincinnati, a charter committee was formed in the church parlor of Christ Episcopal Church, the rector, Dr. Frank Nelson, serving as one of the leaders. This committee issued a trumpet call for civic integrity—a call which shook the pillars of the entrenched regime which had given Cincinnati the reputation of being the worst governed city in the United States. The charter committee, functioning on a non-partisan basis and consisting of religious leaders of all faiths, challenged Cincinnati's political regime and finally turned it out. Murray Seasongood, a leader of Rockdale Avenue Reform Temple, was deeply involved in the work of the Charter League. Not long thereafter, the voters of Cincinnati elected him mayor. Today Cincinnati merits its hard-won reputation as a city of good, clean government.

THE ROLE OF THE SYNAGOGUE

But, it will be said, civic reform means getting mixed up with "politics" and a synagogue should not get involved in "politics."

Such statements assume that politics is a nasty piece of business that must be avoided by respectable folk. But what is it? Webster's Universal Unabridged Dictionary defines politics as: "The science of government; that part of *ethics* [italics ours] which consists in the regulation and government of a nation or state, for the preservation of its safety, peace and prosperity . . . and the protection of its citizens in their rights, with the preservation and improvement of their *morals* [italics ours]."

Obviously, Judaism, a religion grounded in ethics, must be concerned with politics in this sense. The ethical insights of prophetic Judaism must be applied to the specific social and political problems of our time. Such questions as civic reform no less than civil rights, genocide, Point Four, immigration, have political aspects, but they involve ethical concepts on which Judaism must have something to say. It is *partisan* politics that the synagogue must and does avoid. It is not our task to further Republicans over Democrats or vice versa, but it is our task to apply the principles we profess in the world in which we live.

Though local civic reform may appear to be an obvious and immediate area for study and action by the community affairs or social action committee of the synagogue, it should be entered warily. Nothing would be more disastrous for both the synagogue and for the community than a mishandled local crusade. Rabbi Sidney Goldstein properly was against civic crusades led by "immature amateurs and by men who lack a passion for civic righteousness." Both limitations are significant. A half-hearted effort would be pre-doomed to failure. Well meaning but inept amateurs might well harm their cause more than they would help it. And, it must be emphasized, all such efforts *must* be non-partisan in character.

With these warnings in mind, however, the local committee may well decide to study the local pattern of governmental operations, particularly if there are indications of serious mismanagement and corruption.

Every experience demonstrates that the first task must be the amassing of a conclusive body of facts. This task will be difficult and perhaps dangerous. Competent and honest counsel will be required.

Second, the facts must be conveyed to the congregation.

Third, if the facts warrant it, an effort should be made to find a non-partisan, non-denominational forum in which to carry the issue to the public. Hopefully, a citizens committee can be developed which will be broadly representative of the decent forces in the community, and which will address itself effectively to the civic conscience.

BIBLIOGRAPHY

"Ethics in Government; a Report by the Minnesota Governor's Committee on Ethics in Government to Governor Orville L. Freeman." St. Paul, Minnesota. A pamphlet.

GOLDSTEIN, SIDNEY E. *The Synagogue and Social Welfare.* New York: Bloch Publishing Co., 1955.

MAYERBERG, SAMUEL S. *Chronicle of an American Crusader.* New York: Bloch Publishing Co., 1944.

SALTER, J. T. *Boss Rule: Portraits in City Politics.* New York: 1935.

SPITZ, DAVID. *Democracy and the Challenge of Power.* N. Y.: Columbia University Press, 1958.

STEFFENS, LINCOLN. *The Shame of the Cities.* New York: Peter Smith, 1948.

SWARTHOUT, JOHN MAX and ERNEST RANDALL BARTLEY. *Principles and Problems of State and Local Government.* N. Y.: Oxford University Press, 1958.

ZINK, HAROLD. *City Bosses in the U. S.* Durham, N. C.: Duke University Press, 1930.

CIVIL RIGHTS

"Have we not all one Father:
Hath not one God created us?"
(*Malachi 2:10*)

JUDAISM GAVE to the world the concept of the sanctity and dignity of the individual. All men are equal because they are created in the image of God. Respect for the civil rights of others is each man's duty to God. "What is hateful unto thee, do not do unto thy neighbor." (*Babylonian Talmud, Shabbos 8*)

In the Midrash (*Bereshis Rabbah*) it is asked: Why did God create one man, Adam? The answer is pungent and illuminating. "Man was created one so that no one can say to his fellow, 'My father was greater than your father.' " The major objective of synagogue social action and of Jewish community relations is the protection and enhancement of equal rights and equal opportunities for all persons and the creation of conditions that contribute toward vital Jewish living. The security of the Jewish group, like all groups, rests upon the concepts of democratic freedoms, of democratic equality, of individual rights and personal liberties for all, regardless of race and religion.

Jewish organizations have been in the forefront of the struggle to achieve equality of opportunity for the Negro, the Mexican, the Oriental, and members of all groups victimized by discrimination. There is a growing recognition that not only anti-Semitism, which happily is waning in America, but discrimination against any racial or religious group in American life, threatens the ultimate security of the Jew. More important for our purposes is the duty of the synagogue, in order to fulfill itself, to bring to bear the full weight of its moral prestige in the achievement of equality of opportunity for all men, regardless of race, color or national origin. For this principle is the essence of our religious faith as it is the essence of democracy itself.

The term "civil rights," as used in this book, refers to the inherent right of every citizen to equality of opportunity regardless of race, color, or national origin. The area of "civil liberties"—by which are designated freedoms, such as speech, assembly, press, and others, guaranteed to the individual by the Bill of Rights—will be dealt with separately in a later chapter. (See pages 112 ff) While these two areas are related, each has had in recent years a markedly different development.

It may be stated at the very outset that this generation, and particularly the last decade, has witnessed a profound revolution in race relations and in the strengthening of equal rights for all Americans. The U. S. has come a vast distance from slavery, but we have an agonizingly long distance yet to go before the gap between our democratic principles and practices is fully bridged. Yet all Americans are entitled to a justifiable sense of satisfaction in the far-reaching and significant gains we have made in recent years.

Prejudice and bigotry have become thoroughly unrespectable in American life. In the 1930's, when the backwash of Nazi poison infected the thinking of millions of Americans, anti-Semitism was a potent aspect of American life. Anti-Semitic organizations were powerful and active. Nazi Bundists marched through many American streets. The unctuous voice of Father Coughlin, carried over the radio networks, deposited its anti-Jewish propaganda in thousands of homes, and Fascist agitators peddled their bundles of hate in communities throughout the United States. Jews felt profoundly threatened, and it was natural that national Jewish organizations assumed the role of "defense agencies" to seek to protect the Jewish community from calumny and vilification.

A New Era

Now, happily, the picture in the U. S. is drastically changed. Partly as a result of the immense emotional impact of the war against nazism, doctrines of religious bigotry and prejudice have become clearly identified in the American mind as evil. Through the radio, the press, the movies, and television; through the efforts of voluntary human rights organizations and religious groups; through the influence of government; and, of course, through the basic sense of decency of most of the American people, prejudice has become associated in the public mind with un-Americanism. Anti-Semitic organizations today are few, largely ineffective and have no significant influence on the community-at-large. National Jewish organizations have little need to "defend" the Jewish community, for any bigoted attack on Jews is now likely to be rejected spontaneously by most Americans. Nonetheless, social snobbery and discrimination in employment and higher education continue to trouble American Jewry. These practices are usually not organized and are not sanctioned by responsible groups and opinion makers in American society. Herein is reflected the progress in recent decades.

As a result, national Jewish agencies have been able to minimize the "defense" character of their activities. They now conceive of themselves as community relations agencies and have developed broad-ranging positive programs, including the techniques of law and social action, designed to strengthen democracy by the promotion of equality of opportunity for all Americans. These agencies have progressed from a narrow program of Jewish defense to a mature program aimed at broadening the horizons of democracy itself. In this change in the character of Jewish agencies is reflected a profound American victory—won in their hearts and minds by the American people themselves, and no less significant than victories at Tarawa or Bastogne, or Pusan.

This does not mean that prejudice has been eliminated, that feelings of antagonism toward Jews, Negroes, Catholics, and even Protestant minorities do not lurk in many hearts. It means that in *articulating* such prejudice, there is no commonly accepted sanction which can be invoked. Indeed, one collides directly with what is becoming almost a taboo in decent American society. This is particularly true if one seeks to discriminate—that is, to put into action his prejudice against another American because of race, religion, or national origin.

For discrimination has become, in recent years, an odious word. Government on all levels—the Courts, the Executive Branch, the Congress, and individual states and communities—has accented the truth that discrimination solely because of race, color, or national origin is contrary to public policy. One of the most significant developments in American life during the past decade has been the change in our conception of the role of government in the area of civil rights. Today government affirms in principle its positive and active responsibility to protect and enhance the civil rights of all citizens. Our last three presidents—Roosevelt, Truman, Eisenhower—have clearly enunciated this principle and moved to enforce it by executive orders: Roosevelt through an FEP Commission during the war, and Truman and Eisenhower through special commissions set up to enforce non-discrimination under government contracts.* Today many states ** and cities have enacted Fair Employment Practices legislation, designed to prohibit discrimination in private employment. Such effective FEP laws as that operating in New York State, the pioneer in such legislation, have demonstrably reduced discrimination in employment and have opened the job market to many members of minority groups, particularly Negroes, previously excluded because of discrimination. With few exceptions such commissions have been able through conciliation and consultation to persuade employers and labor unions to make merit and not skin color or ancestry the basis of selection. Only rarely have they had to invoke the machinery of compulsion. Unquestionably, these laws have in them-

---

* "In connection with the performance of work under this contract, the contractor agrees not to discriminate against any employee or applicant for employment because of race, religion, color, or national origin. The aforesaid provision shall include, but not be limited to, the following: employment, upgrading, demotion, or transfer; recruitment or recruitment advertising; layoff or termination; rates of pay, or other forms of compensation; and selection for training, including apprenticeship. The contractor agrees to post hereafter in conspicuous places, available for employees or applicants for employment, notices to be provided by the contracting officer setting forth the provisions of the nondiscrimination clause."

** New York State, New Jersey, Massachusetts, Connecticut, New Mexico, Oregon, Rhode Island, Washington, Indiana, Wisconsin, Minnesota, Michigan and 35 cities.

selves broken discriminatory barriers in many areas of our economy. Unquestionably, also, they have exerted a powerful impact on the attitudes of millions of Americans who have come to associate discrimination with wrongdoing and lawlessness.

When President Truman's Committee on Civil Rights in 1948 presented its monumental report entitled "To Secure These Rights," it focused the sharp light of public attention dramatically on the nation's unfinished business in extending equal rights to all Americans. Once in the spotlight, this problem, which some consider our Number One national problem, has remained in the center of the stage of national interest. If anything, the East-West "cold war," with its bitter ideological contest between Communist tyranny and the free world, has invested the problem of race relations in the U. S. with an even stronger sense of urgency.

Legislation has been a formidable tool in the achievement of civil rights in the U. S., but many who only a few years ago, in the flush of excitement over the report of the President's Committee, regarded it as something of a panacea, are now aware of some of its limitations. In the years immediately following the report of the President's Committee, civil rights agencies, including national Jewish organizations, set as their first priority the enactment by Congress of a Federal Fair Employment Practices Act, with proper enforcement powers. Vast energies were expended to achieve this objective which promised to do so much in one broad stroke. But, despite a sympathetic President and evident sympathy and interest on the part of millions of Americans, no FEPC act was ever adopted by the Congress.

Federal Legislation

No federal FEPC act was adopted, primarily because of the undemocratic procedure in the U.S. Senate whereby a small minority of recalcitrant senators is usually able, through the use of the filibuster, to prevent the Senate from voting on crucial civil rights measures. Yet, the momentous racial revolution, set in motion by the U.S. Supreme Court decision on school segregation, has had a deep impact on the Congress as well. This was symbolized in 1957 by passage of the first national Civil Rights measure enacted since 1875. The Civil Rights Law established machinery to protect the voting rights of Negro citizens and it created a Civil Rights Commission, with broad investigatory powers. In many ways, the real teeth of the measure were pulled before the bill reached the floor. But that a civil rights measure, diluted as it was, could get through Congress was an unmistakable herald of a new dawn and a new day.

Almost two-thirds of the American people live in areas covered by either state or municipal Fair Employment Practices legislation. There is ample evidence that these acts have substantially benefited members of some minority groups, particularly Negroes. It is largely a matter of speculation, however, as to the extent to which discrimination against *Jews* has been reduced by such legislation. In most FEPC states, there are ordinarily few complaints of discrimination made by Jews. While this would appear to indicate a small amount of discrimination against Jews, it is more likely to signify that, because of the generally high level of employment, Jews prefer to move on to employment available elsewhere rather than to take the trouble of filing a complaint against a firm which has discriminated against them. In addition, as indicated in a study conducted by Dr. Gerhart Salinger, only 32% of the Jews questioned in New York State expressed familiarity with the N. Y. state law against discrimination and further questioning demonstrated that only about 8% actually understood the provisions of the law.

Experts on Jewish employment problems are aware that discriminatory practices continue to bar Jews from many industries and occupations of their choice. In addition, many FEP commissions understandably concentrate on breaking discriminatory patterns against those groups like the Negro, against whom discrimination is most acute. Jewish organizations, while continuing to join vigorously in campaigns to win additional FEP measures in states and cities not now covered, are giving serious consideration to suggestions for improving the enforcement of such laws already in existence and making them more effective instruments in dealing with the more subtle problems of discrimination against Jews.

Unlike Jews in the past who were prohibited from owning land and from membership in craft guilds, Jews in America face no legal bars to equal economic opportunity. Nor are they hemmed in by legally enforced segregation to which Negroes and other Americans of color are subjected. But discrimination takes many forms. The subtle forms of discrimination against Jewish job seekers have helped shape the occupational structure of American Jewry. Jews have tended to seek employment in Jewish firms or in those professions and operations where they could avoid the rebuffs to which they were subjected in the general labor market.

Paralleling the brightened prospects of civil rights in the federal government is the greatly intensified thrust of many state and city governments to strengthen civil rights guarantees. In 1959, for example, Ohio and California adopted strong FEPC measures. Colorado enacted a far-reaching fair housing law. New York City and Pittsburgh broke new human rights ground by making segregation in *private* housing illegal. Many Northern cities took bold new initiatives designed to reduce de facto school segregation. With one baleful eye fixed on the South, and the other eye fixed squarely on the 13,000,000 Negroes who clearly hold the balance of power in many political contests, Northern politicians are, with few exceptions, clambering aboard the civil rights bandwagon.

How widespread is discrimination against Jews in employment? There is no accurate measure. There are significant evidences, however, that discrimination against Jews, though declining, continues to be perceptible in many fields and widespread in some. In fields like public accounting, firms tend to be "Jewish" or "non-Jewish." For example, in a study made of the fifteen largest accounting firms in Cincinnati, of the 286 accountants working in those firms, only three were Jews. One of the three was a partner in his company. Employment agencies, both governmental and private, continue to report to investigators that Jews are consistently harder to place in many positions than either Protestants or Catholics. Only Negroes and, in the New York area, Puerto Ricans, are more difficult.

Despite local and state FEPC laws, many commercial employment agencies continue to accept discriminatory placement requests. The American Jewish Congress reported this finding after a survey by telephone of such agencies in Manhattan. The callers did not give their identity, merely asked if a "white Protestant" secretary is available. Of the 313 agencies called, 222 gave responses that could be used. Of them, 156 (70.3 per cent) said that they would attempt to fill the discriminatory order. Fourteen accepted the order with a certain amount of hesitation, indicating an awareness of the illegality of the request. The remaining 66 agencies (29.7 per cent) refused to honor the request.

There continue to be some barriers, sharply reduced from two decades ago in education and housing, steadily maintained in that last bastion of exclusivism, the country club and the snob resort. But it is certain that there is a tide flowing in America, with ever-increasing momentum, and that it will not subside until it has cleansed the American scene of all racial and religious barriers separating man from man.

School Segregation

A climactic achievement in the field of civil rights during the twentieth century was the Supreme Court decision of May 17, 1954, in which for the first time in American history, segregation by race in the public schools was declared by the highest court of the land to be illegal. This ruling was extended, shortly thereafter, into the areas of segregation in places of public recreation and interstate transportation. In these historic words, the Supreme Court, by unanimous vote, ushered in a new era in American human relations:

> "Today, education is perhaps the most important function of state and local governments. Compulsory school attendance laws and the great expenditures for education both demonstrate our recognition of the importance of education to our democratic society. It is required in the performance of our most basic public responsibilities, even service in the armed forces. It is the very foundation of good citizenship.
>
> "Today, it is a principal instrument in awakening the child to cultural values, in preparing him for later professional training, and in helping him to adjust normally to his environment.
>
> "In these days, it is doubtful that any child may reasonably be expected to succeed in life if he is denied the opportunity of an education. Such an opportunity, where the state has undertaken to provide it, is a right which must be made available to all on equal terms.
>
> "We come then to the question presented: Does segregation of children in public schools solely on the basis of race, even though the physical facilities and other 'tangible' factors may be equal, deprive the children of the minority group of equal educational opportunities? We believe that it does.
>
> "Such considerations apply with added force to children in grade and high schools. To separate them from others of similar age and qualifications solely because of their race generates a feeling of inferiority as to their status in the community that may affect their hearts and minds in a way unlikely ever to be undone.
>
> "We conclude that in the field of public education the doctrine of 'separate but equal' has no place. Separate educational facilities are inherently unequal."

The education of Negro children has been a subject of controversy since the earliest years of public education in this country. It was actually a crime in some slave states before the Civil War to teach a Negro to read and write, and even some of the "free" states didn't trouble to provide for Negro education. The last century has seen great progress. Even before the Supreme Court decision, every state acknowledged its responsibility to provide equal educational opportunity for every child, regardless of race. Actual practice, of course, was something else again and Negro schools were not only separate but invariably inferior. Seventeen states and the District of Columbia, at the time of the Court's decision, still required racial segregation in their public schools as a matter of law. Four other states made segregation permissible. Nor is this strictly a Southern or regional problem. Even in many cities of the North and West, school segregation has existed as a matter of fact, though not prescribed by law, because it results from residential segregation and local custom.

While the Supreme Court's decision is the blow which ultimately dooms the entire legal basis of segregation in the United States, that structure had already been seriously shaken. As indicated earlier, many racial barriers had been struck down during the previous decade, due in no small measure to the firm determination of Negroes themselves to win full citizenship. Thanks to the vigorous leadership of groups like the National Association for the Advancement of Colored People and the tireless assistance of religious, labor, and other community organizations, racial barriers collapsed with ever-increasing speed. Sympathetic public opinion, court action, and executive orders helped to secure for the Negroes access to the ballot and eliminated all but the vestiges of segregation in the Armed Forces, interstate travel, sports, and higher education. Segregation in the public schools was one of the few pillars of legal segregation still standing, and the Supreme Court has now toppled this pillar, too.

LONG-RANGE PLANS

The school segregation issue will haunt the agenda of the American people for decades to come. By 1959, great strides had already been made. The collapse of segregation in Virginia, which had provided intellectual leadership to the last-ditch resisters, was a harbinger of things to come, even in the solid South. In Montgomery, Alabama, Rev. Martin Luther King and his followers had given the world a shining example of Negro self-discipline and Christian ethics. And in hundreds of communities, where parents did not impose their prejudices upon the young, white and Negro students calmly accepted the challenge of change—and went about their business.

The segregation issue has moved into its most crucial phase, where intelligent and long-range plans must be evolved in states and local communities throughout the South and border states. In this phase, the fullest cooperation of men of good will of all races and religions in every community is indispensable to a harmonious transition from segregation to integration. That the churches and synagogues have a unique role to play in this noble work is evidenced by the earnest pledges of cooperation which have been made by Protestant bodies including the Southern Baptists, Catholic and Jewish religious groups. Typical of these is the statement adopted by the Union of American Hebrew Congregations in 1955:

> "Having consistently opposed every form of discrimination because of our fundamental belief in the equality of all men under God, we rejoice in the unanimous decision of the U.S. Supreme Court in the school segregation cases. We regard this decision as a major chapter in the history of the growth of true equality under the law.
>
> "As proponents of Judaism, which first enunciated the concept of the fatherhood of God and the brotherhood of man, we pledge ourselves to do all within our power to make this decision of the highest court in the land meaningful in our respective communities.
>
> "We therefore urge our congregants and congregations in all sections of the country to join with forward-looking racial, religious, and civic groups in the community in using their influence to secure acceptance and implementation of the desegregation decisions in every community in our land."

Resolutions, of course, are easier than resolution. The segregation controversy has inevitably placed heavy pressure on Southern Jews. Part of a tiny community, usually merchants and therefore susceptible to economic pressure, fearful of rejection by the larger community—Southern Jewry has not played a leadership role in the struggle for desegregation. Many Southern Jewish leaders have urged neutrality on the part of the Jewish community. Neutrality, however, is not only unworthy of a living faith; it is also impossible. The bombings of Jewish institutions in the South should have shattered the illusion that the Jewish community can be "neutral" or "safe" when the fabric of law and order disentangles.

While Jewish groups have not been conspicuous in the South among integration leaders, it is also true that Jews have, with few exceptions, spurned the blandishments of the White Citizens Councils. Moreover, several rabbis have displayed distinctive courage under agonizing circumstances in bespeaking their religious conscience in the accents of the Jewish tradition. As the burden of moral leadership has fallen more and more clearly upon the *religious* leaders of all faiths in the South, there are signs that rabbis will be buttressed by their committed lay leaders in interfaith efforts to restore Negro-white communication, foster a positive climate of opinion, and prepare the way for the "new South" which is agonizingly but surely being born.

But, as with all birth, pain and suffering must precede. The disintegration of Little Rock, Arkansas, at the demagogic hands of Governor Faubus; the abandonment of public schools in several localities; the lynching of Mack Parker in Mississippi; the decay of public ethics and the corruption of civil liberties in the hard-core Southern states; the extra-legal assaults on the right of the NAACP to pursue its lawful purposes; the pandering of cynical politicians; the lengthening shadow of fear over many communities—all these are ugly portents of the hard struggle which lies ahead.

THE ROLE OF THE SYNAGOGUE

Self-understanding would be an excellent starting point in this area, so fraught with deep-seated, often irrational, emotions. The first task of the Social Action or Community Affairs Committee might be a careful study of the real feelings and attitudes of its own members toward other groups—Negroes, Catholics, Puerto Ricans, and others. Many possible techniques can be used in this study: psychodrama, socio-drama, rumor clinic, and others. These same tech-

---

* Not all such legislation provides for enforcement. The laws of Wisconsin and Indiana are known as "voluntary" or "educational" FEP laws which provide for existing agencies merely to "investigate discriminatory employment practices . . . to formulate programs to eliminate such discrimination, and to recommend legislation to the Governor and General Assembly." Will Maslow, director of the Commission on Law and Social Action of the American Jewish Congress and one of the foremost authorities on civil rights, has condemned the Wisconsin and Indiana statutes as "counterfeit measures" which "hold out a semblance of activity, but so far as we can determine, practically nothing is being done in those two states to eliminate discriminatory employment practices."

niques can be used to good advantage in impressing upon the membership of the congregation-at-large the vital importance of gaining insights into one's own prejudices and distorted thinking about other racial, religious, and nationality groups.

In approaching the problems of civil rights, synagogues must bear in mind that they must consider these problems from the standpoint of the ethical principles of Judaism. A synagogue committee should not allow itself to become another civil rights agency. The sole basis for its concern is that equality is a religious principle which is intrinsic to Judaism. The Committee, as well as the congregation as a whole, must be made sensitive to the relevancy of Judaism to the problems of civil rights in their community.

The Social Action or Community Affairs Committee of the congregation must familiarize itself with the civil rights picture in its own community. In a few cases, the committee may find it necessary, because of a lack of available information, to initiate a full-fledged community survey or self-study. Usually, however, it is relatively easy to assemble sufficient information to provide a basis for the committee to develop plans and programs.

The committee should know what civil rights laws have been enacted by the municipal and/or state governments. Where such laws exist, the committee should meet with representatives of the FEP or other administrative agencies in order to learn how the act works and whether it is being effectively enforced. The extent to which Jews are benefited should be explored. Summaries of all these findings should be made available to the congregation using the techniques described earlier.

Where necessary civil rights measures have not yet been enacted, the committee should determine which community groups are active in the campaign to secure such legislation. It should evolve methods of cooperating with such like-minded organizations. Upon the authorization of the synagogue board or membership, it can then proceed to implement its action program in the community.

The committee should become aware of the extent and nature of discrimination in housing, employment, use of public accommodations, and education. It should know the governmental and community resources upon which it can call when complaints of discrimination are called to its attention. For example, reports of discrimination against Jews by national business firms can be referred to the NCRAC, which maintains a central channel for the clearance and reporting of such complaints, thus assembling evidence which is helpful in seeking to eliminate such discrimination.

While in most communities the synagogue committee can follow the lead of other local civic groups, there are some communities in which it will be incumbent upon the synagogue, either directly or through its rabbi, to take the initiative in stimulating community-wide action. A striking example occurred in the State of North Dakota. On the statute books of that state for many years had been a law prohibiting miscegenation. The rabbi of Temple Beth El of Fargo, Rabbi Steven Schwarzschild, initiated a state-wide campaign for the repeal of this discriminatory and undemocratic law. He was joined, first by one Protestant minister, and then by other individuals and groups, including his own congregants. A concerted campaign culminated in a hearing before legislative committees and eventually, in 1954, repeal of the statute.

In 1958, Rabbi Jacob Rothschild joined Christian clergymen in Atlanta in a manifesto of conscience on racial equality, civil liberties, and public education. Many other rabbis found similar occasions for expressing the values of Judaism.

The synagogue in a community making the transition from segregated to integrated public schools has a significant role to play. Together with the local church groups, it can help to create a sympathetic climate of community opinion which will help make a harmonious transition possible. Thus, Temple B'nai Jehudah of Kansas City evolved an interfaith statement on desegregation which helped to foster community understanding of the need to eliminate segregation in the city's public schools. An indispensable step in a congregational social action program on this issue should be education within the congregation on the mandate of Judaism regarding equal rights for all men.

It is neither necessary nor desirable in many cases, particularly in Southern communities, for Jewish groups to carry the ball in local efforts to achieve desegregation. On the other hand, where responsible Christian leadership in the community seeks cooperation from representative groups, Jewish religious leadership must become part of this vital effort.

In its work on civil rights, the Social Action Committee should make sure to make available to the entire congregation the results of its studies and actions. The temple religious school should become involved in the educational process. Excellent materials, especially audio-visual aids, are available for children as well as adults in the areas of racial equality, segregation in public schools, and related issues.

BIBLIOGRAPHY

ASHMORE, HARRY S. *The Negro and the Schools.* Chapel Hill: University of North Carolina Press, 1954.

BARTLETT, ROBERT MERRILL. *They Stand Invincible; Men Who Are Reshaping Our World.* New York, Crowell, 1959.

BELTH, NATHAN C. and HAROLD BRAVERMAN and MORTON PUNER, Editors. *Barriers: Patterns of Discrimination Against Jews.* New York: Friendly House Publishers, 1958.

BERGER, MORROE. *Equality by Statute, Legal Controls over Group Discrimination.* New York: Columbia University Press, 1952.

BLOSSOM, VIRGIL T. *It Has Happened Here.* New York: Harper and Brothers, 1959.

CAMPBELL, ERNEST Q. and THOMAS F. PETTIGREW. *Christians in Racial Crisis.* N. Y.: Public Affairs Press, 1959.

CARMICHAEL, OMER and WELDON JAMES. *The Louisville Story.* N. Y.: Simon and Schuster, 1957.

CARR, ROBERT K., ed. *Civil Rights in America.* American Academy of Political and Social Science. Philadelphia, 1951.

CARR, ROBERT K. *Federal Protection of Civil Rights.* Ithaca, N. Y.: Cornell University Press, 1947.

CLARK, KENNETH BANCROFT. *Prejudice and Your Child.* Boston: Beacon Press, 1955.

COLE, STEWART G. and MILDRED W. *Minorities and the American Promise: The Conflict of Principle and Practice.* New York: Harper and Bros., 1954.

GRODZINS, MORTON. *The Metropolitan Area As a Racial Problem.* Pittsburgh, Pa., 1959. Pamphlet.

HASELDON, KYLE. *The Racial Problem in Christian Perspective.* N. Y.: Harper and Brothers, 1959.

HERSKOVITS, MELVILLE J. *The Myth of the Negro Past.* Gloucester, Mass.: Peter Smith, 1959.

KING, MARTIN LUTHER, JR. *Stride Toward Freedom:* The Montgomery Story. N. Y.: Harper and Brothers, 1958.

KONVITZ, MILTON. *The Constitution and Civil Rights.* New York: Columbia University Press, 1946.

MYRDAL, GUNNAR and staff. *An American Dilemma—the Negro Problem and Modern Democracy.* New York: Harper and Bros., 1944.

National Community Relations Advisory Council. *Jewish Employment Problems.* A pamphlet, 1955.

President's Committee on Civil Rights. *To Secure These Rights.* New York: Simon and Schuster, 1948.

PRICE, MARGARET. *The Negro Voter in the South.* Atlanta, Georgia: Southern Regional Council, 1957. A pamphlet.

RAND, CHRISTOPHER. *The Puerto Ricans.* New York: Oxford University Press, 1958.

WHITE, WALTER. *How Far the Promised Land?* New York: Viking Press, 1955.

CIVIL LIBERTIES

"The God who gave us life gave us
liberty at the same time: the hand
of force may destroy but it cannot
disjoin them"—*Thomas Jefferson.*

JUDAISM TEACHES that each man has the right to express or
keep private the dictates of his soul, for the soul is the divine
element in man and cannot be interfered with by other men or governments of men. "The spirit of man is the light of the Lord"
(*Proverbs 20:27*). The Talmud teaches that where honest differences prevail and agreements are difficult: "These *and* those might
be the words of the Living God." It was that "flaming spirit
within" that impelled the prophet to speak out even at grave personal risk.

The right to speak out without fear has always been cherished in Jewish tradition. The Bible is crowded with examples of persons daring to say the unpopular. During the reign of King David, a beloved monarch, the prophet Nathan publicly rebuked him, but nobody presumed to silence Nathan or to question his right to assert himself. The angry prophets infuriated the people with their scathing denunciations, but the rights of conscience and speech were inviolate. Talmudic authorities considered inclusions into and exclusions from the Bible in open discussion. Heated arguments frequently raged, but the opposing view was always heard and respected. Frequently both the majority and minority views are quoted in Talmudic decisions. The classic example is that of Hillel and Shammai, whose respective schools differed strongly in many of their interpretations, and yet both were and are recognized as great rabbinic authorities. Deep respect for the right of conscience and the right to be different inheres in Jewish reverence for the human personality. In addition, the life experiences of the Jewish people have made us uniquely sensitive to the integral relationship between the survival and well-being of our people and the maintenance and expansion of individual and group freedom.

These rights are also the foundation-stones of American democracy. But they have periodically been under heavy assault, especially in recent years.

What happened in American life to place in jeopardy the basic liberties—freedom of speech, assembly, press, religion—which Americans for generations have taken for granted?

We live in a world split apart by profound ideological conflicts, under the haunting shadow of atomic doom, gripped by confusion, fear and uncertainty. There is a legitimate need for every nation to protect itself against foreign aggression and internal subversion. The American people and their government accept the need to protect themselves from totalitarian infiltration and espionage, whether of the Communist or Fascist variety. How to strike a balance between the sometimes conflicting requirements of national security and individual liberties is one of the awesome questions of our times.

In the post-war condition of national anxiety and irresolution, demagogues found a happy hunting ground. Exploiting for their own cynical purposes the understandable fear and anxiety in the hearts of the American people, they sought to bring about the curtailment of some of our fundamental individual liberties. They cast doubt upon the loyalty and patriotism of our public officials, our teachers, our armed services, our religious leaders, our intellectuals.

In recent years, the American people have regained much of their calm and traditional respect for fair play. Senator McCarthy died, but the air of hysteria had gone out of the balloon before his demise. The U.S. Supreme Court, in case after case, has sought to heal the wounds inflicted upon American liberties by the blood-letting of mccarthyism. The Court's far-reaching decision protecting civil liberties, virtually paralleling the historic school segregation decision, laid the Court open to a heavy battering of abuse from various quarters and touched off repeated legislative efforts to circumscribe and weaken the Supreme Court. Should such ill-conceived efforts succeed, the Court would lose the authority which has made it a bastion of individual liberty at a time of severe pressure for conformity.

Two unanimous decisions affecting freedom of association were handed down in 1958. In one, the Court upheld the right of an individual—Scull, a printer—to refuse to answer questions regarding his membership in or association with various private organizations, including Jewish organizations active in civil rights issues. In another case, the Court asserted the right of an organization—the National Association for the Advancement of Colored People—to refuse to disclose its membership lists. Both decisions had far-reaching significance. The power to compel disclosure of membership is the power to destroy voluntary associations, for individuals can be subjected to severe intimidations and coercion and thus be forced to withdraw from membership or support of such associations.

In contrast to these decisions, the Court has, in a few other cases, moved in the direction of narrowing earlier interpretations of constitutional guarantees. Thus, in the Barenblatt and Uphaus cases in 1959, the Court upheld contempt convictions in two cases testing the right of witnesses to refuse to answer questions put by investigating committees. In a 5 to 4 vote, the majority brushed aside the minority contention that the questioning of the witnesses had been solely for the purpose of "exposure" and not for a valid legislative purpose.

If some of the rulings of the Court in crucial civil liberties cases have been motivated in part by a desire to pacify critics of the Supreme Court, it points up the need for intensified public alertness by lovers of civil liberties to resist further Congressional efforts to limit the Supreme Court's proper jurisdiction and impair its integrity and independence.

The Jewish View

Judaism is fundamentally antagonistic to tyranny of all kinds. Jewish antipathy to communism as an ideology and as a way of life has been explicit and unyielding. Communists and their fellow-travellers are committed to a philosophy that is hostile to the basic beliefs of Judaism and repugnant to its most cherished traditions. Jews and Jewish organizations in the United States have combatted and will continue to combat communism and all other tyrannies both in the country generally and in their special efforts to insinuate themselves into Jewish organizations and activity.

Jewish groups have long recognized the need of protecting American institutions from subversion by persons whose loyalties are directed elsewhere than to the United States. Subversion can and must be effectively opposed, however, without destroying the tradition of individual freedom which undergirds democracy. As Judaism stands opposed to tyranny from abroad, it rejects with equal finality any domestic tyranny foisted on the American people in the name of false patriotism.

Jewish history is an unmatched record of resistance to tyranny of every stripe. Jews in the United States have maintained this unique, almost prescient, sensitivity to forces which actually or potentially threaten human freedom. Strikingly illustrating this special sense were the public opinion polls on the attitude of the American people toward Senator McCarthy. In March, 1954, a Gallup Poll showed that 56% of the Catholics and 45% of the Protestants polled approved of McCarthy, but a thumping 87% of the Jews polled considered him a menace.

The following excerpts from resolutions adopted by Jewish religious organizations over the past 30 years indicate this sensitivity to dangers confronting individual freedom even as they show that threats to individual liberties are nothing new in American life:

> "We declare our abhorrence of all interference, whether by private citizens or by officials, with the exercise of freedom of speech, oral or written, and of freedom of assemblage, both of which are guaranteed by the constitution." (*CCAR, 1920*)

* * * *

> "We commend the American Civil Liberties Union for its courage in taking the stand that while it will at all times protect the rights even of those who would deny rights to others were they in power, has excluded all pro-totalitarians from its officership and governing body." (*CCAR, 1940*)

"We witness with alarm the emergence of post-war hysteria indiscriminately directed against political non-conformists which intimidates the citizen in the exercise of freedom of speech, thought and press." (*CCAR, 1948*)

The United Synagogue of America in Convention Assembled Hereby Resolves:

"1. To petition the Congress of the United States of America to establish and maintain procedures governing all its various committees investigating subversive and un-American activities, so as to protect the fundamental rights of all persons.

"2. To petition the Congress of the United States of America to repeal the McCarran Act (known as the 'Internal Security Act of 1950') recently enacted, which, in many of its provisions, flagrantly departs from American democratic principles and long-established practices." (*United Synagogue, 1950*)

* * * *

"We deplore the wholesale and irresponsible campaign of vilification being conducted against government employees and men and women in public life. The necessary effort to exclude the disloyal from positions of responsibility can be exercised without the defamation of the innocent." (*CCAR, 1950*)

* * * *

"We endorse the proposal of Arthur Hays Sulzberger and others to grant amnesty in public opinion to those who clearly dissociated themselves from Communist fronts before the Berlin Airlift of 1948. We regard such a proposal as being in the highest and noblest traditions of our country and as being consonant with ethical religion which recognizes the possibilities of repentance as ever present." (*Rabbinical Assembly, 1953*)

* * * *

"We deny the validity of the proposition that our government can make itself more secure by denying justice to any man. Absolute security for the State is possible of achievement only in a totalitarian regime and is unattainable in a democracy. There can be no freedom without some measure of risk. In the current demand for absolute security, we must not utilize the totalitarian practices of the enemies of democracy, thus destroying the human and spiritual values which are the mark of civilized man.

"We protest the irresponsible use of political informers by our law enforcement agencies. We deplore the view that citizens should be encouraged to inform against fellow citizens with respect to their opinions and political associations.

"We would defend all constitutional privileges and immunities without regard to the guilt or innocence of those who invoke them. In our view, the preservation of these rights is of greater significance to our way of life than any benefit our law enforcement agencies can derive from curtailment or suspension of these rights.

"We abhor the test oath and its loyalty oath derivations. As did our forefathers before us, we reject the notion that the techniques of the Inquisition, the High Commission and the Star Chamber are to have acceptance by us in any form. . . .

"We re-affirm the recommendation, adopted at our 42nd Biennial Assembly, that the President of the United States be requested to appoint a commission of outstanding citizens representative of the broadest possible cross-section of American life to study the best ways of protecting our nation from totalitarian dangers without subverting our traditional American freedoms." (*Union of American Hebrew Congregations, Feb. 1955*)

Among the major current threats to civil liberties in recent years have been the following:

I. Security Program

Shortly after the end of World War II, with the onset of the cold war, the American public became increasingly concerned by sensational disclosures of the activities of Communist agents in the United States. The result was a sharp public demand for additional security safeguards (there had been a government personnel program since 1940) which led, in 1947, to the Truman Loyalty Program and Executive Order 9385. The program ordered an investigation of all government employees and future applicants. Should "derogatory information with respect to loyalty" be revealed, then a "full field investigation shall be conducted." Moreover, it provided that if "reasonable grounds exist for belief that the person involved is disloyal to the Government of the United States," he was to be dismissed. In addition, the program specified six "activities and associations" which might be "considered in connection with the determination of disloyalty."

The Attorney General was directed to draw up a list of "subversive" organizations without the necessity of holding public hearings. One hundred and ninety seven organizations were designated by November 16, 1950. Under tremendous pressure from sections of the press and from some veterans and civic organizations, together with powerful political demands to harden the government's security program, President Truman in 1951 revised the system, by amending the standard from "reasonable ground of disloyalty" to "reasonable doubt as to the loyalty . . ." This radical departure in the program reduced the burden of proof required by the government and led to the re-opening of many cases and to the dismissal of many additional persons.

President Eisenhower on April 27, 1953, issued Executive Order 10450 which created a new "security risk" system. Covering all agencies of the government, this program gave each agency head the responsibility for dismissal or refusal of employment if he found information indicating that the employment of any official ". . . may not be clearly consistent with the interests of national security . . ." Seven categories of offenses were enumerated as "criteria of security," including such personal weaknesses as drug addiction, sexual perversion and untrustworthiness.

The security program of the government, which was emulated by state and local governments as well as in many large industries and universities, became a bitterly controversial issue in American life. There was no question that the program was poisoned by partisan political considerations. There was clearly a need to lift security out of politics in order to end such immoral spectacles as the so-called "numbers game" involving the number of security risks dismissed by the government and what percentage of these were Communists. There was need for Republicans and Democrats alike to cease exploiting public anxiety about communism for personal and political advantage.

Dramatic events shocked large elements of the public and the Congress into a recognition that the security system had become a kind of Frankenstein which seemed to be running amok. Among the more flagrant of these events was the dismissal as a "security risk" of Wolf Ladejinsky by the Secretary of Agriculture in late 1954 on the basis of "information" which included that elicited by a blatantly anti-Semitic letter. The Ladejinsky case, as well as the Chasanow case and the investigations at Fort Monmouth, illumined for public view some of the dark recesses of the federal security system: the faceless informer, the veil of secrecy, the virtual invitation for malicious gossip and bigotry in security dossiers, the denial to the accused of the right of confrontation and cross-examination, the capriciousness and bias of some security officers, all resulting in the unwarranted destruction of reputations of many decent and loyal government workers.

The Supreme Court, in case after case, has struck down some of the most flagrant evils of the security program. It has restricted the program to sensitive jobs; it has challenged the application of the program to defense plant workers; it has emphasized the importance of confrontation and cross-examination of witnesses in loyalty cases; it has ruled against dishonorable discharges for military personnel accused of improper associations before induction; and it has forced the government to improve its security procedures. But the bitter legacy of the fearful years has still not been fully cleansed away, and the task of the Court will continue to be to reclaim the right of the individual.

II. Congressional Investigating Procedures

Another threat to constitutional liberties arose out of excesses and abuses by Congressional investigating committees. Legislative investigations have traditionally played an important and constructive role in the operation of American democracy. Frequently, they have elicited information which provided a basis for necessary legislative action. Examples include the Wilson Committee probe into the land grant frauds of the Union Pacific Railroad in the 1870's, the explosive Teapot Dome hearings, the Seabury investigations and the tax scandal exposure of recent years.

With the emergence of the cold war, however, and the panicky fear of "subversion" in the United States, some legislative investigating committees assumed a new and strange role. They arrogated to themselves a judicial function and, in effect, substituted themselves for a courtroom and judge in attempting to determine personal guilt or innocence, without in any way accepting the responsibility of acting within the code of fairness demanded by a court. They violated the basic American tradition that a man is considered innocent until proved guilty. They denied to witnesses elementary rights. Professor Zachariah Chafee relates, for example, that "Harlow Shapley was questioned in secrecy by the House Committee on Un-American Activities, his attorney was forcibly ejected from the room, he could call no witnesses, his written statement was torn from his hands by a presiding member of the Committee." They mocked the Fifth Amendment, and converted investigations into inquisitions. Perhaps as significant as all else, they demeaned the important struggle against communism by making their investigations lurid political spectacles designed primarily to win headlines and build political reputations.

No discerning American who has read his newspaper and watched his television set needs more documentation of these charges. One particularly revealing example of the stark irresponsibility of such investigations was the attempt by the House Committee on Un-American Activities to besmirch the memories of the late Rabbis Stephen S. Wise and Judah L. Magnes. Benjamin Gitlow, ex-Communist, appeared before the Committee in executive session. He was bursting with "information" about Communist infiltration of religious groups in American life. In the course of his imaginative catalogue, he came to Rabbis Wise and Magnes, both dead, and solemnly announced that they had been "subject to Communist Party discipline." Having received this information, the Velde Committee did not ask Gitlow to document his charge nor did it seek itself to substantiate or investigate the charge. It merely released Gitlow's testimony to the press, which in turn emblazoned headlines of "Charges Rabbis Were Reds" for millions of Americans to read. The presidents of the Union of American Hebrew Congregations and the American Jewish Congress, in an immediate joint statement, rebuked the committee and attempted to teach it something it had not learned as to what constitutes un-American activities.

Such flagrant abuses of the right of Congressional investigations led to widespread demand for reform of procedures to bring them into harmony with American traditions of fair play and individual rights. Religious groups, such as the Committee on Maintenance of American Freedom of the National Council of the Churches of Christ, and Jewish agencies in the NCRAC have played a prominent role in the effort to improve investigating procedures. These efforts, together with those of bar associations, civil liberties groups, and other organizations, seem to be developing an increasing awareness in Congress of the need for greater restraint and respect for individual rights in connection with Congressional investigations.

III. Legislation

Another threat to constitutional liberties arose from legislation enacted ostensibly as weapons in the battle against communism.

The United States has long had on its statute books laws dealing with the crimes of espionage, sabotage, giving aid to an enemy in wartime, revealing classified government information, bearing arms or assisting those who bear arms against the U. S., attempting to overthrow the government by violence, and entering into a conspiracy to do any of these acts. But in the anxiety produced by the cold war and intensified by the disclosures of undeniable espionage and subversion, sometimes in high places, there was a feeling that new and special legislation was needed to combat communism. The result was a rash of legislation proscribing "Communist," "Communist-front" and "subversive" organizations and their memberships.

There can be no doubt that a sizable segment of the American people supported these measures as "doing something against communism." Consequently, much of the Congress, feeling political heat on its neck, had no inclination to examine seriously the civil liberties implications of these measures. In fact, the small band of courageous legislators who stood up and opposed these measures as being destructive of civil liberties were violently abused as pro-Communists—and have had to justify their votes whenever they stood for re-election since that date. Some have been defeated primarily because of these votes.

Offered as weapons against communism, these measures may well turn out to be more damaging to democracy than to the Communists. Because communism is a danger does not mean that any proposal advertised as anti-Communist is wise. As Justice Louis Brandeis once observed:

> "Experience should teach us to be most on our guard to protect liberty when the government's purposes are beneficent. Men born to freedom are naturally alert to repel invasion of their liberty by evil-minded rulers. The greatest dangers to liberty lurk in insidious encroachment by men of zeal, well meaning, but without understanding."

A. THE SMITH ACT OF 1940

This act makes unlawful any conspiracy to teach and advocate the overthrow of the government by force and violence. Since 1947 the Smith Act has been used against the national leadership of the Communist Party and against "second-string" officers in several parts of the country. The law was upheld by a majority of the Supreme Court in 1951. In its opinion, the majority appears to have held in effect that the historic and long-accepted test formulated by Justice Oliver Wendell Holmes, requiring that there be a "clear and present danger" to the nation before free speech and press could be abridged, was no longer adequate to protect the national security and that "a clear and probable" test was to be used in the future.

Justice Hugo Black, dissenting, articulated the basic objection to the Act:

> "These petitioners were not charged with an attempt to overthrow the Government. They were not charged with overt acts of any kind designed to overthrow the Government. They were not even charged with saying anything or writing anything designed to overthrow the Government. The charge was that they agreed to assemble and to talk and publish certain ideas at a later date. The indictment is that they conspired to organize the Communist Party and to use speech or newspapers and other publications in the future to teach and advocate the forcible overthrow of the Government. No matter how it is worded, this is a virulent form of prior censorship of speech and press, which I believe the First Amendment forbids."

The Smith Act continues to be a controversial issue. Proponents contend that it is indispensable as a weapon against domestic communism. Opponents denounce it as a major breach in the fortress of traditional American civil liberties. None can deny that this measure set off a chain reaction, the final result of which is still not discernible.

B. THE INTERNAL SECURITY ACT (McCarran) of 1950

This law does the following: (1) Declares the existence of a worldwide Communist conspiracy; (2) Sets up categories of "Communist-action" and "Communist-front" organizations; (3) Creates a Subversive Activities Control Board of five men to list these organizations; (4) Requires such organizations to register, file certain information, and follow prescribed procedures; (5) Establishes "Emergency Detention" provisions which include detention camps; (6) Imposes new restrictions on the rights of aliens (later incorporated in the McCarran-Walter Immigration Act of 1952). This act was passed over the veto of President Truman and over the warnings of the Departments of Defense, Justice, State, and the Central Intelligence Agency that the law would do more harm than good in that it would imperil their security operations. Major religious, labor, and civic organizations denounced the measure as ill-considered and loaded with booby-traps endangering traditional American civic liberties.

In a ringing veto message, President Truman excoriated the measure as one which "would put the Government of the United States in the thought-control business . . . would give Government officials vast powers to harass all of our citizens in the exercise of their right of free speech . . . The language of the bill is so broad and vague that it might well result in penalizing the legitimate activities of people who are not Communists at all, but loyal citizens."

Examination of the provisions of the bill, passed over the President's veto, seems to confirm President Truman's harsh indictment. For example, the standards by which Communist-front organizations are to be determined are incredibly vague. The board considers whether the suspect group gives "aid and support to a Communist-action organization." Could not this be used to indict the American Civil Liberties Union, an anti-Communist organization, which extends legal assistance whenever and wherever constitutional rights appear to be violated, irrespective of whether the defendants are Fascists, bigots, or Communists?

Another criterion of judgment asks whether the policy positions of the suspect organization "do not deviate from those of any Communist-action organization." Such vague and careless standards as this can easily be used against liberal non-Communist organizations which, for example, favor public housing, oppose segregation, and are against the Internal Security Act and the McCarran-Walter Immigration Act. The Communist Party, for its own reasons, favors the same policies. That this fear is not fanciful is demonstrated by many events which took place in the mid-century madness such as: inquiries by loyalty investigators into an individual's position on FEPC, the McCarran-Walter Act, segregation; the questioning of James Wechsler, liberal anti-Communist editor, by Senator McCarthy and the latter's charge that Wechsler's position on Congressional investigations "parallels" the Communist line; suspension by the Army of a number of civilian scientists at Fort Monmouth on specifications which ranged from active membership in the American Veterans Committee through sympathy for Max Lerner and the *New York Post*. (Almost all these scientists were later reinstated, after lengthy and costly proceedings.)

The alien provisions expose most starkly the vicious and inhumane character of this act. Any alien who has *ever* been a member of a proscribed organization may be excluded from the United States, or can be deported if he is now here. The record is already choked with cases of persons entrapped in the web of the Mc-

Carran Act for a casual, brief association with an organization a generation or more ago. In one case, an immigrant had joined the Communist Party in the United States in 1932, gave 10¢ in dues to the organization which he was told was set up to fight unemployment. Yet he found himself twenty years later locked in the tentacles of the Internal Security Act. The act is distinguished mostly by the harshness of its provisions and the shocking looseness of its definitions. For example, it excludes those *"likely to engage* [emphasis added] in activities prejudicial to the public interest," whatever that may mean and however it may possibly be determined.

President Truman perhaps did not reflect the impatient mood of the American people at the moment but he may well have anticipated the judgment of American history when he said: "The course proposed by this bill would delight the Communists, for it would make a mockery of the Bill of Rights and of our claim to stand for freedom in the world."

C. OUTLAWRY OF THE COMMUNIST PARTY (Public Law 637, 83rd Congress)

This act was adopted in 1954 by a startling vote of 79–0 in the Senate and 265–2 in the House. As finally approved, the act outlaws the Communist Party but does not include specific penalities for party membership.

At least as significant as the legislation itself is the way it became law. The Administration had disapproved the outlawry of the Communist Party, warning that it would drive the Communist Party underground and make the job of FBI surveillance even more difficult. Attorney General Brownell had testified in opposition to the fifteen bills and resolutions considered by a sub-committee of the House Judiciary Committee. No bill to outlaw the Communist Party was reported out by a Congressional Committee.

On the floor of the Senate, liberal Democrats, apparently seeking to trip up the Republicans on the very Communist issue with which the Republicans had for so long abused them, suddenly proposed outlawry of the Communist Party. Many legislators, with at least one eye on the elections only three months away, practically fell over one another leaping for the bandwagon. With the exception of two courageous congressmen, Rep. Abraham Multer of Brooklyn and Rep. Usher L. Burdick of North Dakota, the people's representatives seemed disinclined to ponder the constitutionality or effect of such legislation upon traditional American civil liberties. In a demonstration of political cynicism and irresponsibility which caricatured the democratic process, legislators went on record in support of a muddled, patchwork bill which apparently none of them had read, the implications of which nobody had had the time to consider seriously.

Perhaps as revealing as the fact that the "liberals" engineered this legislative coup—and insisted upon full credit—was the almost complete lack of opposition from organizations and individuals in American life. Nothing could throw into sharper focus the deep inroads which mccarthyism had made in all strata of American life than the fact that the stamp of "anti-Communist" was enough to stifle criticism and paralyze the nerve at a time when so far-reaching and basic a bill was being considered.

The *New York Times* said editorially on August 26, 1954:

> "The text that went to the White House was never available to the whole Congress nor to the press and public. There were piecemeal drafts of conflicting bills and amendments that had been approved.
>
> "This is the bill President Eisenhower signed with the comment that its full impact 'will require further careful study.' Of one thing we can be certain; it did not receive careful study—or any study at all—by the overwhelming majority of legislators who voted for it. The Democrats proposed it and the Republicans carried it forward not because it represented a serious and well-thought attack on the Communist conspiracy, but because three months before a national election it seemed like an expedient and politically popular thing to vote for. Even though it was modified at Administration insistence and thereby greatly improved, the bill still is so worded as to raise grave doubts over its constitutionality, its desirability and its practical effectiveness . . .
>
> "Legislation to control Communist subversion is necessary because the Communists do represent a conspiracy against our democracy; and some of the legislation to this end listed by the President is undoubtedly desirable and helpful. But the country is not in such internal danger from communism or anything else that it has to plunge ahead with hastily drawn, loosely worded laws that actually may interfere with intelligent Communist control, may do violence to the liberties of loyal Americans and may further shake our confidence in ourselves and the free world's confidence in us."

D. STATE AND MUNICIPAL "ANTI-SUBVERSIVE" ACTS

If the laws described above raise disquieting questions as to the fate of traditional American liberties, the so-called "anti-Communist laws" hatched by many states and municipalities open a Pandora's box of distortions and perversions of constitutional traditions. An excellent pamphlet entitled "We Hold These Truths," published by the Massachusetts Council for Constitutional Rights, describes some of these measures:

"Massachusetts outlaws the Communist Party, by name, sets up provisions for declaring subversive any association of three or more persons advocating overthrow of the government, and bars these bodies from the state ballot, as well as making it a criminal offense for anyone to provide a meeting place for such groups. Michigan's Truck Act is similar, but adds a secret police force to gather information for the act. A Pennsylvania law bars subversives from the benefits of its welfare and public aid programs (although a *blind* Communist may still get relief). Maryland's Ober Law bars 'disloyal' persons from public employment, outlaws organizations advocating overthrow, and provides that membership in such outlawed organizations shall result in the individual's losing his right to vote in Maryland elections. This law also requires all private educational institutions receiving state funds to report on their progress in dismissing subversives, a provision clearly aimed at Johns Hopkins University's position on academic freedom.

"Many states have passed so-called 'little Ober laws.' Mississippi felt the need to meet Communist subversion in their territory by a control law, despite the fact that J. Edgar Hoover testified that Mississippi has one Communist in its borders. Ohio requires unemployment insurance recipients to swear that they have no tie with a party that advocates overthrow; while a Texas law requires all *students* at the University of Texas to take a loyalty oath. Under a Tennessee Act of 1951, a person who is guilty of unlawful advocacy could receive the death penalty.

"At the municipal level, more than 100 cities passed antisubversive ordinances in the period following the outbreak of hostilities in Korea in 1950, among them Birmingham, Miami, Los Angeles, Cumberland, Jersey City, and New Rochelle. Typical provisions require Communist and very broadly defined 'disloyal' types to register with the chief of police, be fingerprinted, file copies of everything they write, and sometimes require them to publish notice of meetings in city newspapers. Another type of ordinance requires the 'subversive' to leave the town immediately. In Birmingham, any person who communicates in any way with a present or former Communist is presumed to be a Communist himself, and must leave town immediately or else face a $100 fine and one hundred and eighty days in jail for each day he remains. Detroit closed down all news-stands selling the *Daily Worker* on the ground that they were a nuisance; Miami Beach now requires a loyalty oath for all candidates running for City Council.

. . . "In all this legislation—federal, state, and municipal —there needs to be an end to single factor analysis. Instead of simply signing up against communism, we might well inquire: Is this law likely to accomplish the end of security without becoming a dragnet? (In Pennsylvania, the loyalty oath law caught several Quakers whose religious beliefs forbade their signing.) Is this need for security best met by registration laws or subversive lists or penalties, or rather by police and FBI detection of unlawful acts? What will be the effect of this law on freedom of speech and association? In short, what is the total impact of this law upon our free society?"

IV. Loyalty Oath

One of the most widespread devices allegedly designed to combat Communist infiltration is the loyalty oath. By 1954, twenty-three states had prescribed such oaths for teachers and eleven applied them to various other state employees as well. In contrast to the positive promise to uphold the Constitution, which had for years been accepted as a proper oath of office, the new procedures require one to swear that he is not disloyal, that he is not, or has not been, a member of any subversive group.

Because they have been vigorously challenged and hotly defended, loyalty oaths have become subject to controversy and misunderstanding. Advocates of loyalty oaths imply, if they do not say so flatly, that opposition to a loyalty oath is evidence of pro-communism. The fact is that many loyal, anti-Communist teachers and others have resigned their jobs rather than sign them. Others, while signing, have protested the oath and demanded its elimination. Why do such persons object to signing such an oath? The reasons are many.

In the first place, many of the oaths are so hazily drawn that they may constitute a violation of due process. A notable example was the Oklahoma loyalty oath which was declared unconstitutional by the Supreme Court because of its arbitrary and "indiscriminate classification of innocent with knowing activity."

Secondly, various religious groups, such as the Society of Friends (Quakers), are constrained by their religious principles from signing such an oath or, in some cases, to various sections of the oath, such as a promise of military service.

Another basic objection brought against the loyalty oath is that it is based on the concept of guilt by association inasmuch as it is conceived in terms of "membership in" or "affiliation with" certain organizations. Guilt by association undermines the best traditions of American justice. The Supreme Court has said that "under our traditions, beliefs are personal and not a matter of mere association, and . . . men in adhering to a political party or other organization notoriously do not subscribe unqualifiedly to all of its platforms or asserted principles."

Perhaps the paramount objection to the loyalty oath is that it is an instrument for enforcing conformity. "Test oaths are notorious tools of tyranny," said Justice Black in the Oklahoma case. "When used to shackle the mind they are, or at least they should be, unspeakably odious to a free people." To be required to swear to one's beliefs and associations is a drastic departure from American tradition. Honorable men find it insulting, just as doctors would resent any law that required them to swear they are not quacks, or wives that they are not unfaithful to their husbands.

Are loyalty oaths effective in tracking down subversives? President Truman, in vetoing the McCarran Act of 1950, pointed out that requiring the Communist Party to register is a little like asking all thieves to register with the sheriff. So it is with loyalty oaths. Herbert Philbrick, F.B.I. counterspy, has frequently testified that real subversives would not hesitate a minute to sign such an oath. The net usually ensnares a handful of obviously loyal, sometimes distinguished, persons who refuse as a matter of conscience or religious scruple to sign the oath.

Religious groups have been particularly concerned with a recent innovation in loyalty oaths which is directed specifically at churches, synagogues, and other bodies claiming tax exemption on their property. The California legislature, implementing a constitutional provision adopted in 1953 after a popular referendum, required every church, synagogue and other tax-exempt body, if it wished to continue its tax exemption on property, to sign an oath, swearing that it does not advocate the overthrow of the government by force and that, in the event of hostilities, it would support the United States. Several Protestant churches refused to sign the oath and accepted the loss of tax exemption. Other churches and synagogues signed the oath under protest. A number of organizations, including the California Council of Churches (Protestant), the Board of Rabbis of Northern California, the Quakers, Southwest Region of the United Synagogue, contended that the new law is dangerous because it casts suspicion by innuendo upon the loyalty and integrity of churches and synagogues and their leadership. The law was ruled unconstitutional by the U.S. Supreme Court. This decision, it is to be hoped, will put an end to the outrageous suggestion that Houses of God must certify their "loyalty" to the state as the price of tax exemption.

V. Vigilantism and Censorship

As important to the fate of our civil liberties as what goes on in the nation's Capitol and in state legislatures is what is happening in each individual community in the United States—in the schools, the public forums, the libraries, the newspapers, the theatre, bookstores, synagogues and churches. The pressures toward censorship, conformity, and suppression, some of which have been described in this section, bear on our local communities, too, and sometimes with crushing impact.

In Sapulpa, Oklahoma, books were removed from the high school library and burned on the request of a women's civic group which objected to their "socialistic" content.

In Los Angeles, the Board of Education virtually suspended the use of UNESCO material in the public schools because, they said, use of such materials implied endorsement of the UN and UNESCO, whereas both should be considered controversial.

In Englewood, New Jersey, the Board of Education urged that textbooks selected for use must "not advocate the support of a foreign power" nor "advocate a principle or doctrine inimical to the American system of free enterprise."

In Norwalk, Connecticut, a local chapter of the Veterans of Foreign Wars set up a special committee to watch residents of Norwalk and report possible Communists and Communist sympathizers to the FBI.

In Arkansas, a religious publication, the *Arkansas Methodist*, reported that self-appointed local vigilante groups who claimed to be fighting communism entered objection to an Easter prayer which asks that Jesus "be our fellow-traveler along the Emmaus Road of Life." They claimed this prayer had Communist overtones.

Not all of these and other civil liberties episodes in local communities are resolved on the side of the vigilantes and censors. Where the decent forces in the community—including the churches and the synagogues—are on their toes and aroused, the assault can usually be turned back.

In Scarsdale, New York, would-be censors carried out a whirlwind campaign in an effort to label as "communistic" some public school textbooks and library books. The good sense and devotion to freedom of the Scarsdale community-at-large led to the formation of a Citizens Committee of prominent people from all walks of life which succeeded in resisting the attacks.

In Tennessee, the state legislature authorized a committee to investigate textbooks in the public schools. Immediately a host of vigilante groups and super-patriots tried to expand this limited inquiry into a full-fledged investigation of "subversive" library books, teachers, and others. Rabbi William B. Silverman, of Vine Street Temple, Nashville, didn't like the pattern of unproved accusation which was developing. He urged a reporter of the Nashville *Tennessean* to dig into the story. The reporter's documented exposé revealed that the source of the explosive material circulating through the community was Allen A. Zoll, once head of the extremist organization, American Patriots. With the help of the newspaper accounts and a courageous radio address by Rabbi Silverman, the citizens of Nashville were jolted to the realization that the book burners and enemies of the public school were at it in Nashville—and that they had to be repelled.

In Englewood, New Jersey, the late Mary McLeod Bethune, distinguished Negro educator and college president, was scheduled to speak before the American Legion Women's Auxiliary in the local high school, until a local "anti-Communist" charged that she was or had been a member of organizations on the Attorney General's list. The Auxiliary canceled its invitation and the school board denied use of the building. Dr. Bethune spoke instead at a privately sponsored meeting in the local Presbyterian Church. However, the vigorous protests of aroused citizens caused the school board to reverse its decision and permit Dr. Bethune the use of the auditorium for a second visit to the community.

In Indianapolis, a public meeting hall was denied to the American Civil Liberties Union after charges were made by the American Legion that the ACLU was pro-Communist. Immediately, a local Catholic priest offered the ACLU the facilities of his church where the meeting was held.

In Pennsylvania, a Quaker group which refused to fire the librarian of its library, despite demands of an American Legion post and a D.A.R. chapter, was awarded $5,000 by the Fund for the Republic.

In the local community as much as on the national scene, our civil liberties must be maintained. If we permit them to be corroded, we will have nothing of real significance to defend against communism. The distinguished jurist, Learned Hand, put it eloquently:

> "I believe that that community is already in the process of dissolution where each man begins to eye his neighbor as a possible enemy, where non-conformity with the accepted creed, political as well as religious, is a mark of disaffection, where denunciation, without specification or backing, takes the place of evidence, where orthodoxy chokes freedom of dissent; where faith in the eventual supremacy of reason has become so timid that we dare not enter our convictions in the open lists to win or lose."

CENSORSHIP

The problem of censorship—by which is meant an infringement upon the right of the public freely to exercise selection—has been aggravated by the effects of the "Communist" question in American life. But censorship has always been an issue in American life and would continue to be even were communism to disappear.

Censorship takes many forms. Much of it is official; that is, governmental. The Postmaster General of the United States, for example, has broad latitude in banning from the mail a publication which he deems obscene. Several state censoring agencies have the power to ban the showing of motion pictures they deem offensive. Many cities have censorship bodies which judge what books may not be entrusted to its citizens. Judgment seems to vary geographically. For example, a San Francisco jury concluded in ten minutes that the people of the city could safely read *The Memoirs of Hecate County,* while the judges of a New York court concluded that the book was too obscene for its citizens. The people of New York were permitted to read *God's Little Acre* by Erskine Caldwell, but this "privilege" was refused to the population of Sioux City, Iowa.

Censorship is widely used in the selection of books and textbooks for public libraries and public school curricula. Increasingly, political pressures seem to be outweighing educational considerations in such selections. The *Nation* was banned from New York City school shelves. The *New Republic* and other such publications were banned in Oklahoma and a librarian was fired for displaying "subversive" material. In Boston, the *Post* launched a campaign to eliminate all "Communistic propaganda" from the city's public libraries. There are indications that many librarians played it safe in the selection of books so as to protect themselves in advance from know-nothing criticism and attack and possible censure.

Attempts at censorship by private organizations are also common in American cities. Here, a veterans organization seeks to prevent the showing of a Charlie Chaplin film. There, a civic organization seeks to prevent the circulation of literature it labels "bigoted." Somewhere else, a church committee organizes a "decency in literature" campaign, which lists many of the established literary classics along with allegedly obscene magazines and comic books, and seeks to enforce its censorship by pressure and threats of boycott directed against local newsdealers.

Jewish groups, including those of the synagogue, must be very clear in analyzing this problem because Jewish organizations have themselves sometimes blundered into acts of censorship. On the national level, major Jewish agencies, despite their protestations to the contrary, laid themselves open to the charge of censorship in connection with the movie, *Oliver Twist*. Locally, several Jewish groups have used pressure tactics to achieve such defensive purposes as securing the withdrawal from classroom use of such books as *Merchant of Venice,* denying the use of public facilities to notorious anti-Semites, preventing the public appearance of well-known artists whose backgrounds were pro-Nazi. This does not mean that Jewish groups do not have the right of protest against, for example, the showing of a film they regard as anti-Semitic. This right is inviolable. But this right does not extend to pressure tactics which, however rationalized, have as their purpose the denial of the public's right of selection and of judgment. As a group of distinguished citizens of Scarsdale, New York, wrote, in spiking a local book-banning: "Surely we have not, as a people, lost the courage to take the risks that are necessary for the preservation of freedom." Certainly Jews, who cherish the traditions of civil liberties, should not be so short-sighted as to sacrifice these ultimate principles for the sake of an immediate advantage. It is heartening that Jewish agencies are increasingly exercising wisdom and restraint in eschewing the short cuts of censorship in favor of the necessary risks of liberty. Censorship has proved to be not merely undemocratic; it is also invariably a boomerang.

RELIGIOUS GROUPS

These are days of sharp inter-religious controversy. One of the most crucial issues, upon which the religious groups divide, is that of the propriety of censorship of literature, movies, and other materials. In hundreds of communities, Committees on Decent Literature have been organized. Their ostensible purpose is to "clear obscenity and pornography" from the news-stands by voluntary means. Usually, the local committees are stimulated by the NODL (National Organization for Decent Literature) and the initiative is commonly, although not always, taken by local Roman Catholic leaders. Despite the well-intentioned nature of such groups, coercion has been exerted against many storekeepers to compel them to eliminate such allegedly "obscene" authors as Faulkner, Hemingway, Caldwell, O'Hara, and many other renowned novelists and authors of classical works.

In several communities, Protestant leaders have joined with Roman Catholic representatives in such campaigns and efforts have been made to enlist rabbis and Jewish laymen in interfaith campaigns along these lines. Whether or not to associate in such projects has posed difficult problems for Jewish communal leaders. How can responsible religious representatives of the Jewish community refuse to join in the struggle against pornographic and obscene materials which are made available to youngsters? Despite the very obvious pressures and difficulties, many Jewish leaders have politely declined to associate themselves with any project which has the potentiality of becoming a cultural vigilante committee, arrogating to itself the powers of censor and cultural arbiter for the community. Every community is protected by statutes which permit the city to deal effectively with the problem of pornography by lawful, official procedure, without opening the Pandora's box of private censorship and arbitrary lists of "objectionable" materials. This seems to be the best solution to the problem.

Censorship of movies has also become an increasingly significant battleground for American liberties. Religious groups have sought to ban various films on the grounds of "sacrilege" and "obscenity," frequently threatening exhibitors with permanent boycott for exhibiting an "objectionable" film. While any group has the right to protest against and the right to urge its own members not to see a movie, no group has the right to impose its views upon the total community, thus denying to others their right to make up their own minds. Fortunately, the courts—in the *Miracle* case, *Lady Chatterley's Lover,* and many other tests—are speaking out with increasing vigor against arbitrary censorship.

Events of recent years have demonstrated that there are sharp differences among American religious groups in their attitudes toward civil liberties. These differences were highlighted vividly during the brief period of Senator McCarthy's "reign." Even now, however, years after the demise of the Senator, it is clear that American Catholicism continues to conceive of the menace of domestic communism as an over-riding national issue in American life. To the Roman Catholic, this menace is so urgent and immediate that, if necessary, even traditional civil liberties should not necessarily be allowed to stand in the way of vigorous anti-communism. All branches of Judaism, and many major segments of Protestantism, are as concerned with encroachments upon civil liberties as they are with the danger of domestic communism. Indeed, these Protestant and Jewish groups tend to believe that the Roman Catholic press exaggerates the actual significance of domestic communism and contributes to an atmosphere of continuing hysteria which is injurious to civil liberties.

All religious groups are strongly opposed to communism, but the differing value judgments among them can have crucial consequences. Thus Protestants and Jews have been concerned with maintaining respect for the Fifth Amendment, with fairer government security procedures and tighter controls upon congressional investigating committees. Roman Catholic spokesmen, on the other hand, usually commend sweeping congressional investigations, applaud the House Un-American Activities committee, demand restrictions on use of the Fifth Amendment, and join in efforts to compel ex-communists to inform upon their former associates. Many Catholic leaders, of course, attribute these differences to an underestimation on the part of Jews and Protestants of the danger inherent in domestic communism.

THE ROLE OF THE SYNAGOGUE

The Social Action or Community Affairs Committee must begin its work in the area of civil liberties by becoming well informed itself on current issues involving civil liberties, particularly those present in its own community.

Through careful program planning, the committee must educate the membership of the synagogue and its affiliates to a religiously motivated concern for the preservation of civil liberties. This can be achieved through the rabbi's sermon, the congregational bulletin, special religious services, distribution of materials, discussion groups and forums.

The committee must establish close and continuing contact with other groups in the community sharing its concern and interest in these problems. These include the Jewish Community Council, the local chapter of the American Civil Liberties Union, the League of Women Voters, the National Council of Jewish Women, the American Jewish Congress, the National Association for the Advancement of Colored People, labor organizations, possibly fraternal associations such as Elks and Masons, and similar bodies. Many communities are blessed with special coordinating councils on civil liberties which include representatives of all these groups. The Synagogue Social Action Committee should be represented in these bodies.

Close and continuing communication should be maintained between the synagogue and Christian churches in the community. Where possible, joint interreligious activities should be undertaken, such as the holding of institutes on the religious stake in the defense of civil liberties, joint statements on important local issues, etc.

The committee should study local, state, and federal bills which impinge upon civil liberties and give the membership of the congregation the benefit of their thinking, so that individuals may exercise their rights of citizenship in reacting to legislative proposals. The committee must be alert to guard against tendencies in the community which lead to censorship and suppression. It must be especially careful not to be guilty of such practice itself.

BIBLIOGRAPHY

American Civil Liberties Union. Annual Reports.
BACHRACH, PETER. *Problems in Freedom.* Harrisburg, Pa.: Stackpole Co., 1954.

BARTH, ALAN. *The Loyalty of Free Men*. New York: Viking Press, 1951.

CHAFEE, ZECHARIAH. *The Blessings of Liberty*. Philadelphia, Pa.: Lippincott, 1956.

CHAFEE, ZECHARIAH, ed. *Documents on Fundamental Human Rights*. 3 vols. Cambridge, Mass.: Harvard University Press, 1951–2.

COMMAGER, HENRY S. *Civil Liberties Under Attack*. Philadelphia: University of Pennsylvania Press, 1951.

COMMAGER, HENRY S. *Freedom, Loyalty, Dissent*. New York: Oxford University Press, 1954.

CUSHMAN, ROBERT EUGENE. *Civil Liberties in the United States*. Ithaca, N. Y.: Cornell University Press, 1956.

DAVIS, ELMER. *But We Were Born Free*. New York: Bobbs-Merrill, 1952.

DAVIS, JEROME. *Character Assassination*. New York: Philosophical Library, 1950.

DOUGLAS, WILLIAM O. *An Almanac of Liberty*. New York: Doubleday and Doran, 1955.

DOUGLAS, WILLIAM O. *The Rights of the People*. Garden City, N. Y.: Doubleday, 1958.

EMERSON, THOMAS and DAVID HABER. *Political and Civil Rights in the U. S.* Buffalo: Dennis and Co., 1952.

HUNT, ALAN REEVE and PAUL A. LACEY. "Friends and the Use of the Fifth Amendment." Philadelphia: Civil Liberties Committee of Philadelphia Yearly Meeting of Friends, 1957. Pamphlet.

HYMAN, HAROLD M. *To Try Men's Souls:* Essays in the History of American Loyalty. University of California Press, 1959.

KONVITZ, MILTON R. *Fundamental Liberties of a Free People:* Religion, Speech, Press, Assembly. Ithaca, N. Y.: Cornell University Press, 1957.

LASSWELL, HAROLD D. *National Security and Individual Freedom*. New York: McGraw-Hill, 1950.

MACIVER, ROBERT. *Academic Freedom in Our Time*. New York: Columbia University Press, 1955.

"Report of the Special Committee on the Federal Loyalty-Security Program of the Association of the Bar of the City of New York." New York: Dodd, Mead and Co., 1956. Pamphlet.

STOUFFER, SAMUEL A. *Communism, Conformity, and Civil Liberties*. New York: Doubleday and Co., 1955.

RELIGIOUS LIBERTY

"Congress shall make no law respecting an establishment of religion or prohibiting the free exercise thereof."

IN THESE simple words of the First Amendment to the Constitution of the United States was set forth a revolutionary doctrine, unique in history, called by Thomas Jefferson "a wall of separation between Church and State." The founding fathers and the generation that adopted the Constitution were haunted by the spectre of religious conflicts and persecutions which invariably followed unions of church and state and from which many of them had fled to seek religious liberty. They sought to achieve "disestablishment" of church and state and to protect the United States from the "unholy alliance of church and government."

Under this system of separation of church and state, religious freedom has been secured in the United States to a degree unequalled in any other land. Far from being harmed by separation, religion has flourished in America. Experience has confirmed the judgment of the founding fathers that complete separation of church and state is best for both church and state and secures freedom for both. This grand experiment elicited the following judgment from a great American—David Dudley Field—a judgment in which many students of world history concur:

> "The greatest achievement ever made in the cause of human progress is the total and final separation of church and state. If we had nothing else to boast of, we could lay claim with justice that, first among the nations, we of this country made it an article of organic law that the relations between man and his Maker were a private concern, into which other men have no right to intrude. To measure the stride thus made for the emancipation of the race, we have only to look back over the centuries that have gone before us, and recall the dreadful persecutions in the name of religion that have filled the world."

The principles of religious freedom, giving every person the right to worship God in accordance with the dictates of his conscience, conform to the spirit of both the Old and the New Testament. The Bible commands obedience to both civil and ecclesiastical authorities, but when they are in conflict, as in the life of Daniel, "we ought to obey God rather than men." It is man's God-given right to worship or not as his conscience impels him.

Freedom of religion was undertaken for mankind more slowly and with more difficulty than was freedom of opinion and political expression. For centuries governments had acted on the assumption that control of religion was a responsibility of the state and that the state had a duty to defend and maintain the official religion against heresy and non-conformity. State-supported religions were still the rule in the seventeenth century, in Britain as well as in the American colonies. Religious persecution declined in England in the eighteenth century as a result of a growing secularism, but the residue of such attitudes was still strong enough to elicit shouts of "No Jews, no Jews" in the streets of London when an abortive statute was considered in 1753 to grant toleration to members of the Jewish faith. Nor were Jews the only victims of religious discrimination. Not until 1829 did Parliament rescind disabilities against Roman Catholics and put them on a level of equality with other persons.

Religious liberty expanded more rapidly in the United States, but not without a struggle. In most of the colonies the Church of England was established and one had to be a member to qualify for political status. The Puritans of Massachusetts Bay, who had been hounded in England for their religious ideas, now sought to impose their views with equal harshness on all other faiths. But the ideals of religious freedom were vigorously advocated by Roger Williams and William Penn and later by Jefferson and Madison, and, under the impact of the American Revolution and the radical spirit of the age, soon brushed aside old laws curbing religious liberty. By the end of the Revolution, the new nation was ripe for full religious toleration and separation of church and state. It is significant that these principles were set down in the very First Amendment to the American Constitution.

Even after 1787, it was a long struggle before all civil disabilities against Jews and some others were removed. In Maryland, no Jew could hold office until an arduous campaign led by a Catholic, Thomas Kennedy, who risked his political life for the so-called "Jew bill," resulted in an amendment of the state constitution rescinding the religious test. The long struggle was finally crowned in Maryland in 1825. Seventeen years earlier in North Carolina, Jacob Henry, a Jew, who had been elected to the House of Commons, was denied his seat because the state constitution required its officials to accept the divine authority of the New Testament. Inspired by a ringing and historic address on religious toleration by Henry, the House gave him his seat and later changed the constitutional provision.

Since 1787, the principle of religious liberty has been frequently attacked in the United States but the American people have repeatedly shown that they hold the right of each individual to worship or not and to suffer no civil disabilities as a result to be one of America's magnificent and indispensable triumphs.

It is not surprising that Jews, perhaps more often than any other group, the persecuted victims of church-state unions in many lands, have dedicated themselves zealously to the maintenance of the principle of separation of church and state in America. Rejoicing in an atmosphere of religious liberty unparalleled in history, American Jewry has been sensitive to all efforts and movements which would weaken the wall of separation which has served as the cornerstone of religious liberty in America. The Central Conference of American Rabbis, in the year 1904, established a Committee on Church and State, which is still active, one purpose of which is to take all steps necessary to preserve the nonsectarianism of the public schools and to safeguard "the absolute necessity of separation of Church and State."

Of course, we have never had complete and absolute separation of church and state. Indeed many practices existed at the time of the adoption of the First Amendment, and many more have developed since, which involve some governmental support of religion. Such practices include chaplaincies in Congress and in the Armed Forces; Presidential Thanksgiving proclamations; tax exemption for religious institutions; compulsory chapel attendance at West Point and Annapolis; and the inscription "In God We Trust" on our coins. Despite practices such as these, some of which are minor in significance, the gap between principle and practice in the area of government-religion relations has continued to be far narrower than it is, for example, in the areas of civil liberties and civil rights. The validity of the essential principle itself is well established in American life.

The constitutional guarantees of religious liberty and separation of church and state do not, of themselves, solve every problem in this sphere. The struggle to maintain these principles is continuing and evolving. Moreover, there is a twilight zone where it is argued that the right to religious liberty must yield to the larger common welfare. Some of the issues which lie in this zone are of special significance to Jews. The following illustrations are intended merely to suggest the complex nature of these issues.

Sunday Laws

Compulsory observance of Sunday as the Sabbath is established by law in most states throughout the United States. Such laws were frequently justified by legislators and the courts on the grounds that they go back to Mount Sinai and the commandment to keep the Sabbath holy, and that they have been established aspects of American life since Colonial days. Sunday laws have always been religious laws. A New York court frankly declared: "The Legislature has authority to protect the Christian Sabbath from desecration by such laws as it may deem necessary. . . ."

Sunday laws are invariably hodge-podges of contradictions and inconsistencies which defy both logic and reason. Writing about the New York State law, which is rather typical of such measures,

Leo Pfeffer says: "There is no reason discernible to the present writer for permitting the sale of bread, milk and eggs on Sunday but not meat or fish; or for permitting the sale of gasoline, oil, and tires but not anti-freeze, tire jacks, or batteries; or the sale of beer, but not butter; or of real property but not personal property; or (before the 1952 amendment) permitting professional football and hockey, but not bicycle or roller-skate racing." (*Church, State and Freedom,* page 233) Actually, what is allowed and not allowed depends less on principle or the desirability of the particular trade involved than on the strength of one pressure group as against another. Enforcement of Sunday laws is usually as illogical as the law itself.

A serious problem confronts Jewish merchants as well as some others who observe Saturday or a day other than Sunday in the enforcement of Sunday laws. They are subjected to discrimination solely because of religious conscience. Having closed their stores on Saturday to observe their Sabbath, they find themselves compelled by law to close on Sunday, thus imposing a competitive handicap which, in effect, penalizes them for their religious beliefs. Vigorous efforts by Jewish and other groups in New York State to secure a fair Sabbath law had not succeeded by 1956, although a growing number of legislators seem to recognize the inequity and discrimination which result from present legislation. The Supreme Court may ultimately reconsider the basic constitutional issue as to whether, under American principles, the church has the right to invoke the power of government in this way to insure compliance with sectarian beliefs.

Flag-Salute Cases

The recurrent controversy over flag-salute cases illustrates another situation in which the right of the individual to religious liberty has been weighed against the right of state—in this case, to maintain national unity and loyalty. The flag-salute issue stemmed from the refusal of children of the Jehovah's Witnesses faith to join in the ceremony of saluting and pledging allegiance to the American Flag in the public school. It is Jehovah's Witnesses' doctrine that "to salute the flag would be a violation of Divine Commandment stated in Exodus 20:3–5, to wit: 'Thou shalt have no other Gods before me. Thou shalt not make unto thee any graven image or any likeness of anything that is in heaven above, or that is in the water under the earth. Thou shalt not bow down thyself to them nor serve them . . .' Salute to the flag means in effect that the person saluting the flag ascribes salvation to it, whereas salvation is of Jehovah God."

For many years, the courts, including the Supreme Court, denied to Jehovah's Witnesses petitioners the right to abstain from flag-salute exercises in the public schools. The courts contended that the freedom of religious conscience is qualified and that, in this situation, the claims of religious freedom must yield to the paramount need of the state to foster national unity as the pre-requisite of national security. Despite a series of negative judicial decisions and intermittent physical attacks upon them and their Kingdom Halls in various parts of the country, the Witnesses stead-fastly refused to surrender the struggle. Gradually, important lead-ers in American life—law professors, editors, religious and civic leaders—began to protest against the idea that American security demanded that a small group had to be coerced into violating their conscientious principles about the propriety of saluting.

In 1943, the Supreme Court, by a vote of 6 to 3, reversed its previous decision and sustained an injunction granted to Witness Walter Barnette which enjoined the West Virginia State Board of Education from enforcing a compulsory flag-salute regulation. Said Justice Jackson, who wrote the historic majority opinion: "If there is any fixed star in our constitutional constellation, it is that no official, high or petty, can prescribe what shall be orthodox in politics, nationalism, religion, or other matters of opinion, or force citizens to confess by word of mouth or act their faith therein . . ."

Zoning Regulations

There is no question of the right of the state to regulate the use of property by zoning ordinances. Difficulties arise, however, when the ordinance is used to exclude houses of worship from the zoned area. Until recently, most courts in all parts of the land have acted on the assumption that whatever minor inconvenience might be occasioned for home owners residing near a church or a synagogue is not sufficient to warrant excluding such buildings.

Recently, however, there have been increasing tendencies by zoning boards, frequently sustained by the courts, to interpret the term "residential areas" narrowly to mean homes and to exclude houses of worship. Sometimes the zoning bodies seem to be desir-ous of keeping all religious institutions out of certain areas. It must be noted that the motivation of local government is frequently to protect residential areas from public buildings in general, with their attendant noise, parking problems, traffic and related problems. In certain specific cases, however, the zoning regulations seem to have been deliberately interpreted in such a way as to exclude a synagogue.

The right of the municipality or state to regulate the use of property is unquestioned but the right must not be used arbitrarily or unfairly to deny necessary places of worship for members of all religious faiths.

Child Adoption

Few issues have evoked as much interreligious tension and conflict in recent years as has the question of child adoption across religious lines. In most of the cases reaching the court in recent years, the religion of the child's natural mother has been Roman Catholic. Lawyers representing the Catholic Church have vigorously contended that the state should prevent such children from being adopted by persons of another religious faith. Since it is Catholic doctrine that the spiritual well-being of the child is the paramount concern, the motivation and consistency of the Catholic position are readily apparent. The problem arises when the state— through the courts or the legislature—is called upon to pass on the issue.

Several states have adopted legislation which provides that "whenever practicable" the judge shall allow adoption only to person of the same religious faith as the child. The courts have witnessed bitter tests of the interpretation of "whenever practicable." Catholic groups and lawyers have argued that this is virtually mandatory. Others have contended that it merely means that religious faith is one of the factors to be considered by the court in its discretion in determining the best welfare of the child. At stake in this interpretation is whether the material and psychological welfare of the child will be the paramount considerations in determining who shall be allowed to adopt a child, or whether these considerations will be subordinated to the rigorous requirement that the child must be placed in a home of the same religion as his natural mother. That this is not an academic issue has been demonstrated repeatedly in the last five years when children, placed with adoptive parents of another religion by the decision of the natural mother, and raised with love and security, have suddenly become the centers of bitter legal and religious disputes when the state was called upon to separate the child from his adoptive parents. The emotional damage that results to the family, and particularly to the child, as well as to interreligious amity, point to the need for careful study of state legislation to assure that child adoption laws are grounded in humanity and concern for the welfare of the child and not in religious compulsion.

A Principle in Controversy

Recent years have witnessed profound developments in the area of church-state relations. Formidable pressures have been brought to bear in efforts to breach the wall of separation of church and state. Indeed the very meaning of the First Amendment has been called into question, and various groups have tried to demonstrate that what was intended by the First Amendment was not an absolute wall but merely a prohibition against the setting up by law of an official Church in the United States. This view, advocated most vigorously by the Roman Catholic hierarchy in the United States, was clearly expressed in a statement issued on November 20, 1948, through the National Catholic Welfare Conference:

> "To one who knows something of history and law, the meaning of the First Amendment is clear enough from its own words: 'Congress shall make no laws (sic) respecting an establishment of religion or forbidding (sic) the free exercise thereof.' The meaning is even clearer in the records of the Congress that enacted it. Then and throughout English and Colonial history 'an establishment of religion' meant the setting up by law of an official Church which would receive from the government favors not equally accorded to others in the cooperation between government and religion—which was simply taken for granted in our country at that time and has, in many ways, continued to this day. Under the First Amendment, the Federal Government could not extend this type of preferential treatment to one religion as against another, nor could it compel or forbid any state to do so.
>
> "If this practical policy be described by the loose metaphor 'a wall of separation between Church and State,' that term must be understood in a definite and typically American sense. It would be an utter distortion of American history and law to make that practical policy involve the indifference to religion and the exclusion of cooperation between religion and government implied in the term, 'separation of Church

and State' as it has become the shibboleth of doctrinaire secularism."

That the Roman Catholic Church in the United States is committed to this view should not be surprising. The Catholic Church is dedicated to the principle that the ideal state is the Christian state in which the Catholic faith is the established religion and the only one entitled to governmental recognition. At the same time, its leaders are well aware that such an ideal is not attainable in the United States in the foreseeable future. Roman Catholic spokesmen believe that governmental support of the Church under these circumstances should be extended as a matter of moral right. They have thus sought to persuade the American people and the courts that the First Amendment does not mean a blanket prohibition against governmental aid to all churches and *does* permit such governmental aid so long as it is done on a non-preferential basis.

Support of this view of the First Amendment is not limited to Catholics. Many prominent Protestant leaders feel similarly. Within the Jewish community, there is a broad area of agreement that, in the words of Justice Frankfurter, "separation means separation, not something less." The Jewish community has demonstrated that it wants to see a constitutional wall—and not a moat—between church and state. Through the Joint Advisory Committee on Religion and the State of the NCRAC and the Synagogue Council of America, Jewish religious bodies and community relations agencies have jointly addressed themselves to important developments in the church-state area, have developed policy positions as new issues arose, and have taken appropriate legal and public action where it felt it was needed to safeguard the principle of maximal separation of church and state.

The question of the proper relationship between religion and the state in a democratic society is complex and takes many forms. It is involved, for example, in such issues as the expenditure of public funds for denominationally-controlled hospitals, as provided in the Hill-Burton Act of 1945. Is such public aid compatible with the principle of separation?

One of the more dramatic conflicts involving the question of church-state relations in the U. S. was occasioned by the nomination by President Truman on October 30, 1951, of General Mark Clark as a full-ranking "Ambassador Extraordinary and Minister Plenipotentiary" of the United States to Vatican City. This nomination was later withdrawn because it generated furious opposition on the part of non-Catholic religious and civic leaders who insisted that the establishment of diplomatic relations with one church would accord that church special favor above all others and would flagrantly violate the guarantees set forth in the First Amendment. If it accomplished nothing else, this abortive effort to send an ambassador to the Vatican served to throw a spotlight on one of the most important and least-understood of our constitutional principles and led Americans of all religious faiths to consider some of the implications of the principle of separation of church and state.

Religion and the Public Schools

Despite the importance of many issues involving church-state relations, it seems clear that the crucial battle-ground in this area has been and will continue to be the public school. The problem of religion and public education has become not only the paramount issue agitating the field of church-state relations, it is one of the momentous questions before the American people today.

Until recent years, the struggle for the principle of full separation seemed to have been won in the field of public education. Whereas a century earlier the denominational school had been virtually the only kind of school on the American scene, it had through the years been almost completely displaced by the secular public school. Most states had rigid prohibitions against sectarianism in the public school system. There seemed ample ground for satisfaction that the protracted and frequently bitter fight to separate the church and the public school had been successfully resolved in the United States.

The divorce of church and public education caused increasing consternation among some church groups. With the passing of the denominational school from the scene, church groups were faced with the question of how to provide religious education for children of school age.

One possible solution seemed to be the establishment of parochial schools, parallel with but independent of the public school system, which the church bodies would maintain. Such schools would provide both secular and religious education. The United States Supreme Court in 1925 declared parochial schools constitutional and immune from legislative attack but parochial schools proved incapable of solving the problem confronting most church bodies since few denominations were prepared to undertake their establishment. Only the Roman Catholic group among the major faiths seemed to be affected appreciably by the growth of parochial schools. Religious censuses reveal that more than half the Catholic children of school age attend parochial schools, while a negligible percentage of Protestant children and a tiny but growing percentage of Jewish children are enrolled in parochial schools. For the Jewish community, Sunday and after-hour weekday religious schools provided a partial solution. But none of these solutions went any significant distance toward meeting the problem facing Protestant leaders determined to provide adequate religious education for children of Protestant faith, which their Sunday schools were obviously not doing. (See pp. 51 ff)

RELEASED TIME

Out of this sense of need was born the suggestion of "released time"—releasing children from public school one or two hours weekly to enable them to attend church schools for religious instruction. This suggestion was first put into practice in Gary, Indiana, and it soon spread to other communities. Attempts to introduce the program in New York City actually led to riots at public hearings. Elsewhere, apathy stymied the program in many communities. In the 40's and 50's, and especially with the renewed interest in religion which accompanied the Second World War, the program was invested with fresh public interest, providing an impetus to its further expansion. By 1950, the program was widespread and the number of pupils enrolled in released time programs in all public elementary and secondary schools in the country was estimated at around 1,500,000.

American Jewry is virtually unanimous in its opposition to released time. This unanimity was evidenced by the filing, in 1947, of a brief *amicus curiae* in the historic McCollum Case which challenged the constitutionality of the released time program in Champaign, Illinois. The brief was filed by the Synagogue Council of America, representing the three rabbinic and three congregational bodies in Jewish religious life, and the National Community Relations Advisory Council, then comprising the American Jewish Committee, American Jewish Congress, B'nai B'rith, Jewish Labor Committee, Jewish War Veterans, and the Union of American Hebrew Congregations, as well as Jewish community councils in all the major cities in the United States. Their brief, acclaimed by the *St. Louis Post-Dispatch* as an historic contribution to the cause of religious liberty, pointed out the reasons that led them to intervene in this case:

". . . We regard the principle of separation of church and state as one of the foundations of American democracy. Both political liberty and freedom of religious worship and belief, we are firmly convinced, can remain inviolate only when there exists no intrusion of secular authority in religious affairs or of religious authority in secular affairs. As Americans and as spokesmen for religious bodies, lay and clerical, we therefore deem any breach in the wall separating church and state as jeopardizing the political and religious freedoms that wall was intended to protect. We believe, further, that our public school system is one of the most precious products of our American democracy. We are, therefore, impelled to voice our opposition whenever attempts are made to compromise its integrity . . .

"Our opposition is not to religious instruction as such. In Jewish history and tradition religious instruction has always been regarded as a most sacred responsibility. The overwhelming majority of Jewish children voluntarily attend after-hour and Sunday schools conducted by the local Jewish communities where they receive their religious education wholly independent of the public school system. We believe that the responsibility for religious education may not and should not be shared by the public school system. American Jewry is not prepared to concede the spiritual insolvency implicit in such a division of responsibility.

"Since the adoption of the First Amendment, the United States has escaped much of the bitter religious conflict and sectarian strife which have risen in other parts of the world, and driven men to violence and bloodshed. That good fortune has been due largely to two of the truly great contributions the American people has made to Western civilization: the concept of the separation of church and state and the free public school system. The first, by protecting religion against the intrusion of civil authority and by making it impossible for the state to become a battleground for sectarian preference and favor, has preserved both our political freedom and our religious freedom. The second, by providing for the education of our children on terms of complete equality and without cognizance of their differences in religious beliefs or disbeliefs, has been the cornerstone of our American democracy. The intrusion of sectarianism upon the public school system . . . both threatens the separation of church and state and challenges the traditional integrity of the public schools. That intrusion, if permitted and sanctioned . . . will destroy the institutions which have preserved religious and political freedom in the United States and which have prevented religious warfare in this nation . . ."

It is not surprising, then, that there is little participation by Jewish communities in released-time programs and that in some cases Jewish groups have even gone to court to enjoin continuation of such programs. Jewish leaders share the conviction that the responsibility for religious education must rest with the family, the church, and the synagogue and should not be thrust upon the public school. They believe that exploitation of the public school influence and machinery for the purposes of obtaining attendance for religious instruction impairs the integrity of the public school and the principle of separation which secures religious liberty. In addition, Jewish leaders have observed that the released time program, far from promoting interfaith amity, may do considerable damage to interfaith understanding. Jews do not feel that the public school should be asked to bail out the church and synagogue which fail to do their job of religious education. We take satisfaction in the fact that, through Jewish religious schools and without the aid of released time, almost three out of every four Jewish children in this country receive religious education at some time or another.

The Jewish position of opposition to released time and support of a strong line of separation of church and state is in conflict, and sometimes in sharp conflict, with the Roman Catholic Church and almost all Protestant denominational bodies. Some Protestant leaders who disagree with the prevailing Protestant positions on church-state matters have organized themselves into an organization called Protestants and Other Americans United for Separation of Church and State. But this militant body lacks the prestige and stature of the church groups themselves.

Notwithstanding the almost unanimous support of released time by Christian religious organizations, it is by no means certain that the American people as a whole shares these views. Occasionally we get a revealing glimpse of how others besides official church bodies feel about these questions. Such a glimpse was afforded at the 1950 Mid-Century White House Conference on Children and Youth, attended by 4,620 delegates. These included distinguished leaders from all parts of the country in the fields of religion, education, health, and welfare, together with representatives of labor unions, fraternal organizations, service clubs, business associations and other major groups. The delegates represented a fair cross section of American life.

At this conference, the committee on religion—made up wholly of religious representatives—submitted a report, which had been preceded by months of intensive preparation, describing government responsibility for religious education and endorsing public aid to religious education and released time. The report triggered an intense, sometimes fiery, debate which finally led to rejection of the committee report and, by a vote of two to one, adoption of the following resolution which was introduced by Dr. Abraham Franzblau, Dean of the Hebrew Union College School of Education:

"Recognizing knowledge and understanding of religious ethical concepts as essential to the development of spiritual values and that nothing is of greater importance to the moral and spiritual health of our nation than the works of religious education in our homes and families and in our institutions of organized religion, we nevertheless strongly affirm the principle of separation of church and state which has been the keystone of our American democracy and declare ourselves unalterably opposed to the use of the public schools directly or indirectly for religious educational purposes."

THE COURTS

An examination of recent U. S. Supreme Court decisions indicates that the church-state boundary as drawn by the court has been moving back and forth and is not yet clear or fixed insofar as public education is concerned.

In 1947, the United States Supreme Court, in the Everson Case, upheld the constitutionality of a New Jersey local law which provided for the reimbursement of children's transportation expenses to a Catholic parochial school. Constitutionality was upheld by a 5–4 majority, but the majority declared that the New Jersey law was at "the verge" of the power of the states under the "establishment of religion" restrictions. The minority thought that the verge had been crossed. Even more significant than the decision itself was the insistence by all the Justices that the First Amendment was to be given a broad interpretation precluding any governmental aid to religious groups or dogmas. Speaking for the Court, Justice Black voiced this insistence in the following now-historic words:

"The establishment of religion clause of the First Amendment means at least this: neither a state nor the Federal Government can set up a church. Neither can pass laws which aid one religion, aid all religions, or prefer one religion over another. Neither can force nor influence a person to go to or to remain away from church against his will or force him to profess a belief or disbelief in any religion. No person can be punished for entertaining or professing religious beliefs or disbeliefs, for church attendance or non-attendance. No tax in any amount, large or small, can be levied to support any religious activities or institutions, whatever they may be called, or whatever form they may adopt to teach or practice religion. Neither a state nor the Federal Government can, openly or secretly, participate in the affairs of any religious organizations or groups and vice versa. In the words of Jefferson, the clause against establishment of religion by law was intended to erect a wall of separation between church and state."

In the din of sectarian controversy which followed this decision—Catholics hailing it, Protestants condemning it as an infringement of the principle of separation of church and state—only a few immediately recognized that the broad principle which the Court enunciated was far more important than the majority's specific ruling on the law under attack. One who discerned this and didn't like it was James M. O'Neill, Professor of Speech at Brooklyn College, who characterized the Court's interpretation of the First Amendment as "historically and semantically indefensible" and wrote an influential book to support his argument that the Constitution did not prohibit non-preferential government aid to all religions.

Several months after the Everson decision, the Supreme Court was confronted with the necessity to pass upon another state law which had been attacked under the "establishment of religion" clause of the First Amendment. The famous McCollum Case involved a suit challenging a program of released time for religious education in the public school system of Champaign, Illinois—a program operating in school buildings, during school hours, under teachers provided for sectarian groups by their respective authorities. This system was challenged as violating the principles articulated by the court in the Everson Case. Every major Jewish organization joined in a brief amicus which argued that the released time program violated the Constitution. Counsel for the Champaign Board of Education, drawing on the manuscript of Professor O'Neill's book, urged the court to re-interpret the First Amendment as advocated in the O'Neill thesis. By a vote of 8 to 1, however, the court invalidated the Champaign released-time program, reaffirming the Everson interpretation of the First Amendment. The decision did not make clear what the court would hold in other released-time systems where the specific elements of the released-time program might differ from those in Champaign.

There followed a vigorous all-out campaign to persuade the American people and the courts that the court's interpretation in the McCollum Case was not only wrong but even un-American. Some Roman Catholic leaders posed the issue in terms of secularism vs. godliness in the American public school and spokesmen frequently equated secularism with atheism and communism. Abuse was heaped upon the concept of "a wall of separation," upon the Supreme Court, and upon all groups, including religious bodies, which insisted upon a broad interpretation of the First Amendment. The O'Neill thesis gained widespread acceptance in sectarian circles and provided ideological ammunition for those who opposed a firm interpretation of separation of church and state.

In 1952, the Supreme Court considered another released-time case, which was sponsored in 1952 by 11 organizations and instituted jointly by the Protestant father of a child attending the public schools, and the Jewish mother of two public school children. Known as the case of Zorach vs. Clauson, it challenged the New York City released-time program which differed from the Champaign system in several respects, most importantly in that classes met outside the public school building. Here, the majority of the Supreme Court, by a 6–3 vote, upheld the released-time program as practiced in New York, placing great weight upon the fact that classes were not held in the public school system and that it found in the record no evidence of compulsion. The dissenting judges strongly criticized the majority decision, branding it a reversal of the court's own doctrine in the McCollum Case. Justice Jackson characterized the majority's distinctions between Champaign and New York as "trivial, almost to the point of cynicism." It must be noted that the majority expressly stated that the McCollum ruling was in no way vitiated by the Zorach decision. The majority, however, seemed unwilling to uphold a doctrine of rigid and absolute separation, declaring: "When the State encourages religious instruction or cooperates with religious authorities by adjusting the schedule of public events to sectarian needs, it follows the best of our traditions."

Jewish organizations continue their opposition to the released time program. The legal setback in the Zorach Case was followed by a clear reaffirmation by NCRAC agencies of this principled opposition which is based on several grounds, of which the constitutional aspect is only one. These arguments were summarized by Leo Pfeffer, a leading authority on the problem of church-state relationships and author of the monumental volume entitled *Church, State, and Freedom,* as follows:

"1. The plan [released-time] constitutes a violation of the principle of the separation of church and state. This is the most frequently advanced argument.

"2. The plan constitutes an entering wedge which the church may exploit to regain control of education.

"3. The plan emphasizes religious differences and therefore is a divisive influence.

"4. The time allotted under the plan is entirely inadequate.

"5. Released pupils may discontinue regular after-hour or Sunday school attendance in churches and synagogues.

"6. There is an ever-present danger of proselytizing.

"7. The plan entails substantial cost to the city and administrative difficulties to public school authorities.

"8. The plan is unfair to the non-released children if the time is used merely for 'busy' or similar work; or it is unfair to the released children if the time is used for positive educational activity.

"9. Many people believe that there is much in present-day religious instruction that encourages religious prejudice and particularly contributes to anti-Semitism. While the state may not constitutionally prohibit such instruction, it should not facilitate children's being subject to it."

BIBLE-READING

Bible-reading in the public schools is undoubtedly widespread, although precise information as to the extent of this practice is not available. At least twenty-four states permit the practice of Bible-reading, according to a survey made in 1946 by the National Education Association, and in twelve states and the District of Columbia, Bible-reading in the public schools is specifically required by statute. Like the released-time programs, Bible-reading in the public school was largely Protestant-inspired and developed within the past forty years as a reflection of growing Protestant disaffection with the secularity of the public school.

In those states in which Bible-reading is either required or permitted, the laws provide that the teacher may not comment on the passages read. This requirement reflects the belief that, since the Bible itself is non-sectarian, the danger of sectarian comment can be prevented by disallowing all comment. Sometimes the statute limits the reading to the Old Testament, and in some cases provision is made for excusing a pupil whose parents do not wish him to participate. While state laws seldom specify which version of the Bible should be used, local school boards almost invariably select the King James version (Protestant) rather than the Douay (Catholic).

Protestants are the principal advocates of Bible-reading in the public schools. With the exception of such denominations as the Unitarians, Universalists, and Seventh-Day Adventists, and some Southern Baptist and Lutheran groups, Protestants are overwhelmingly in support of this practice. Although historically the Roman Catholic Church in the United States has been the most important conscientious objector to the practice of Bible-reading in the public schools, it appears that the Catholic position is undergoing a change in the direction of supporting this practice, just as it did in the case of released time.

Most Jews look upon Bible-reading in the public school with the same cool eye fixed upon all sectarian intrusions into public education. When Isaac Mayer Wise, founder of the institutions of American Reform Judaism, was a rabbi in Cincinnati, the Board of Education of the City voted to introduce Bible-reading in the public schools. Rabbi Wise had dedicated his life to the advancement of the teachings of the Bible. Because of his experience in Bohemia, where the union of church and state existed and where the establishment of a school for Jewish children was difficult and Jewish marriages limited, he knew that the introduction of religious literature in the public schools would undermine the principle of separation. He appeared before the Board of Education despite the organized opposition of the clergy. He lost his appeal before the Board and took it to the courts. The courts sustained the rabbi. Rabbi Wise did not believe he was fighting only for Jews when he took his stand. He knew that he was fighting to preserve religious freedom on the American scene and to prevent the recurrence here of the religious intolerance which marred the history of Europe and which he had personally experienced. Rabbi Wise found considerable sympathy for his stand because his generation, many of whom were immigrants, remembered their own sufferings when they lived in lands where church and state were one. They appreciated the importance of maintaining that principle even at a sacrifice.

The Central Conference of American Rabbis has consistently contended that exclusion from the public school of Bible-reading is indispensable to the preservation of the principle of separation of church and state and religious liberty. The view is shared by the major Jewish organizations associated in the Synagogue Council of America and the NCRAC. They deny that the Bible is nonsectarian and declare that the New Testament, which attributes divinity to a human being, violates the religious conscience of any Jewish child devoted to his religious faith. Equally fallacious, they contend, is the assurance that Bible-reading is voluntary and not compulsory. There are more subtle and more common forms of compulsion than that which, several years ago, consigned a Jewish child to a closed wardrobe while the rest of his class read the Bible. Courts have come to recognize the subtle compulsions toward conformity, as evidenced in Justice Frankfurter's concurring opinion in the McCollum Case:

> "That a child is offered an alternative may reduce the constraint; it does not eliminate the operation of influence by the school in matters sacred to conscience and outside the school's domain. The law of imitation operates, and non-conformity is not an outstanding characteristic of children. The result is an obvious pressure upon children to attend . . ."

The attitude of the courts on the constitutionality of Bible-reading in the public schools is not yet clear. The U. S. Supreme Court has not passed on the question, having dismissed the Doremus Bible-reading Case on a technicality without consideration of its merits. The decisions of the state courts are mixed, although the majority of such decisions have upheld the validity of Bible-reading in the public schools. The final decision by the U. S. Supreme Court will hang on whether and to what extent the doctrine it laid down in the McCollum Case was vitiated by that in the Zorach decision.

BIBLE DISTRIBUTION

The aggressive campaign of the Society of Gideons to place a copy of the New Testament and Psalms in the hands of every public school child in the country has raised another troublesome issue in the problem of religion and public education. The Gideons is a missionary society which aims at conversion to Christianity through distribution of the Bible in hotels, hospitals, institutions and schools.

The book which the Gideons distribute to public school children is a small paper-backed volume containing all of the New Testament, the Psalms, and Proverbs. The usual procedure in getting these books into the hands of the school children is the following: a Gideon representative gets permission from the school authorities to appear before the student body. Addressing the students, he describes the benefits of Bible distribution and instruction. He tells the students that they are to be given a copy of the Bible at no cost provided they obtain their parents' consent. Printed forms are distributed to the students at the end of the meeting, and when the signed form is returned by the student, he receives from his teacher a copy of the Gideon Bible.

Unlike other sectarian practices in the public schools, the distribution of the Gideon Bible has little support from responsible religious denominations. Roman Catholic parents and clergy take strong exception to the Gideon Bible which they regard as an unacceptable version. In Boston, for example, Catholic public school children who had received the Gideon Bible in the public schools were ordered to return them on instructions from the Archdiocesan Superintendent. Jews are unitedly opposed to the perversion of the public school machinery for distribution of the Gideon Bible, and rabbis have frequently taken the lead in protesting such proposals. Many Protestant leaders are uneasy about the Gideon campaign. Their reactions were well summed up in an editorial in the influential *Christian Century:*

> ". . . Protestants have no more right to use the public schools for sectarian purposes than have Jews, Catholics, or atheists . . ."

Fortunately, the courts appear to feel the same way. In the Rutherford, New Jersey, case, brought jointly by a Catholic and a Jewish parent, challenging the distribution of the Gideon Bible in the public schools, the New Jersey Supreme Court held unanimously that such distribution through the public schools is unconstitutional. The U. S. Supreme Court rejected the appeal of this case, thus settling for the present the question of law.

PRAYERS

Many public schools which require Bible-reading also require the recitation of prayers. Usually the prayer used is the "Lord's

Prayer" which is certified, sometimes even by the courts of the land, as non-sectarian. This characterization is somewhat incredible since there are differences between the Protestant and Catholic versions of the "Lord's Prayer"; the text of the prayer derives from the New Testament; and the prayer itself, by investing a human being with the term the "Lord," violates the conscience of religious Jews.

In November, 1951, the New York State Board of Regents evoked sharp controversy when it proposed its own non-sectarian prayer for recitation in the New York public schools. "We believe that at the commencement of each school day," the Regents declared, "the act of allegiance to the flag might well be joined with this act of reverence to God: 'Almighty God, we acknowledge our dependence upon Thee, and we beg Thy blessings upon us, our parents, our teachers and our country.' "

Protestants generally hailed the proposal, although several individual churches attacked it. Roman Catholic Church spokesmen commended the recommendations of the Regents. John F. Brosnan, a member of the Board of Regents and an influential Catholic layman, declared that "the only criticism came from those who do not believe in God." Mr. Brosnan thus cavalierly consigned to atheism not only several Protestant churches and individual leaders but the entire Jewish community of New York State. Every Jewish organization which took a position on this proposal—including the Synagogue Council of America, the American Jewish Congress, New York Board of Rabbis, B'nai B'rith, Brooklyn Jewish Community Council—opposed the Regents' proposal. Their opposition was largely based on the following grounds:

(1) The Regents' prayer will prove ineffective because moral and spiritual values cannot be conveyed by rote recitation in the classroom.

(2) The proposal would employ the state's compulsory education system to promote religious worship.

(3) Adoption of the proposal may lead ultimately to bringing into the public school influences and pressures which would endanger the existence of the non-sectarian public school system.

(4) Children pray in different ways, and such religious differences should not be brought into the public school where all children must be regarded as Americans without divisions based on race, color, or religion.

(5) The proposal violates the principles of religious liberty and separation of church and state.

While some communities in New York State have adopted the Regents' proposal, a much larger number of communities have not acted on it at all. The vigilance and courage of Jewish groups throughout the state, including Jewish religious bodies, have been important factors in this result.

HOLY DAY CELEBRATIONS

The most widespread religious activities in the public schools are those associated with the celebration of Christmas. Christmas trees bedeck almost all schools, carols are sung; frequently Nativity plays are presented by the children.

Only the naive and the fatuous can deny that these are religious observances celebrating the birth of Jesus of Nazareth. Certainly the more Christological carols and celebrations violate the sensibilities of members of the Jewish faith, of atheists, and of others. And yet some of these practices are so deeply imbedded in the American school pattern that they can be eliminated only with great difficulty if at all. While Jewish parents are frequently able to moderate the deeply Christological elements of the celebration through frank and friendly consultation with the school authorities, the general pattern remains substantially the same. Almost every year in one community or another there is an ugly public explosion at Christmas time which inflames once again the dark passions which the introduction of religion into the public schools can evoke. Among others, Waterbury, Connecticut; Camden, New Jersey; White Plains, New York; Kingston, New York; and Brooklyn, New York, have experienced such situations in recent years. The Brooklyn episode is sufficiently typical to be summarized here.

On November 24, 1947, Isaac Bildersee, assistant superintendent of schools in Brooklyn, circulated a memorandum to the principals in his district, an area approximately 80% Jewish in population. The directive read in part:

"1. The use of Christmas trees or other inflammable decorations in the class rooms and in any part of the building is prohibited by order of Superintendent Jansen and the Fire Department.

"2. Christmas and other similar occasions may be celebrated only as seasonal, pre-vacation occurrences. There must not be any references, any dramatization, song or other aspects of the occasion to any religious significance involved. Christmas carols with reference to the nativity may not be sung, nor may decorations include religious symbols of any faith."

The immediate chorus of outraged cries left no doubt that Bildersee had struck an aching nerve. The flabbergasted educator became fair game for violent brick-bats hurled by preachers, politicians, editorial writers, radio commentators, organizations. Public protests poured in from the Catholic War Veterans, the National Conference of Christians and Jews, the National Apostleship of Prayer, Episcopal Bishop Charles K. Gilbert, the New York City Protestant Council, the Rev. Norman Vincent Peale, Mayor William O'Dwyer and the New York State Knights of Columbus, the latter of which branded the order "an insult to Christians" and called for an immediate investigation. One of the sorriest notes in the episode was struck by Kate Smith, popular singer, who publicly erupted in a nationwide radio editorial that was shot through with such language as the following:

"... disgust ... right from the Moscow book ... Never in my memory have approximately 135 million Christians of this country been so insulted ... utterly stupid ... If (Bildersee) is still being permitted to occupy his office ... it is a further insult ... He should be barred from any further educational activities until this incident receives a thorough airing."

Three days after Bildersee's letter became public, it was revoked by Superintendent of Schools William Jansen. Seeking to rescue the situation, Jansen sought to invoke the spirit of good will associated with the Christmas season. He cancelled the Bildersee directive in a letter to all principals which began:

"We are approaching that happy season of the year when the minds of all men are filled with thoughts of brotherhood and peace, of peace within themselves, peace within their homes, peace within their community, their nation, and the world. As teachers of the young, we are again privileged to place before our children this joyous message and to bring through our daily work brightness and hope into the lives of the school children of New York City . . ."

JOINT RELIGIOUS HOLIDAY OBSERVANCES

The problem of the reactions of Jewish children to the celebration of Christmas in the public school has given rise in the past decade to the approach of joint Christmas-Chanuko celebrations in the public schools. Conceived and sponsored for the most part by the B'nai B'rith, largest Jewish fraternal order in the United States, the idea of taking advantage of the calendar coincidence of Christmas and Chanuko in joint celebrations in the public schools appealed to many Jewish parents who are resigned to the fact that Christmas in the schools is here to stay and feel that Jews ought to make the best of the situation. B'nai B'rith has contended that such joint holiday observances need not be sectarian events but, rather, inter-cultural observances which can build mutual respect among Jewish and Christian students.

Virtually every other major Jewish organization opposes such joint holiday observances. Both the Synagogue Council of America and the NCRAC are on record against such practices. These groups believe that neither Christmas nor Chanuko belongs in the public schools, since they are both religious holidays. Combining Chanuko with Christmas merely compounds the evil of religious celebrations in the public schools. Moreover, experience has shown that Christmas-Chanuko celebrations in the schools tend to impair the integrity of the Jewish observance of Chanuko and subordinate it to the Christmas celebration.

Interestingly, many leading Christians, particularly Roman Catholics, strongly resent such joint celebrations. The *Boston Pilot* referred to such joint observances as "hodge-podge mixtures of very different observances" and declared they contribute nothing to interfaith relations. Many Christian groups have criticized the trend toward de-religionizing the Christmas celebration in the public school and have joined in militant campaigns to "put Christ back into Christmas." It would seem that, far from making a positive contribution to intercultural relations, Jewish sponsorship of joint religious holiday observances in the public schools is more likely to harm such relations. Be that as it may, there can be little doubt whatever that, by asking for the inclusion of Chanuko into the public schools, we betray a principle on which Jews have stood and gravely weaken our position in other church-state issues.

A NEW FRONT

During the last decade there has been an ever-accelerating campaign to integrate the study of religion and religious values directly into the public school curriculum. In this effort, churchmen have been joined by many educators, including some associated in the American Council of Education and the National Education Association. Some contend that there should be introduced into the curriculum a "common core" of religious beliefs. Others, perhaps feeling that it is impossible to formulate such a common core, plead for a "factual study of religion," or "objective teaching about religion." A slightly different course is advocated by the National Education Association which has evolved a platform calling for the inculcation of "moral and spiritual values" in the public schools. While there are slight differences among these various approaches, all flow from the basic conviction that the public school must do more than it is now doing to integrate religious values in its curriculum. The mounting pressure behind these approaches has thrust upon the Jewish community the necessity to evaluate each of them and to evolve positions on them in the same way that positions were adopted earlier on such programs as released time and Bible-reading. As a result, the Synagogue Council of America and the NCRAC, evolved a statement of principles which sets forth principled objections to each of these programs. The full text of this and earlier statements on religion and public education is published in the Appendix. (See pages 261 ff)

THE ROLE OF THE SYNAGOGUE

What can the Committee on Community Affairs or Social Action do to help safeguard the principle of separation of church and state? The committee can make sure that members of the congregation understand what is meant by this principle and what stake Jews have in it. Through the rabbi's sermon and all the channels of communication which the temple affords, the congregation-at-large should be made aware of the implications of such programs as released time and school prayers, and why Jewish organizations have opposed their introduction into the public schools. Too often, congregants have been so uninformed as to what is involved in the principle of separation that they actually opposed their own rabbi when he has spoken out against infringements of this principle in the local public schools. The responsibility of being watchdogs rests not only upon the rabbi, but equally upon the members of the congregation as represented in the Social Action Committee.

Through close cooperation with the Jewish Community Council and the agencies of the general community, including the schools themselves, the committee must be familiar with the practices actually being used in the schools. Is there a released-time program? Do the Jewish children participate? If not, what is done with them while the other children are engaged in released-time classes? Is the right of non-participation fully respected? Is there Bible reading? Prayers? Nativity plays?

The committee must develop its own positions on various issues which confront the Jewish community. For example, should the temple support or oppose the idea of joint Christmas-Chanuko celebrations? The Social Action Committee should study both sides of this question, read the relevant material, possibly invite advocates of both points of view to debate the topic before them, and then decide its own position. The Community Affairs Committee of Temple Avodah, Oceanside, Long Island, developed such a study process, culminating in adopting a statement of principles by the entire congregation at a congregational meeting. The committee, having developed a position, should be prepared to present it to public school officials when it is deemed necessary to do so. It should be constantly borne in mind, however, that the area of religion in public education is acutely sensitive and must be dealt with wisely and carefully.

The committee should be vigilantly alert to the introduction of sectarian intrusions into the schools. When the Board of Education is considering the adoption of a prayer, of a released-time program, or making possible the distribution of the Gideon Bible, the opposition of the synagogue should be made clear, whether through the Jewish Community Council or in the name of the synagogue.

In dealing with the area of church-state relations, the Synagogue Social Action Committee should be aware of the resources available to it within the Jewish community. The Commission on Social Action of Reform Judaism, the American Jewish Congress, and the Committee on Church and State of the CCAR have had considerable experience in dealing with these problems and will be glad to offer assistance and counsel. The most representative instrumentality is the Joint Advisory Committee on Religion and the State of the Synagogue Council of America and the NCRAC, a special committee created in 1947 "to make available to local Jewish communities such guidance and direction as they may request, and local Jewish communities are urged to consult with the Joint Advisory Committee about such problems." Under the auspices of the Joint Advisory Committee, a series of national and regional conferences on church-state problems have been held and statements of positions on all types of sectarian practices in the public schools have been evolved. The committee has provided legal and public relations assistance to innumerable Jewish communities and synagogues throughout the United States on the problems raised in this section.

BIBLIOGRAPHY

BANKER, SIR ERNEST. "Church, State and Education." Ann Arbor, Michigan: University of Michigan Press, 1957. Pamphlet.

BLANSHARD, PAUL. *American Freedom and Catholic Power*. Boston: Beacon Press, 1958 (revised).

BLAU, JOSEPH L. *Cornerstones of Religious Freedom in America*. Boston: Beacon Press, 1949.

BRAITERMAN, MARVIN. "Religion and the Public Schools." New York: UAHC Commission on Social Action, 1958. A pamphlet.

BROWN, NICHOLAS C., Editor. "The Study of Religion in the Public Schools; an appraisal." Washington, D. C.: American Council on Education, 1958. A pamphlet.

Central Conference of American Rabbis. *Summary of CCAR Opinions on Church and State,* 1948.

DAWSON, JOSEPH M. *America's Way in Church, State and Society*. New York: Macmillan Co., 1953.

JACOBSON, PHILIP. "Should the Ayes Always Have It; Majority Rule Cannot Decide Questions of Religion." N. Y.: American Jewish Committee, 1958. A pamphlet.

JOHNSON, ALVIN W. and FRANK H. YOST. *Separation of Church and State in the United States*. Minneapolis: University of Minnesota Press, 1948.

Joint Advisory Committee. "Safeguarding Religious Liberty." A pamphlet.

National Education Association, Educational Policies Commission. "Moral and Spiritual Values in the Public Schools." A pamphlet. Washington, D. C., 1951.

NELSON, CLAUD D. "The American Pattern of Interaction between the Forces of Religion and of Government." A study and discussion guide published by the National Council of Churches of Christ.

O'NEILL, JAMES M. *Catholicism and American Freedom*. New York: Harper and Bros., 1952.

O'NEILL, JAMES M. *Religion and Education under the Constitution*. New York: Harper and Bros., 1949.

PFEFFER, LEO. *Church, State, and Freedom*. Boston: Beacon Press, 1953. Available to synagogues through Community Service Department, American Jewish Congress.

WALTER, ERICH A. Editor. *Religion and the State University*. Ann Arbor, Michigan: University of Michigan Press, 1958.

WHIPPLE, LEON. *Our Ancient Liberties*. New York: H. W. Wilson Co., 1927.

INTERRELIGIOUS ACTIVITIES

"Behold how good and pleasant it is for brethren to dwell together in unity." (Psalm 133:1)

AMONG MANY kinds of community activities, the synagogue can usually pick and choose those it wishes to pursue in accordance with its desires and resources. The individual rabbi does likewise in his role as teacher of Judaism not only to his congregation but to the community in general. But there is one area of social concern which, by its very nature, is mandatory upon the synagogue: interfaith activities. For the synagogue is the repository of the principles of Judaism and their exemplar in the community. If a fundamental principle of Judaism is the achievement of the brotherhood of man, then the synagogue has an unavoidable obligation to help members of the community to achieve a positive understanding not only of Jews but of all religious groups. This process is interfaith activity.

In every community, some forms of interfaith activity already exist. At the very least, some recognition is accorded each year to Brotherhood Week, which is observed between Lincoln's and Washington's Birthdays. It is one of the activities sponsored by the National Conference of Christians and Jews, the major intersectarian agency in this field. The NCCJ carries on a year-round program of educational, research, and project activities designed to further the ideal of human brotherhood.

It should not be necessary to point out that, at all times in interfaith work, the appropriate counterpart of the church is the synagogue, rather than any grouping of Jews organized on purely civic lines in the community. Whether it wills it or not, whether it discharges its obligation effectively or not, every synagogue is, by its nature and by the image it projects to the community, involved in interfaith activity. It may work cooperatively with other Jewish agencies, especially within the Jewish Community Council framework, but the primary responsibility for interreligious activities is and must be the synagogue's.

As new research findings and insights based on actual experience have emerged in recent years, an uneasiness has begun to develop within the Jewish community as to the validity and efficacy of some ways in which "interfaith" or "good will" programs have been carried out. Searching questions have been asked, such as: What is accomplished by programs based mainly upon exhortation toward good will? Do brotherhood programs really affect attitudes and reduce bigotry or do they merely achieve verbal acquiescence? Is the "common denominator" approach to religions healthy? Or is it preferable to encourage a frank facing of the real differences among religious groups? Is it a fact that one of the primary factors in evoking anti-Judaism is the charge, perpetuated in some Christian teaching, that Jews, by crucifying Christ, have called down upon themselves eternal damnation? If so, what are the implications of this fact for an interreligious program? Shouldn't a realistic interreligious program take into consideration also the impact on interreligious tensions of conflicts among various religious bodies on basic social issues such as religion in the public schools, birth control, censorship of mass media? How can Judaism best be interpreted to the non-Jewish community?

These are basic questions and they are under constant study by many of the organizations, both Jewish and intersectarian, which expend enormous energies and substantial resources to promote understanding and amity between Jew and Christian. Constructive answers to these questions should result in a significant improvement in the character of interreligious activities and in interfaith relationships in the United States.

The questions posed above were among the subjects studied at a three-day meeting in June, 1953, held under the auspices of the Committee on Re-Assessment of the National Community Relations Advisory Council. The subject of the conference was "The Community Relations Values of Interreligious Activities," which was defined as "promoting good community relationships and combating anti-Semitism, by working with or through non-Jewish or interfaith groups organized primarily on a religious basis." Participants included clergymen and scholars drawn from Christian circles as well as rabbis and lay leaders from the three branches of Judaism, together with eminent social scientists.

There were, as was to be expected, many honest differences among the participants in the conference. In fact, the opening presentations—by Rabbi Maurice N. Eisendrath, president of the Union of American Hebrew Congregations, and by Dr. Robert MacIver, Professor Emeritus of Sociology, Columbia University—immediately posed a basic difference of opinion on perhaps the most fundamental question of all: to what extent is anti-Semitism based on Christian doctrine? Rabbi Eisendrath associated himself with the views of Thomas Sugrue, a Catholic layman, who wrote the following in his introduction to Malcolm Hay's *Foot of Pride*:

> "Nothing can be done about anti-Semitism until something is done about Christianity. It is as illogical for a follower of Jesus to persecute a Jew as it is for him to commit any other sin of hate; the process by which he rationalizes his anti-Semitism should be identical with the process by which he rationalizes his other breaches of the code according to which his religion orders him to live. The fact that the two processes are not identical is the essence of the matter; the fact that a Christian is able to feel that anti-Semitism is not a sin, and indeed may be a virtue, a participation in the divine chastisement of a race of God-killers, is the evil which spreads and maintains and strengthens this Christian violation of the law of love. As long as so cool and Luciferian an assumption is

resident in Christian thinking, the Jew is a marked man, with a yellow patch on the arm of his identity."

"In America, too," Rabbi Eisendrath declared, "while scholars may believe that 'some Jews' were responsible for the death of Christ, the vast majority of the people have been infected through their religious school texts and home teaching with the doctrine that Jews are accursed by God."

Having made his diagnosis, Rabbi Eisendrath suggested several approaches in working toward an amelioration of the sickness of religious anti-Semitism. He urged Jewish leadership to grasp the opportunity to make use of the great potential of television in order to convey to the Christian population the true nature of Judaism and the Jew. He called for an intensification of the "constructive and promising," though still fragmentary, work being done with Christian scholars in the revision of Christian textbooks. He urged that such books as those by Malcolm Hay and James Parkes, Christian scholars who accept the heavy responsibility of Christianity for historic anti-Semitism, should be printed in paper editions and distributed in vast quantities. Scholarships should be established, theses should be encouraged at universities and in the more liberal seminaries, in order to increase understanding of the Jew and his religion. Similarly, Institutes for Christian Clergymen, such as those in which the UAHC has pioneered, should be expanded along with Institutes for religious school teachers and leading lay men and women of the churches.

In his presentation, Dr. MacIver sharply dissented from Rabbi Eisendrath's thesis:

> "I believe that attribution of present-day anti-Semitism mainly to the religious issue is entirely mistaken. I could adduce various kinds of evidence to support this conclusion, but will here be content to point out that the major outbreaks of anti-Semitism in our times have not been bred in religious circles, but often in anti-religious ones, particularly the Hitlerian horrors and the recent developments in Soviet territories.
>
> "I would suggest that we get a better perspective on anti-Semitism if we regard it as a particular manifestation of a tendency inherent everywhere in human nature, group egoism with its corollary of aversion to other groups. Certain conditions strengthen this tendency, above all any conditions that engender the sense of distance or aloofness between the two groups, any customs or ways of living, for example, that pre-

vent normal social relationships. Differences of economic interest may also strengthen bias. But it seems to me a serious mistake to make any specific factor, economic interest, religious separation, or any other, the key to the understanding of prejudice."

Although the differences of opinion on this basic issue of the effect of Christian dogma on anti-Semitism remained unresolved, there was a substantial body of agreement within the conference on almost every other point. The participants unanimously agreed that, alongside those Christian doctrines which conduce toward anti-Semitism, are many positive teachings common to Judaism and Christianity which can motivate religious people to foster good community relationships. They stressed the vast potential for good community relationships residing in the churches and synagogues in American life. They urged that programs of interpreting Judaism to non-Jews should be based upon a full recognition of the distinctiveness of Judaism and on the essential pluralism of American life. They warned that efforts of religious groups to work together on the basis of the lowest common denominator of agreement are doomed to disappointment and frustration, but affirmed that interdenominational cooperation on the basis of complete acceptance and frank facing of difference can be valuable. They placed great emphasis on the importance of cooperation with non-Jewish religious groups in working toward shared civic and social goals, such as the extension of civil rights, achievement of a fair immigration policy, combating juvenile delinquency, and other such programs. "Any program of interreligious activities aimed at achieving the goal of more harmonious living together in America must be directed increasingly toward social action."

The recommendation that Jewish religious groups cooperate with Christian bodies in social action for the achievement of shared civic objectives is nothing new. There is a long and fascinating history of such interreligious cooperation on the highest national level in connection with major issues in American life. In the 1920's there was continuing and significant joint activity by Protestant, Catholic, and Jewish agencies—the then Federal Council of Churches of Christ, National Catholic Welfare Conference, and Commission on Social Justice of the Central Conference of American Rabbis—in the furtherance of economic justice and other social objectives. These were not mere desultory statements and gestures. They represented arduous and systematic efforts which left an imprint on contemporary American life. Among many such joint activities were on-the-spot investigations by representatives of the three groups of certain national labor disputes, resulting in reports to the public; the holding of conferences on unemployment; a campaign to win the eight-hour day in the steel industry; legislative efforts in Washington to curb the depression; development of a platform on economic justice and, in 1943, "A Pattern for Peace," a statement of basic moral principles developed as a guide to planning for the post-war world.

It is interesting to note that interreligious cooperation of this high calibre has now declined to the point of virtual disappearance from the national scene. Infrequently, there is now a perfunctory joint statement by Protestant, Catholic, and Jewish religious agencies on a specific public matter which is timely at the moment. Seldom do such statements flow from the kind of intense and continuing common planning and thinking which invested the actions mentioned above with the significance with which they were received by the American public. While meaningful cooperation in areas of social justice continues to be evident in many local communities throughout the United States, depending on a host of local factors, there is little doubt that on the national scene there has been a sharp falling off of such activity. Why? It would seem that the following are among the more influential of the many factors involved:

(1) Interreligious tension has increased significantly in American life. Protestant-Catholic relationships, in particular, seem to be under severe strain. Evidence of deteriorating Protestant-Catholic relationships include the embittered conflicts stirred by such issues as the appointment of an ambassador to the Vatican, federal aid to education, the writings of Paul Blanshard, birth control, divorce legislation, gambling, censorship, and mccarthyism. The heated controversy about mccarthyism, in particular, resulted in angry charges and counter-charges between leading Protestant and Catholic leaders. The latter contended among other things that Catholicism is the only safely anti-Communist religion; the Protestants retorted that actually communism flourishes in Catholic countries while a dedication to democracy tends to characterize Protestant cultures. Against the backdrop of such acrimony, it is not surprising that positive interreligious cooperation has been rare.

(2) There has developed a strong tendency on the part of such overall religious bodies as the National Council of the Churches of Christ and the National Catholic Welfare Conference to prefer

separate and parallel, rather than joint, action even where there is agreement among the religious groups. The NCWC, for example, apparently conceives of its responsibility primarily in terms of addressing its own churches and constituents from the standpoint of Catholic doctrine rather than joining nationally with other religious groups in joint statements and actions. Within the National Council this tendency probably reflects the growing conservatism of many Protestant denominations today, together with the complex processes of policy formulation involved in a council of some thirty sovereign denominations.

(3) The last two decades have seen a drastic change in the kinds of issues which command the deepest public attention. In the latter part of the 1920's and in the 1930's, national economic issues were uppermost in the public mind. Today the problems of world peace, communism, internal security, civil liberties, public schools, church and state, the family—these loom among our central pre-occupations as a nation. And on many of the issues involved in these problems, fundamental differences of principle separate America's religious groups from one another. The stresses which are invariably created by these deep differences inevitably serve to weaken whatever disposition there is to work together on other issues.

Because of these factors mentioned and others, interreligious cooperation for social justice on the national level increasingly takes the form of statements and action by Jewish, Protestant, and Catholic religious leaders as individuals rather than as representatives of *organizations*. This is infinitely easier. It does not require cumbersome organizational procedures for policy approval. It makes it possible to work directly with those religious leaders who are likely to see eye to eye on the specific issue under consideration. An excellent example of such an action was a statement on the moral implications of America's food abundance in a hungry world which was published by eighty-eight religious leaders of all faiths in May, 1955.

THE ROLE OF THE SYNAGOGUE

What does all this mean for the individual synagogue and its Social Action or Community Affairs Committee? It means that the synagogue must exert its influence to make sure that, on the national level and in the local community, the Jewish religious bodies play their proper role in interreligious activity; that the synagogue, and not the secular Jewish organizations, acts as the counterpart of the Christian church nationally and locally. The voice of the synagogue must be felt in every Jewish Community Relations Council and the synagogue should play its proper role in the interreligious program of the councils. But the responsibility for such a cooperative relationship with the local Jewish Community Council rests not only with the council itself, but also with the synagogue, which must demonstrate a deep and abiding interest in the community relations issues facing the Jewish community and the Council.

The Committee on Social Action of the synagogue must keep itself posted on the real nature of interreligious relations nationally and in its own community. It must know the general positions and attitudes of Christian religious bodies in major areas of social action. It must know which of these positions are in conflict with those of other Christian or Jewish groups, thus giving rise to interreligious tension; and it must know which are generally agreed to, thus offering a basis for effective interfaith action on the local level. Some examples may be useful.

Catholic, Protestant, and Jewish religious bodies share a determination to achieve full equality of opportunity for Americans regardless of race, creed, or national origin. Each of the groups has made significant contributions toward this goal. The Roman Catholic Church, for instance, has set an example for the rest of the nation in the bold and determined way it has gone about the elimination of segregation from its Southern churches and parochial schools. Agreeing on the need for vigorous action to break down the barriers of discrimination and segregation, groups representing the three faiths have frequently worked effectively together in local communities throughout the country to secure municipal and state FEP legislation, to pave the way for harmonious desegregation in public schools, to end discrimination in housing, and in many similar ways. Much depends on the views and personality of the local minister and priest and the attitude of the archdiocese. In general, however, the synagogue and the church locally can find activities directed toward the achievement of civil rights a rich and productive area of effective joint activity.

There are many other issues on which churches of all Christian denominations and synagogues can cooperate effectively on the local level. An outstanding example in recent years has been the effort to achieve an American immigration policy more in harmony with religious principles and American traditions than the Mc-Carran-Walter Act. All major religious bodies in the U. S. found the McCarran-Walter Act inadequate. In Rochester, New York, the Roman Catholic Diocese, the Church Federation, and the Jewish Community Council joined in an interfaith statement on the need for a humane U. S. immigration policy. When the President's Commission on Immigration and Naturalization held public hearings in cities throughout the United States, local religious groups were frequently able to arrange for a joint statement to be presented for all by one spokesman. In Indianapolis a Catholic priest, Reverend Raymond Bosler, was the spokesman for groups representing the three faiths.

That there are also some social issues, many of great importance, on which religious bodies are divided, should never be concealed in a misguided effort to present a united front where none exists. Unlike the area of civil rights, for example, there are issues as has been indicated earlier, where the Jewish groups may be separated from their Christian neighbors by deep ideological differences. In such cases, there should be frank and full discussion of differences, not for the purpose of converting one another, but in the hope of developing a respectful understanding of varying points of view. For a synagogue to swallow its principles because, in a particular matter, it has few allies in the Christian community is not only cowardly, it is even bad public relations.

The fact is that there are some social goals which the Catholic Church pursues, and some which various Protestant bodies seek to attain, with which Jews are in sharp disagreement. No interfaith program is worth maintaining which requires that any religious group surrender its principles to be considered a partner. Various Catholic bodies have been actively engaged recently in creating intersectarian bodies against "obscene literature" and, however meritorious the objective, have sometimes engaged in censorship of literary classics through threats of boycott. (See page 129 ff) Yet, in some communities, rabbis and Jewish groups have gone along with the creation of such non-sectarian committees, apparently out of a feeling of: "How can we say no to the Christians who may then believe we are *for* obscenity?" But is there not also something obscene about replacing principle and courage with obsequiousness?

Similarly, in various communities, rabbis have been invited to sit with ministers and priests to formulate a "common core" of religious beliefs which can be used as a guide for the local public schools. Feeling constrained to cooperate, several rabbis soon found themselves facing the even more difficult alternative of either having to endorse a formulation offensive to Jewish religious principles or of opposing it and thus seeming to sabotage the entire time-consuming effort. Certainly it would appear more self-respecting, and even better public relations, to have said at the very outset: "Sorry, gentlemen, I do not think I can participate in this effort. You see, I don't believe it is possible to develop a 'common core' of religious principles common to the three faiths that will be anything more than a platitude. But, even more important, as a Jew and as an American, I am dedicated to the principle of separation of church and state, and I think it is contrary to the spirit of that principle for clergymen of any and all faiths to develop a religious formulation for our public schools. I would, however, be delighted to meet with you to discuss ways of strengthening our religious schools, our churches and synagogues, and of making religious principles more applicable to the life of our community." The Christian clergymen would probably not have agreed on the merits of the argument, but they would have understood and respected such a forthright position.

The Synagogue Social Action Committee must keep its finger on the pulse of interreligious relations in its own community. Working with the rabbi, it must maintain continuing contact with Catholic and Protestant church leadership, so that it knows what factors in the local community contribute to interreligious harmony and which to interreligious tension. Only by becoming aware of the forces at work beneath the surface of the community can the synagogue group evolve and carry through a worthwhile program of interreligious activity.

There is for the synagogue an indispensable aspect to a rounded interreligious program—the positive interpretation of Judaism to the community at large. It is interesting that both Rabbi Eisendrath and Dr. MacIver, beginning from almost diametrically-opposed premises, agreed on the importance of reciprocal education between Jews and Christians which will lead each better to appreciate the religious creed of the other. The amazing popularity of mass-circulation magazine articles and television programs about the meaning of major religions indicates a widespread hunger of Americans for a better understanding of their fellow Americans of other religious faiths.

A valuable project in this regard is the Institute on Judaism which is designed to bring the basic tenets of Judaism to Christian leaders on a face-to-face basis. Many synagogues have undertaken, with the assistance and guidance of the Union of American Hebrew Congregations and the National Federation of Temple Sisterhoods, to hold Institutes on Judaism for local Christian clergymen, religious school teachers, and lay church men and women. The enthusiastic response to such Institutes has shown that many of the Christians participating in such Institutes were getting, perhaps for the first time, a glimpse at Judaism and Jewish practice in a way far different from that in which they were presented in their seminaries or religious schools. Such Institutes afford useful opportunities to develop friendly relationships with Christian leaders in the community and to develop reciprocal exchanges of information about Judaism and Christianity. Planning for such Institutes, and following through on the interest generated in them, may well be undertaken by the Synagogue Social Action Committee, as part of its overall program of activity.

An extremely popular and successful technique has been developed over many years by the Jewish Chautauqua Society, sponsored by the National Federation of Temple Brotherhoods, an affiliate of the Union of American Hebrew Congregations. The program consists of sending rabbis, upon request, to speak to Christian students at colleges and universities on the nature of Judaism. It also involves camp programs for Christian students where information about Judaism is conveyed.

In addition to such Institutes and Chautauqua activity, information about Jews and Judaism is available from national Jewish religious bodies in the form of pamphlets as well as audio-visual materials. Such materials include information depicting the stake of the church in combating anti-Semitism. The Synagogue Social Action Committee should be familiar with these materials and disseminate them to clergymen and church leaders in the community.

Radio and television, of course, provide unparalleled opportunities for reaching wide non-Jewish audiences with positive information about Jews and Judaism. The national Jewish religious bodies are devoting themselves to the task of finding how best to make use of television time being made available by the networks. Such programs as the "Message of Israel," sponsored by Reform Judaism and the "Eternal Light," presented by the Conservative Jewish movement, have pointed the way to programs which will be both informative and interesting. Local synagogues can secure films from the National Federation of Temple Brotherhoods and kinescopes of "Frontiers of Faith" television programs from the Jewish

Theological Seminary at low cost for showing to the congregation or by local television stations. In addition, individual television stations are usually eager to arrange for local religious groups of all faiths to utilize available public service time. A friendly and co-operative relationship should be developed between the synagogue and the local TV and radio station.

Working in the field of interreligious activities, synagogues should be aware of the many resources available to them. Guidance and assistance can be secured from the NCRAC Interreligious Committee. Information and material on Reform Judaism is available from the UAHC; on Conservative Judaism, from the United Synagogue of America; information regarding Orthodox Judaism is available from the Union of Orthodox Jewish Congregations. Materials from the Catholic standpoint can be secured from the National Catholic Welfare Conference; Protestant, National Council of Churches of Christ. The intersectarian organization in this field is the National Conference of Christians and Jews.

In addition, the American Jewish Committee and the Anti-Defamation League maintain departments on interreligious activities. These departments also distribute information and films about Jews and Judaism, cooperate with Christian groups and scholars in seeking to cleanse religious textbooks of anti-Jewish references and to promote positive human relations values in such materials, and maintain day-to-day contact with Christian religious bodies in the area of social action. There continues to be deep-seated controversy within the Jewish community on the basic question as to the propriety of interreligious programs being conducted by Jewish secular agencies, as distinguished from the Jewish religious bodies themselves. This controversy notwithstanding, the above-named agencies make available resources and materials which many synagogues have found useful in connection with their social action programming.

All activities in the interreligious field, as in other areas of Jewish community relations, should be coordinated by the Jewish Community Council in each locality. If a JCC does not exist, the Synagogue Social Action groups would do well to explore the need for such a coordinating body, and to take the initiative in calling together representatives of all organized Jewish groups for the purpose of establishing a council. In small towns, where few Jewish organizations may exist, care should be taken at all times to include all local synagogues and rabbis in interreligious planning and action. No one synagogue or rabbi should attempt to monopolize this field. Interreligious work is the concern of the total Jewish community. The role of the synagogue in it is a primary and vital one.

BIBLIOGRAPHY

BLANSHARD, PAUL. *American Freedom and Catholic Power*. Boston: Beacon Press, 1958 (revised).

HAY, MALCOLM. *The Foot of Pride*. Boston: Beacon Press, 1950.

KAGAN, HENRY ENOCH. *Changing the Attitude of Christian Toward Jew*. New York: Columbia University Press, 1952.

MILLER, MILTON G. and SYLVAN D. SCHWARTZMAN. *Our Religion and Our Neighbors*. New York: Union of American Hebrew Congregations, 1959.

MYER, GUSTAVUS. *History of Bigotry in the United States*. New York: Random House, 1943.

National Community Relations Advisory Council. "Community Relations Values of Inter-Religious Activities." A pamphlet. A report of the NCRAC Special Committee on Reassessment.

O'NEILL, JAMES M. *Catholicism and American Freedom*. New York: Harper and Bros., 1952.

PARKES, JAMES W. *The Conflict of the Church and the Synagogue*. London: Soncino Press, 1934.

PFEFFER, LEO. *Creeds in Competition,* A Creative Force in American Culture. New York: Harper and Brothers, 1958.

RAY, RALPH LORD. *Apostles of Discord*. A study of organized bigotry and disruption on the fringes of Protestantism. Boston: Beacon Press, 1953.

VAN TIL, WILLIAM. "Prejudiced—How Do People Get That Way?" New York: Anti-Defamation League, 1958. A pamphlet.

WILLIAMS, ROBIN M., JR. *American Society*. New York: A. A. Knopf, 1951.

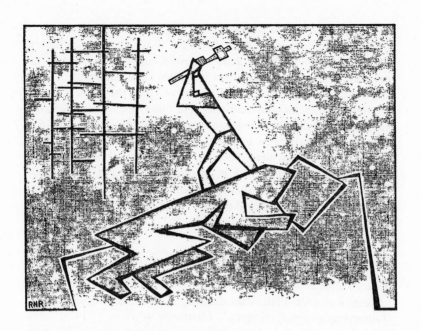

ECONOMIC AFFAIRS

"Seek justice, relieve the oppressed.—" *(Isaiah 1:17)*

"Judaism has always emphasized that our ethical ideals must also be applied to the economic processes of society. Our society must be judged by the extent to which men are enabled to achieve, through their work, a decent standard of living, and to provide for themselves and their families the fullest possible protection of their mental and physical health."—*UAHC, 1955*

NOTHING COULD be more foolish than to attempt to identify religion—and especially Judaism—with a particular social or economic system. Too frequently is religion invoked in support of pre-conceived economic views. There are those who fashion highly-rationalized arguments designed to prove that maintenance of the free enterprise capitalistic system is a stern commandment of God, and there are others who seek to derive from the Bible a moral sanction for the socialist economy. At other times God, religious teachings, and the Bible are summoned as witnesses by opposing sides in controversies as to whether this or that approach to the problem of unemployment, housing, labor, or health is best. None-theless, certain fundamental principles are inherent in Judaism. What follows is a brief survey of some of the major economic problems of contemporary American society, and the relevance of such Jewish religious principles to them.*

Labor

Judaism conceived of labor as dignified and noble. Unlike the ancients and even Plato who disparaged labor, the rabbis taught: "Labor lends dignity to man." (*Nedarim 49b*) and "Love labor and hate lordship." (*Aboth 1:10*) The prophets and rabbis were workers and artisans. While divine blessing was invoked upon the works of man's hands (*Deut. 28:12*), the Bible has no patience with the indolent rich:

> "Sweet is the sleep of the laboring man,
> Whether he eat little or much;
> But the satiety of the rich
> Will not suffer him to sleep."
>
> (*Ecclesiastes 5:12*)

The Mosaic Law is solicitous for the rights of the laborer. The hired servant must not be mistreated. He must be given rest on the Sab-bath. He must receive his wages before sunset. The employer had a right to the work of the laborer but could not presume to control his body or his soul. And, together with other groups, the hired servant was guaranteed free access every seventh year—the year in which cultivation of the soil was suspended—to whatever grew in the fields spontaneously. When laborers were not fairly treated, the prophets excoriated the evil-doers. "Woe," inveighed Jeremiah against King Jehoiakim,

---

* For more detailed information on these topics, see pamphlet on "Juda-ism and Economic Issues" published by the Commission on Social Action of Reform Judaism.

"Woe unto him that buildeth his house with unrighteousness,
And his chambers by injustice;
That useth his neighbor's service without wages,
And giveth him not his hire."

(Jeremiah 22:13)

In modern times, individual Jews and the organized Jewish labor movement have played significant roles in the building of a strong American labor movement. Jews, together with other immigrant groups in our urban centers, helped form the basis for much of organized labor in the United States. Samuel Gompers, an immigrant English Jew, was a founder of the American Federation of Labor in 1886. He served as president until his death. Adolph Strasser, an immigrant German Jew, helped to lead the early AFL. Jews were active in the founding and growth of many labor unions; the International Ladies Garment Workers, and the Amalgamated Clothing Workers, unions which set standards for labor statesmanship, are but two outstanding examples. The continuing close link between the Jewish community and the American labor movement is reflected in the existence of the Jewish Labor Committee, an organization of Jewish trade unionists which, since its inception in 1934, has worked side by side with all labor unions in the struggle to achieve equality of opportunity in employment and all other aspects of life for all Americans, regardless of race, creed or color.

Not enough Americans are aware that during the past two generations—and particularly in the last generation—we have passed through a peaceful revolution in terms of the status of the laboring man. Sixty years ago the average American laboring man worked sixty hours a week and took home $11 each week. The sixty hours were brutally hard. Moreover, the status of the worker in society was low. Few of the nation's workers were organized. Rarely were existing labor unions able to bargain collectively with their employers; for the most part, they were still struggling to secure recognition. Employers, by and large, had no concept of the benefits to be derived by themselves and the economy in general from high wages, decent working conditions, and a measure of social security.

The laborer is no longer a pariah in American society. His average pay is sufficient to make possible a standard of living which, to most of the world, seems lavish. Generally, he has clean, safe working conditions; a paid vacation; security for his old age guaranteed by both the government and his employer; protection against illness and disability. He has, moreover, a militant labor union which looks out for his interests. It is not the millennium, but it is the attainment of a new dimension for the American laborer. Samuel Gompers once summed up labor's demands in one word—"more." But this does not merely mean more money. It means more dignity, more security; it means more justice not only for the worker but in American society in general.

It was the labor union which, probably as much as any other single factor, brought this increased measure of security and dignity to the American worker. As a nation, we have come a long way since the early 1800's when American courts banned union organization as a criminal tendency "to exact and procure great sums of money for their work and labor . . . to the damage, perjury, and prejudice of the masters employing them." The struggle for the rights of labor was long and difficult, culminating in the Wagner National Labor Relations Act, enacted in 1935, which has been regarded as the Magna Carta of American labor.

The Wagner Act was designed not merely to protect the rights of workers to form labor organizations. It was clearly and admittedly intended to encourage the growth of labor unions, in the conviction that labor's poor bargaining power results in low wages and therefore depressions which cut production and commerce. Under the stimulus of a sympathetic law and administration, labor flourished. Membership in trade unions grew from 2,973,000 in 1933 to 8,500,000 by 1947. Today 16 million working men belong to an estimated 75,000 local unions and through these to 215 national or international unions. One out of every three workers in non-agricultural establishments is a member of a union in mid-twentieth-century America.

Despite the revolutionary progress of the past few decades, there are still hard problems confronting labor. Labor leadership regards the Taft-Hartley Law of 1947 as an essentially anti-labor instrument which seriously hampers the further development of labor unionism. Supporters of the measure contend, on the other hand, that the Wagner Act had been one-sided in its pro-labor bias and that the public welfare required the redressing of the balance. Many major religious organizations—such as the National Catholic Welfare Conference, the National Council of Churches of Christ in the U. S., and the Synagogue Council of America—have criticized the law as inequitable and, in some respects, unworkable. The Central Conference of American Rabbis came out flatly for repeal of this legislation. While experience with the law would seem not to bear out the extreme charges made by some labor leaders that this is a "slave law" which will wreck labor unions, it is also true that even some of the supporters of the original act are now willing to acknowledge the unfairness and unworkability of some provisions of the law. Synagogues and churches should familiarize themselves with the provisions and operation of this legislation and should evaluate it in terms of the ethical insights of religion.

In recent years, labor unions have become increasingly concerned about so-called "right-to-work" laws being adopted by state governments. Some labor leaders acknowledge that these state laws now represent a more serious threat to the labor movement than does the Taft-Hartley Law. By the end of 1955, eighteen states had adopted such legislation whose single common feature seems to be an effort to restrict and hamper labor unions. While the much-criticized Taft-Hartley Law permits union discipline of and discharge of any employee who fails to pay his union dues, even this minimum discipline is denied to unions under "right-to-work" laws. Union maintenance-of-membership clauses are outlawed. It would appear that such legislation, invariably adopted in states where unions are weakest, is designed to keep labor weak.

Further complicating labor's position were the startling revelations of racketeering brought to public attention by the investigations of the Select Committee on Improper Activities in the Labor or Management Field, under the leadership of Senator John L. McClellan. These investigations led to a widespread public demand for legislation to prevent such abuses. With President Eisenhower taking an active role in pressing for strong labor-reform legislation, a law was enacted in 1959, in the white heat of public controversy, establishing new and far-reaching controls on labor unions. Labor leaders condemned the act as a "killer measure" and protested that the well-publicized malfeasance of James R. Hoffa and a few other power-mad labor leaders had been utilized as a pretext for drastic anti-labor action by the Federal Government.

The full effect of the labor reform law's 16,240 words will not be clear until the legislation is tested by experience. The law represents a significant change in federal policy by severely restricting secondary boycotts and picketing for union recognition; and by extending state jurisdiction over labor cases.

Thorny problems continue to beset labor, but they are more than matched by new and exciting opportunities and challenges. The vision of a united labor movement has been achieved. New horizons are being glimpsed as a result of the achievement of a guaranteed annual wage in some industries. The drive to organize Southern workers, agriculture workers, and white-collar workers is being stepped up. Within the framework of unity, labor is striving to strengthen its power in political action. It is intensifying its present efforts to shape a society which will be increasingly liberal, humane, and responsive to human needs. This augurs renewed vigor in labor's legislative drives for civil rights legislation, a fair American immigration law, increased minimum wage and social security coverage, a comprehensive and effective medical program for all Americans, federal aid to education, and for a dynamic and imaginative foreign policy. With greater power, however, also comes greater responsibility for labor in keeping its own house in order. Just as it vigorously met the challenge of Communist-dominated unions, the labor movement will have to come to grips effectively with such internal problems as jurisdictional strikes, continued discrimination against Negroes in some unions, and corruption in a few unions such as the International Longshoremen Association.

The American labor movement has achieved a large measure of maturity. Through the leadership of such statesman-like figures as Reuther, Meany, Dubinsky, and others, American labor has demonstrated its recognition that it has a profound stake in and responsibility for the strengthening of a democratic and just society and the achievement of a peaceful and forward-looking world society.

Social Welfare

A principle which has always been characteristic of Judaism is that it is not only a good thing but a positive religious duty to help the weaker members of society—the widow, the orphan, the stranger, the sickly, and the downtrodden. This quality continues to be a distinctive attribute of Jewish life. Concern for the unfortunate members of society goes back to the Bible, to the pleas of the prophets, to social legislation: "Who is kind to the poor lends to the Lord." (*Book of Proverbs, 19:17*) So persuasive was the rabbinic teaching about the imperative of charity that a rabbinic council of the second century actually felt constrained to apply a slight brake by decreeing that no person should devote more than a fifth of his fortune to charity.

Jewish communities from ancient times to the present have maintained collections for charitable institutions and agencies to meet the needs of the unfortunates. The generosity and self-sacrifice which makes Jewish philanthropy unique has been a source of amazement and admiration to many non-Jews. Jewish philanthropy in the U. S. has also in certain respects, pointed the way for the non-Jewish community. The Community Chest campaigns were consciously modeled on the operation of the Jewish federation idea. In applying the principle of Jewish responsibility for the weak to modern-day realities, it is certainly fair to say that one can find no sanction in the Jewish religious tradition for a philosophy of complete laissez faire, of each man for himself regardless of the consequences. Judaism insists that society has an inescapable obligation to safeguard the security of its weaker members.

The American economic system is generally characterized as a "free enterprise" system of individual initiative and individual responsibility. But it no longer bears any resemblance to the concept of "laissez faire"—every man to himself, and the government taking the least possible responsibility for the social welfare of its citizens—which was formulated by Adam Smith in 1776 and which provided the economic framework for our early development as a nation. As reformers, muck-rakers and Congressional investigations focused attention on the economic misery which resulted from unbridled free enterprise, as Presidents like Theodore Roosevelt and Woodrow Wilson affirmed the government's social responsibility toward its citizenry, as industrialization and its attendant human problems compelled federal action, the conception of the role of government underwent drastic revision. The *coup de grâce,* however, was the stock market crash of October, 1929, which brought about the complete and final destruction of the amoral concept of "laissez faire" as an American economic philosophy.

On the ruins of the crash was erected the living proposition that not only has each man a responsibility to his fellows and to his society but that society is responsible to some extent for his social welfare and security. In a sense it was Herbert Hoover, faced with the greatest economic crisis in American history, who in desperation inaugurated elements of the New Deal, such as public works programs. His successor, Franklin Delano Roosevelt, fully and firmly accepted the government's responsibility for the social and economic welfare of its people. Through relief, recovery, and reform—the famous "three R's"—the government set out to provide funds for the basic necessities and then to provide, and sometimes to create, jobs for the millions of unemployed. Through a complex of social legislation—to secure minimum wages, to abolish child labor, to extend credit to the farmer, to regulate the sale of securities and the activities of public utilities, to combat unemployment

—the full weight of the prestige and power of the U. S. Government were brought to bear for the first time on the economic process of the nation.

Regardless of sharply differing assessments of the New Deal, there can be no doubt that it left a deep, and perhaps permanent, imprint on our economic life. A good example is the Social Security program adopted in 1935. This measure was the first comprehensive admission by the federal government that the overall welfare of every individual was the responsibility of the community through its government. In effect, it ruled out for all time the possibility of leaving these problems to chance, charity or caprice. The American people accepted the general premise that the community as a whole benefited when the welfare of each individual was secure. The Social Security Law provided the final blow to the nineteenth century concept that each man was responsible for himself and to himself alone. Rugged individualism was replaced, in large measure, by the recognition that each man had the right to a just share of the fruits of his labors and that no man should overly profit at the expense of another man's poverty. The new law provided for old age annuities, unemployment insurance, and more adequate care for the needy, dependent, and the disabled. In large measure, with the exception of old age insurance, these measures were based on federal-state cooperation with the states usually administering the program. By 1937, every state, along with the District of Columbia, Alaska and Hawaii, had fulfilled the requirements of the Social Security Act. Payment of benefits began the following year. Subsequent legislation extended social security coverage to government employees, farm laborers, and domestic servants, so that the bulk of the American labor force is now included. In the spirit of this trend, individual states have also enacted social legislation in these and other areas, such as unemployment compensation and industrial accident insurance.

Without question the concept of the government's responsibility for social welfare is here to stay. This fact was demonstrated after 1952, with the virtually unquestioned acceptance by a Republican Administration of every major aspect of the fabric of social welfare initiated by its predecessors. In some cases, in fact, social welfare measures were expanded by the Eisenhower Administration. In all probability, the areas of social responsibility will continue to increase as the public's definition of what constitutes the "general welfare" is expanded.

There are still new frontiers of social welfare to be explored.

One of the basic needs toward which future social welfare legislation will undoubtedly be directed will be that of insuring that all
Americans, irrespective of income, receive basic medical services
—as a matter of right and not of charity. As a nation, we have
made notable progress in the past twenty years, chiefly because
these were decades of unparalleled prosperity. In addition, we have
witnessed a rapid growth of voluntary health insurance programs.
According to a recent survey, more than 87 million people, or 57%
of our population, have some hospital insurance; more than 74
million people, or 48%, have some surgical and other medical insurance. But, despite these advances, we have not yet eliminated
the ethical failure which led the Union of American Hebrew Congregations in 1948 to declare:

> "We recognize that medical care is unavailable to many rural
> communities and that in large metropolitan centers the cost
> of medical care has become prohibitive to large masses of
> people. We urge government help, so that adequate medical
> care would be available to all at a cost within the reach of
> all."

The American people spent $10.2 billion in personal health
services in 1953. Of this, only 15% was covered by health insurance. Approximately 1 million families a year paid out almost
half their incomes for medical services while ½ million families
paid amounts equalling or exceeding 100% of their incomes. Of
all American families, 15% were in debt to hospitals, physicians,
dentists and other providers of medical services; their total debt
was $900 million. Of the 7½ million families with medical debts,
a million families owed $195 or more in the year cited.

What these figures suggest is that, despite the mushrooming of
voluntary health insurance programs, we are far from the goal of
medical care available to all at a cost within the reach of all. A
substantial group of low-income families are not covered by such
programs at all. Moreover, the coverage made possible by these
programs is, in the overwhelming majority of cases, far short of
taking care of total charges. Few even begin to protect against the
crushing financial burden of serious and protracted illness. The
stark truth is that only a small percentage of American families can
cope with a major illness, involving costly surgery, for example,
without falling into heavy debt. It requires little imagination to
imagine the emotional strain generated when a medical crisis is
compounded by such financial strictures. While there is legitimate

ground for differing views as to the proper role of government in this realm of social concern, it is certain that empty oratory and sterile negativism will not solve the problem of providing adequate medical care for all Americans "at a cost within the reach of all." It would appear that the federal government, as it has in so many other areas, will have to help safeguard the right of the American family to such medical services in accordance with elementary principles of justice and humanity.

A related and equally serious challenge lies in the field of mental health. As more Americans become aware of the great benefits to be derived from psychiatric and psychological services, the question of the availability of such facilities at prices all families can afford becomes increasingly acute. For mental health, there is no voluntary health insurance. Private psychiatric treatment is usually more costly than the average family can afford. While some of the slack is taken up by community agencies and clinics such as the Jewish Family Service, which charge moderate fees, such facilities do not begin to meet the staggering need and invariably maintain hopelessly long waiting lists. The federal government has indicated an increasing concern for the vast problem of mental health, but there would appear to be no alternative to substantial federal legislation to assist communities to meet their local needs in this vital regard.

Concentration of Economic Control

The attitude of Judaism toward the rights of property was succinctly expressed in a judgment from ancient literature: "He who saith, 'what is mine is mine, and what is thine is mine' is a wicked person." (*Aboth 5:13*) The right to property was always affirmed in Judaism, it being conceived as a sacred trust from God which was attained through industry and which was to be used for the benefit of all. Throughout the period of the Old Testament, the Talmud, and the Middle Ages, the right of the individual to property was always acknowledged. A whole complex of laws and institutions was developed dealing with the maintenance of private property.

Along with the rabbis' injunction that "Thy neighbor's property shall be as precious to thee as thine own" (*Aboth 2:17*), Judaism has always been equally insistent that property and wealth must not be used for evil purposes. Prophetic literature is filled with examples of angry condemnation of those who abuse their wealth and property. "Woe unto them that join house to house, that lay field to field, till there be no more room, and ye be made to dwell alone in the midst of the land." (*Isaiah 5:8*) The right to acquire property and wealth acknowledged, it was the way in which they are secured and the purposes to which they are put that evoked the approval or disapproval of God's spokesmen. The right of private property, in rabbinic teachings, was never placed on as high an ethical level as was the sacred quality of human life. "One human being," said a rabbi, "is worth the whole of creation." Likewise in the social teachings of the prophets, the rights of property are relative, while human rights are absolute.

In America, the need to prevent monopolies was always felt to be inherent in the free enterprise economic system. "Competition is the life of trade" was the common adage. But unbridled, bitter competition in the rapidly industrializing United States was the very force which led to business consolidation. The age of the small business in America lasted until just before the Civil War. Ever since that time, with the emergence of the transcontinental railroad, the development of a national market, and the speeding up of industrial mechanization, the United States has been faced with the problem of industrial concentration.

The problem of monopoly—its extent, the social and economic consequences which flow from it, and what should be done about it—poses a serious challenge to the American people. It is an economic problem and, as such, raises questions which strike at the fundamentals of the limits of freedom in a free enterprise economy. It is a political problem, and, as such, raises questions about the relationship between economic and political power in a democratic order. And it is an ethical problem involving the protection of the small and the weak against the acquisitive power of the economic giant.

The trend in the direction of industrial concentration in the U. S. has been uneven. The first great movement of this kind took place in the 1880's and 1890's with the rise of the giant trusts—Standard Oil, sugar refineries, etc. Public outcry led to the Sherman Anti-Trust Act, but it turned out to be a futile instrument in preventing monopoly. Monopolies and trusts flourished. The First World War stimulated the trend further as the government winked at cooperation between corporations as a necessary aspect of the war effort. With the depression of the 30's, the movement was accelerated further as small firms fell into bankruptcy and others became absorbed by large industrial units in order to survive. During the

Second World War, contracts were largely siphoned to the larger concerns, fifty companies receiving two-thirds of the total dollar value of defense expenditures.

In 1947, following the war, as a result of these various trends, there were in this country 273 non-financial corporations, each with assets of over $100 million. The top two hundred of these corporations, less than one-hundredth of one per cent of all corporations, held 40% of all corporate assets, and between 20 to 25% of the total national income-producing wealth, excluding assets held by government and individual consumers. The largest two hundred corporations employed one-eighth of the total civilian labor force and one-fifth of all employees of business outside of agriculture. Half of the total assets of the 273 non-financial corporations were held by public utilities alone; four industries— steel, automobile, chemicals, and oil—all of them heavily concentrated, accounted for almost two-thirds of the remainder.

Among our public utilities, one corporation today holds a practical monopoly of the telephone business and another of the telegraph business of the country. Great holding and investment corporations control much of our electrical industry, while a major part of the mileage of the nation's railways is directed by a handful of large railroad systems and banking groups.

In the field of natural resources, one corporation—U. S. Steel— owns one-half to two-thirds of the iron ore resources of the United States. One company possesses most of the bauxite used in the making of aluminum. Four corporations control the majority of our copper production.

THE NATION'S SHAREHOLDERS

As far as the *ownership* of the country's publicly held corporations is concerned, Brookings Institution in 1953 declared that the shares were owned by 6½ million Americans (4% of the population), representing 4½ million families. The top 3% of that 6½ million, it asserted, owned 65% of the dollar value of the shares outstanding. In many corporations where wide distribution of stocks prevails, a small group of officers to whom proxies are sent at the time of the annual meetings are able to elect the directors they desire and determine the corporations' policies.

In many industries where a few great corporations dominate the market, the *price leadership* practice prevails, and prices are set by one or more of the leading corporations, the remaining firms, through fear or otherwise, following the lead. "Price leadership" is now standard practice according to Professors Stocking and Watkins, in the processing of steel, oil, glass, brass, anthracite coal, tin cans, corn products, salmon, biscuits and crackers, agricultural implements, fertilizers, industrial alcohol, copper, lead, newsprint, sulphur, plaster, and bananas, among others. In these and many other industries, the days of free competition as formerly understood are past.

DEFENDERS AND CRITICS OF BIG BUSINESS

Concentration of industry has been defended on the ground that giant corporations furnish a better basis for mass production and low costs of production, make possible greater efficiency, more fruitful industrial research, better financing, sales, personnel, distribution, and planning policies, and aid American industry in its competition with foreign products.

On the other hand, the rise of monopoly has been attacked on the ground that it leads to the concentration of too great power in the hands of the few over the economic life of the nation, and leads too greatly to the restriction of competition, to the crushing of small competitors by fair means and foul, to the development of monopolistic and rigid price practices, with resulting greater economic instability, to the weakening of individual initiative, and the increase of inequalities in wealth and income.

Declared the Federal Trade Commission a few years ago: "If nothing is done to check the growth in concentration, either the giant corporation will ultimately take over the country, or the government will be impelled to step in and impose some form of direct regulation." Whether this dire prediction is correct or not only time will tell. Certain it is that the problem of monopoly has not yet been solved by the American people. Its solution will require not only the best judgments of our economists but the firm application of moral principles and the vigilance of public-spirited groups and citizens.

The trend toward mergers and concentration of economic control continued to increase in tempo through 1955 with no signs of abatement. From banking to textiles, small firms continued to be absorbed into larger and more powerful units. Small retail businesses were increasingly being squeezed by the rapid rise of larger discount houses on the one hand and giant and growing department store syndicates on the other. However, counter-pressures which have been present within trade groups, government, and civic organizations also began to increase in tempo. They were highlighted at the end of 1955 by the widely-publicized Senatorial investigation into alleged monopolistic practices by the General Motors Corporation.

Both vigilance and concern will be needed on the part of every concerned citizen to maintain America's diversified economic system on a democratic and expanding basis.

Other Economic Problems

While the statement of the Union of American Hebrew Congregations, which prefaces this chapter, properly declares that "our ethical ideals must be applied to the processes of society," the fact is that few American synagogues seriously examine contemporary economic issues from the standpoint of Jewish ethical ideals. Where such examination and discussion have taken place, they have dealt largely with those issues already discussed in this chapter—labor relations, social welfare, or possibly the problem of industrial concentration and monopoly. There are, however, a number of economic problems, less dramatic in nature perhaps, which ought also to be receiving the concerned attention of all who believe that society should reflect our highest ethical values. This chapter can do no more than to suggest in broad outlines a few of the many such problems.

NATURAL RESOURCES

The vast productivity of America would not be possible without the lavish riches of God's bounty called our natural resources. Forests, rangeland, water, coal, gas, power—seemingly limitless resources lay before our pioneering forebears. But they used them with the profligacy of the wealthy spendthrift. Forests were logged without thought of re-seeding. Topsoil was turned to dust by excessive and unwise cropping. Rangeland became desert. Sources of water were polluted and exhausted. Minerals, fish, wildlife, and recreational sites were expended with no thought to the future.

For the past half century, conservationists—of whom President Theodore Roosevelt was a symbol—have struggled to preserve our natural resources from private exploitation in the conviction that God's resources are the property of all men. The late Justice Louis D. Brandeis spoke for these forces in 1910, before a Congressional Committee investigating the Department of the Interior, when he said:

"Conservation, in its very essence, is preserving things public for the people, preserving them so that the people may have them. It is the aim of our great democracy that men shall, so far as humanly possible, have equal opportunities, and that the differences in opportunities to which men have been subject elsewhere shall not prevail here. That is what conservation means."

In the past half century, we have come a long way in the direction of responsibility and intelligent planning in the many areas of conservation and the judicious use of our natural resources. But many problems remain. Nearly 3,300,000 square miles of land at one time belonged to the federal government; more than 60% of this land has been transferred to the states or to private owners—and the pressures on the government for sale of range and grazing lands in parts of the West and Alaska to private interests continue. We have been even more wasteful with our usable timberland; we are, for example, using our available saw-timber at a rate 40% greater than its yearly rate of growth. Our soil is being used up; 100,000 acres have become untillable as a result of exploitative methods of land-use and millions of additional acres are being damaged each year by erosion. Despite the undeniable benefits of the Tennessee Valley Administration and other public power projects, we have not extended this concept to the Missouri Valley and to the Columbia River Basin which desperately need such development. Lack of effective public regulation has resulted in serious wastage of oil, natural gas, and coal.

It is apparent that "planning" is the key word in the preservation and sensible development of our natural resources. We must recognize the social responsibility we have to preserve and develop all our resources for the benefit of the greatest number, not only for today but for hundreds of years to come. It is the duty of the citizen to weigh all plans in the light of the results which they are likely to produce for all people.

Hell's Canyon, the prospective public power project in Idaho, is not just a name. It pinpoints a fundamental difference in philosophy between two great forces. In every area dealing with natural resources we shall find the same conflicts—whether in the development of atomic energy or in regulating the number of sheep which may graze public lands. Neither exponents of public development nor adherents of private enterprise may question the supremacy of the public interest.

The solution to the pressing problems of conservation cannot be found in slogans or shibboleths. No magic attaches to the labels of "public power" as against "private power," and neither formula is sacrosanct. The duty of the conscientious citizen is to look beyond the labels to the reality. More important than who is doing the particular development programs are such questions as:

Is it in the public interest?
Will the development find new resources?
Will it make fuller use of those we have?
Will there be less waste of our resources?

These are the acid tests by which the religiously motivated citizen can judge the morality of our stewardship of God's bounty.

FARM POLICY

During the past century, the sole concern of the American Jewish community in the area of agriculture and farm problems has been the various attempts made, both on an individual family and on a colony basis, to settle immigrant Jewish families on land. The Jewish Agricultural Society continues to be concerned with this task.

Otherwise, however, the urban-dwelling Jews of the United States and Canada have not been in close contact with the complex problems of agricultural life and work. There are, of course, good historical reasons for the neglect of this area and for this pre-occupation with other problems of society, but it has become clear to increasing numbers of American Jews that the situation of America's farmers must be a social concern to the religious Jewish community.

Historically, Jewish rootage in the soil runs very deep. The history of the ancient Jewish people for many centuries was the story of an agrarian people. At times nomadic, again enslaved in Egypt, and subsequently entering into the more settled community life of the Promised Land, throughout that period, and to a considerable extent in later centuries in Europe, the great preponderance of the Jewish people were farmers.

In the more specialized society of modern America relatively few Jews are directly engaged in agriculture. Only about 2% of American Jews are farmers. All of us, however, in common with all other human beings of whatever faith and whatever occupation, have a direct and vital stake in the effective operation of the agricultural economy. That is to say we all eat food, virtually all of which comes from farms; and we all wear clothes, a great proportion of which originate as cotton, wool or some other farm commodity.

The simple and fundamental fact of human dependence on the products of agriculture for physical subsistence needs to be reemphasized in a day of highly urbanized living. Otherwise it is too easy for city-dwellers to fall into the fallacy of the well-intentioned but ignorant city housewife who was heard to exclaim: "But I don't really care what happens to the farmers. You see, I buy all my food at the A & P."

We cannot afford not to care what happens to the farmers. Not only because of the ethical problems involved in farm policy, but also because our economic history indicates that depressions are frequently farm-led and farm-fed. The lessons of our recent history bear remembering. After World War I, agriculture suffered a severe deflation, and it did not share in the much-publicized prosperity of the late 20's. Most economists believe that the persistent depression in agriculture contributed strongly to the economic collapse of 1929. It seems certain that the U. S. cannot maintain a prosperous economy if this crucial sector of the economy is permitted to languish in depression.

For more than 25 years, the federal government has recognized this problem and has assumed the responsibility of providing some measure of price stability and income support to the farmer. Why should the government contribute to the support of the farmer? Approached from the ethical viewpoint of the public interest, the argument is developed somewhat along these lines: it is in the public interest that farmers shall protect the nation from famine and weakness by producing abundantly of food and fibre. Because of the uncertainties of production, farmers must produce more than is presently required in order to assure that year in and year out there will be an adequate supply. If we require farmers to produce in such abundance, is it not simple justice that we protect them by a public program from the economic havoc which inevitably results when a surplus is thrown on an unprotected market?

Our farm programs of the past two decades are based on the concept of parity. Parity is a ratio between a farmer's prices and his costs. Architects of the original farm program selected 1910–14 as an historic period when farm prices and farm costs were deemed to be in reasonable balance. They said in effect, if a bushel of wheat would buy a pair of overalls in 1910–14, it should do the same in 1935, 1945, or 1955. Both political parties, in general, agree that farmers are entitled to 100% parity. The issues at controversy revolve about: What percentage of parity should the government support? By what means? And for whom?

Proponents of the high-level price supports (90% to 100%) of parity argue that parity is no more than equity and if the program is really going to help farmers, it should establish these reasonable and equitable floors. They point out that consumers are not injured by this level of support, because an hour's labor in industry would buy more of the basic foods at 100% of parity during World War II than at any previous time in history. Moreover, between 1947 and 1955, farm prices declined to 84% of parity, —a drop of almost 30%,—but virtually none of this decline has been passed through to the consumer of food or clothing.

On the other hand are the defenders of lower levels of support and of the so-called "sliding-scale." Under this policy for basic commodities, as the supply rises, the price support level falls. Advocates say this will reduce regimentation of farmers, make the market operate more like a "free" market, and discourage production of surpluses.

In rebuttal, it is argued that farmers have repeatedly voted in wheat, cotton and tobacco referenda for whatever acreage and marketing controls are necessary to maintain a firm price support program; that it is the harshness of the "free" market that the price support program is designed to get away from; and that lowering prices does not reduce production, but actually, as explained above, tends to increase it.

How shall prices be supported? We have become accustomed to a system under which the government purchases and stores or encourages the farmer by a non-recourse loan to store that portion of the commodity that will not sell at the established price. This has worked rather well with grains, cotton and tobacco which are non-perishable. Even with these commodities, however, and more especially with dairy and livestock products and other perishable commodities, the ethics of huge storage programs in a world still haunted by hunger have been gravely questioned. One of the great moral challenges confronting our nation is how to utilize our mountainous surplus of foods in the solution of world-wide hunger.

There are many additional problems of ethical significance in relation to the farmer. Of the 15% of our population now engaged in agricultural activity, 4½ million people are wage workers in agriculture, many of them migratory and seasonal workers. All evidence demonstrates that the great bulk of this group are caught in a pattern of poverty, insecurity and despair. A study in 1949 indicated that the male non-migratory farm worker earned a gross annual income of $818. Migratory workers had averaged yearly earnings of $739. To make matters even more desperate, farm laborers have been excluded from the benefits of social legislation, including minimum wage legislation and unemployment compensation. The plight of the migratory group is well summarized by the following description quoted from the Report of the 1951 President's Commission on Migratory Labor:

> "Migrants are children of misfortune. They are the rejects of those sectors of agriculture and of other industries undergoing change. We depend on misfortune to build up our force of migratory workers and when the supply is low because there is not enough misfortune at home, we rely on misfortune abroad to replenish the supply.
>
> "Migratory farm laborers move restlessly over the face of the land, but they neither belong to the land nor does the land belong to them. They pass through community after community, but they neither claim the community as home nor does the community claim them. Under the law, the domestic migrants are citizens of the United States but they are scarcely more a part of the land of their birth than the alien migrants working beside them.
>
> "The migratory workers engage in a common occupation, but their cohesion is scarcely greater than that of peoples on the seashore. Each harvest collects and regroups them. They live under a common condition, but create no techniques for meeting common problems. The public acknowledges the existence of migrants, yet declines to accept them as full members of the community. As crops ripen, farmers anxiously await their coming; as the harvest closes, the community, with equal anxiety, awaits their going."

These problems are of importance not only to the farmer. They have an urgent claim upon our social conscience.

Taxation

Taxation has been part of man's economic burden since governments were first organized to lead and to serve society. There are few examples in human history of taxless societies. Certainly, the ancient Hebrews of Biblical days paid taxes in various forms. Before the establishment of the monarchy under King Saul, taxes were paid "to God," both on a voluntary and on a compulsory basis. Moses exacted a head-tax of every male Israelite. Priests, Levites, the poor—all received compulsory offerings which amounted to more than 20% of the produce of land and flocks. Under the monarchy, taxes to the Temple continued, and levies were also exacted by the King. At times these were "free will" offerings; under other monarchs, farmers and merchants alike were taxed to pay for wars, to aid the poor, and to fill the king's coffers.

During the medieval period, Jews paid double taxes. They were heavily taxed by their secular rulers: coronation taxes, dress taxes, and the infamous *Judengeleitsgeld* or *Leibzoll* (travel or safe-conduct pass required of and paid for by Jews alone), and many others. In addition, however, the well-organized Jewish inner community (*kehillah*) exacted taxes for internal Jewish needs: the upkeep of the synagogue and other communal institutions like hospitals, orphanages, homes for the aged; relief for the poor, ransom funds for captives, and the like. Even today in America, many Jews think of their annual contributions to welfare funds and federations not as philanthropy but almost as a form of taxation. In any democratic society, taxation is the means by which, in the words of the late Justice Oliver Wendell Holmes, citizens are "bearing their share of the institutions upon which their well-being, if not their life, depends."

Taxation performs indispensable functions in a democracy. But to many Americans it is a dry, technical business with which they are concerned only on or about April 15th of each year. And yet, underlying the technicalities and the complexities of tax laws, are public policies which have profound moral significance. The limitations of space permit us merely to suggest a few such questions:

(1) Which type of tax is fairer and wiser from the standpoint of public policy—consumption (or sales) taxes or taxes on income?

(2) Although the graduated income tax is recognized as the core of our American tax structure, large numbers of otherwise reputable citizens not only cheat in computing their income tax returns but feel no pangs of conscience about so doing. Why is this so and what can be done about it?

(3) There is sharp controversy about the proper form which tax reductions should take if and when they are feasible. Businessmen tend to advocate relief to business and industry, on the argument that the benefits therefrom filter down to the public through increased investment opportuni-

ties, business expansion, productivity, and employment. Other experts urge tax relief largely for the lower income groups, on the argument that benefits will accrue to the entire population through increased purchasing power and consumption of goods. Is either attitude more correct morally? Why?

(4) Interest is mounting in a proposal to provide some averaging procedure for those individuals whose incomes inevitably fluctuate sharply from year to year (professional men, entertainers, writers, baseball players, and others). Such a procedure already exists for business and industry in the form of "operation loss carryback" and "carry forward deductions." Does such a proposal conform to principles of fairness and good public policy?

(5) Our tax laws have, over the years, increasingly rewarded so-called "risk capital" with tax write-offs for plant expansion and speculative investments supposedly in the national interest (like oil-well drilling). Are such deductions both fiscally and morally sound? Is there, morally at least, as much justification for such tax benefits as there is for proposals to increase deductions for the mass of American taxpayers on such items as dependents, medical expenses, domestic help for working mothers?

In addition to all these moral and ethical questions in the area of taxation, primary problems are involved in the pressures leveled against legislators in the writing of our tax laws. Even more serious are the problems involved in the enforcement of tax laws by the various governments. Periodically, scandals erupt involving public officials and, usually, substantial citizens who have conspired to defraud the government of tax monies. Public complacency in the face of these scandals seems to be symptomatic of a dichotomy between our principles and our practices in the area of taxation. This dichotomy must be a concern to all Americans, Jews and Christians alike, who wish to live in accordance with ethical values.

Rabbis and Economic Justice

One of the earliest comprehensive Jewish pronouncements on economic justice in the United States was the platform adopted by the Reform rabbis in 1918. In this document, the rabbis urged adoption of a minimum wage, eight-hour day, one day of rest in seven, and the right of workers to bargain collectively. The progressive positions on economic issues charted by the Central Conference of American Rabbis were parallelled in large measure by the ideas advocated over the years by the Rabbinical Assembly of America, representing the Conservative rabbinate. In one case, the Conservative group took an even more radical stand, calling in 1933 for a reduction of the work week to thirty hours.

The concern of religious bodies in American life with the ethical implications of economic issues has not consisted of mere pontificating. In some cases, their concern has been brought to bear upon the current scene with powerful effect. A notable example was the campaign waged by the three major faiths in the 1920's to abolish the twelve-hour day and the seven-day week in the steel industry. President Harding had urged the industry to put an end to the twelve-hour day. Pointing to an investigation it claimed it had conducted, the Iron and Steel Institute announced that a shorter working period in the manufacture of steel was not feasible. Here, the late Rabbi Horace J. Wolf, chairman of the Social Justice Commission of the CCAR, entered the controversy, enlisting the cooperation of the National Catholic Welfare Conference and the Federal Council of the Churches of Christ. The three groups issued a joint statement addressed to the conscience of America. Due in no small measure to the moral influence of organized religion, the steel industry on July 6, 1923, announced plans for reducing the inhumanly long work period.

The right of labor to organize has long been vigorously advocated by Catholic, Protestant, and Jewish religious bodies in the United States. Both the Reform and the Conservative rabbis, at their annual conferences, denounced yellow-dog contracts, company unions, industrial espionage, and injunctions against striking workers. The Reform rabbis hailed the steps taken to unionize sleeping car porters in 1928 and social workers in 1936. Together with the Protestant and Catholic groups, Reform rabbis conducted on-the-spot investigations into the lockout on the Western Maryland Railroad in 1926 and, the following year, into the mistreatment of the Real Silk Hosiery workers. The CCAR commended the National Labor Relations Act; in 1949 and subsequently, it urged repeal of the Taft Hartley Law. Consistently, Reform rabbis, like their Conservative colleagues, urged the CIO and the AFL to heal the breach in organized labor and restore labor unity. They rejoiced, in December 1955, when the merger was consummated.

Many rabbis have risked much in supporting the principles of economic justice. Rabbi Stephen S. Wise, who strode across the first half of the twentieth century like a latter-day Isaiah, was one such. "The sermon I shall preach this morning will light a million-dollar blaze," he said to his wife one morning in 1919. Already a leader with wide influence, Rabbi Wise was the spiritual head of a congregation which, after a decade of renting quarters, was then planning to build its own structure. The rabbi knew full well that what he planned to say in his sermon would evoke angry protests from some of his biggest contributors. The background for this sermon, assessed at a million dollars, was the bitter struggle of the steel workers, protesting the twelve-hour day, to organize. The companies resorted to black lists and labor spies to prevent union activities and to smearing to confuse the public: "Let us ferret out the Bolshevists," said U. S. Steel leaders, "and peace and contentment will return to the American factories."

Rabbi Wise took dead aim on the situation and fired his heaviest volleys from the pulpit:

> ". . . The men in the iron and steel industry are striving for
> a fundamental right of industry . . . the right to organize
> and deal organizedly with their employers . . . I charge
> Mr. Gary with having made it impossible for me as an Ameri-
> can citizen to know what the thought and what the will of
> the workers in the steel industry is. They have never been
> free to utter them themselves. They are not free today. I
> charge the United States Steel Corporation with resorting to
> every manner of coercion and even of violence . . . in order
> to avoid the organization of the workers . . ."

Rabbi Wise's prediction was accurate. Enough wealthy congregants resigned to force postponement of the building project for many years.

American rabbis have consistently advocated the use of mediation, conciliation and arbitration to settle industrial disputes. Frequently, rabbis have served as mediators and arbitrators, many of them with great distinction. The Social Justice Commission of the CCAR was asked on two separate occasions by striking workers to mediate their conflicts. In 1916, the CCAR heaped criticism, for refusal to arbitrate, on various employers in New York and on some striking workers on the Pacific Coast.

The rabbinate, in its pronouncements on economic matters, has constantly been in the vanguard of the liberal forces seeking a broader measure of economic justice for all. Many, though not all, of the specific proposals of the CCAR and the Rabbinical Assembly were, over the years, adopted as national policy. Suggestions for compensation for industrial accidents, workmen's health insurance, public housing, a national system of employment agencies, unemployment insurance, abolition of child labor, social security, public works as a means of reducing unemployment—these measures are now, for the most part, recognized parts of the American scenery. The important function of religious bodies has been to apply the insights of religion to economic injustice, to dramatize the needs, and to prod the conscience of the public and the law-maker.

In viewing the current situation, it seems safe to say that the religious passion for economic justice which marked the 20's and 30's has certainly abated. There are understandable reasons for this. We have been living for years in the glow of national prosperity. Inevitably, energies have been directed to the solution of other problems in our national life which have loomed larger than the economic. While it is true that the National Catholic Welfare Conference and the National Council of the Churches of Christ maintain effective departments on economic affairs, that the Religion and Labor Foundation continues to function, and Jewish and other denominational groups continue to adopt occasional resolutions on economic issues, the truth is that few synagogues or churches have genuinely accepted economic problems as being within the sphere of their own religious concern. And this is the heart of the matter and of the challenge to religion: to make congregants aware that the moral issues involved in our economic processes justify, indeed require, study and concern on the part of the individual church or synagogue.

THE RABBI AND THE LAYMAN

Most laymen found it possible to agree with many, if not all, the rabbinic proposals outlined earlier. There were, however, other more advanced and far-reaching recommendations by the rabbis which left many laymen cold—and left a few others decidedly hot. Such pronouncements included the CCAR proposal for a steeply progressive taxation of "the higher brackets" and its endorsement of the socialization of banking, transportation, communication and power plants. These specific proposals flowed from the expressed conviction of both the CCAR and the Rabbinical Assembly that the profit system of commerce and industry is not completely compatible with their interpretation of reverence for human personality. The Conservative rabbis characterized the free enterprise system as "a denial of human brotherhood," while their Reform colleagues called for "a fundamental reconstruction of our economic organization" as indispensable. These resolutions were developed at a time when the American economic system was obviously failing to provide an adequate standard of living for most Americans. While these resolutions have not been withdrawn, recent years have not revealed the same kind of anxiety on the part of the rabbinic groups.

It is frequently asserted and widely believed that there is a deep gulf between the laymen on the one hand and rabbis on the other in terms of attitudes toward major social issues of our time. That there are some differences is undeniable, but the extent and depth of these differences has been subject to considerable exaggeration. A review of the social positions adopted over the years by the rabbis, through the Central Conference of American Rabbis, and the laymen, through the UAHC, reveals an impressive measure of agreement on a large number of issues, including opposition to restrictive immigration policies, support of the League of Nations and later the United Nations, support for civil rights measures including a federal FEPC, concern at threats to civil liberties, opposition to religious practices in public education, and many other important issues.

Revealing also has been the experience of the Commission on Social Action which is made up of rabbis representing the CCAR and laymen and women representing the UAHC and its affiliates. In considering the many issues which have come before this joint body, there have frequently been differences of opinion among the members. In no case, however, has a division developed between rabbis on the one side and laymen on the other. Individual rabbis have frequently been somewhat surprised to find themselves arguing for more moderate or conservative points of view than those being advocated, and with vigor, by one or another lay person on the commission.

And yet there are obvious differences. Because of their greater opportunities for study and understandably sharper sensitivity to Jewish values, rabbis as a group have been much more preoccupied with their responsibility to apply religious principles to social justice than have most laymen. The Social Justice Commission was one of the first permanent committees of the CCAR and one to which the most prestige attached. In fact, the records of the conference indicate an occasional remark by a rabbi that the Social Justice Commission was becoming so important in the total conference program that the tail threatened to wag the dog. But the interest of the conference in social justice has not appreciably diminished as a result of these occasional demurrers.

The only sphere in which differences between the rabbis and laymen appear to be deep is that of economic justice. Where the rabbis during the depression years were preoccupied with labor-management relations and the problems of unemployment, the UAHC adopted few positions on economic matters and these were general in nature. This, too, is understandable. The membership of a synagogue is anything but homogeneous in its social outlook; on economic issues it is bound to be sharply divided. It is not surprising, therefore, that a few laymen raged like wounded cougars when they learned that the rabbinic conference condemned the free enterprise system and, on another occasion, came out for a compulsory national health program.

What does this mean for the individual synagogue and its social action program? In the first place, the right of the rabbis to speak out in conference must be as zealously safeguarded as the right of the individual rabbi to a free pulpit. Individual Jews are under no compulsion to agree with the rabbinic pronouncements, nor are the national and local congregational bodies under obligation to associate themselves with the views of the rabbis or even to consider the particular position, if they choose not to.

Insofar as individual Social Action Committees in congregations are concerned, they too are free to decide upon their own positions and upon the particular spheres of activity in which they wish to engage. It may be the better part of wisdom for most such committees, at least at the outset when they must win genuine acceptance by the entire congregation, to concentrate on those issues where there is a greater measure of agreement within the Jewish community and the synagogue.

But certainly the Social Action Committee should assist the congregants in studying major current issues in economic affairs, such as the status of employer-employee relations, unemployment, and the spread of social security. Individual members of the congregations should be informed and should be helped to examine current problems in accordance with the insights of Jewish ethical principles. The Social Justice Platform of the CCAR, adopted in 1928 put it eloquently: "Religion must be in all things or it is in nothing. Religion must be everywhere or it is nowhere. It must touch life at every point or it does not touch it at any point."

BIBLIOGRAPHY

ADAMS, WALTER and HORACE M. GRAY. *Monopoly in America: the Government as Promoter.* New York: Macmillan Co., 1955.

BOGEN, BORIS D. *Jewish Philanthropy.* New York: Macmillan Co., 1917.

BOWNE, HOWARD R., JOHN C. BENNETT, WILLIAM ADAMS BROWNE, JR. and G. BROMLEY OXNAM. *Christian Values and Economic Life.* New York: Harper and Brothers, 1954.

BURSK, EDWARD C. Editor. *Business and Religion.* N. Y.: Harper and Brothers, 1959.

CHILDS, MARQUIS W. and DOUGLAS CATER. *Ethics in a Business Society.* New York: Harper and Brothers, 1954.

Commission on Social Action of Reform Judaism. "Judaism and Current Economic Issues." A pamphlet.

Conference on Economic Progress. "Full Prosperity for Agriculture." A pamphlet.

Federal Council of the Churches of Christ in America. Series on the Ethics and Economics of Society. Harper and Brothers.

FLEISCHMAN, HARRY and RORTY. "We Open the Gates: Labor's Fight for Equality." New York: National Labor Service, 1958. A pamphlet.

GOLDSTEIN, SIDNEY. *The Synagogue and Social Welfare.* New York: Bloch Publishing Co., 1955.

Health Information Foundation. "National Family Survey of Medical Costs and Voluntary Health Insurance," 1954. A pamphlet.

MARCUS, JACOB. *Communal Sick-Care in the German Ghetto.* Cincinnati: Hebrew Union College Press, 1947.

MAY, HENRY F. *Protestant Churches and Industrial America.* New York: Harper and Brothers, 1949.

National Association of Manufacturers. "Moral and Ethical Standards in Labor and Management." N. Y.: NAM, 1958. A pamphlet.

SELEKMAN, DR. BENJAMIN M. *A Moral Philosophy For Management.* New York: McGraw-Hill, 1959.

STEIN, EMANUEL, JEROME DAVIS and Others. *Labor Problems in America.* New York: Rinehart & Co., Inc., 1940.

VELIE, LESTER. *Labor, USA.* New York: Harper, 1959.

WARD, A. DUDLEY, ed. *Goals of Economic Life.* New York: Harper and Brothers, 1953.

IMMIGRATION

"Neither let the alien,
That hath joined himself to the Lord, speak,
    saying:
'The Lord will surely separate me from His
    people;'
. . . the aliens, that join themselves to the
Lord . . .
To be His servants . . ." (Isaiah 56:3, 6, 7)

I N JEWISH TRADITION, since all men are fashioned in the
image of God, not even the stranger, sojourning in the land, is
beyond the pale of God's protection. Maltreatment of the alien is
intolerable. When the people violated God's will and oppressed
the stranger, they visited upon themselves the angry lash of the
prophet's rebuke.

The stranger is guaranteed the same protection in the law court as is extended to the native. "Judge righteously between a man and his brother, and the stranger that is with him." (*Deut. 1:16.*) He must not be discriminated against in the payment of wages (*Deut. 24:14, 15*) nor in the apportionment of land (*Ezek. 47: 21–23*). Like other needy persons, the stranger had free access to the grain which, according to the Law, had to be left unharvested in certain parts of the field, and to the grapes which fell from the vine. (*Lev. 19:9, 10; 23:22; Deut. 24:21*) Even with regard to divine forgiveness, the stranger stood with the native in God's compassion. (*Num. 15:26*)

While it would go too far to assert that the stranger was in every respect accorded equality of privileges with the Israelite, nonetheless the spirit of compassion and kindliness for the stranger, concern for his welfare, and recognition of his godliness illumines the Bible, as reflected in those glowing passages.

In modern times, America has been the chief exemplar of the open door and the hearty welcome to the immigrant. Between the years 1820 and 1937, a tide of 40-million immigrants poured into the United States, giving concrete meaning to the vision expressed by the Jewish poetess, Emma Lazarus, inscribed on the base of the Statue of Liberty:

> "Give me your tired, your poor,
> Your huddled masses yearning to breathe free,
> The wretched refuse of your teeming shore,
> Send these, the homeless, the tempest-tost, to me;
> I lift my lamp beside the golden door."

Of course this vision of the "golden door," open to everybody, was never completely realized. The colony of Massachusetts, as far back as 1647, excluded any person "ordained by the Pope." Orientals were largely excluded from the U. S., beginning in 1882, and contract laborers were barred from immigration in 1885. Yet, until the dawn of the twentieth century, the United States properly regarded itself as a nation of immigrants and, by and large, viewed more immigrants as necessary to the further growth and development of the nation. It was a genuinely composite people which built America into greatness.

Jews were among the major beneficiaries of the open-door policy. Between 1825 and 1910, the original chiefly Spanish immigration was augmented by two far greater waves. Following abortive liberal revolutions in Central Europe, a tide of more than

200,000 Jews, mostly German, poured into the United States. When pogroms once again flared in Czarist Russia beginning in 1871, a mounting flood carried over two million Jews to American shores by 1910.

The Closed Door

As has been pointed out by Dr. Oscar Handlin, a foremost student of American immigration, the traditional American immigration policy rested on the assumption that American institutions were so strong and so good that they would have a positive effect on all immigrants to this land, regardless of the land and circumstances from which they came. Thus, the American people welcomed millions of immigrants who streamed in between the mid-nineteenth century and the end of the century, because they didn't feel threatened by newness—contact with "new" people, "new" cultures. They felt supremely confident in the ability of their own culture to prevail. By the turn of the century, however, as immigration reached nearly a million people a year, this confidence began to give way to an anxious fear that "the uniquely American culture" might be drowned in the flood of strangers.

Underlying this drastic change in attitude toward the immigrant was a new set of assumptions which, by 1900, had begun to permeate American thinking. These assumptions were that mankind is made up of several biologically separate races and that racial origin significantly shapes culture, political views, and status in society. From these assumptions, it was easy to differentiate among the various groups of immigrants seeking admission to the United States. One group seemed to descend from the same stock as the original Anglo-Saxon Americans. The others were racially different—therefore inferior—and seemed to represent a threat to the "American way of life."

Since immigration had been so much a part of the American scene, it did not seem possible to shut it off immediately. Instead, efforts were directed to selecting from various kinds of immigrants. Advocates of restrictive immigration seized upon the device of the literacy test, hoping to admit those who descended from the same stock as old Americans and to keep out the Eastern and Southern Europeans. The literacy test was finally enacted during the First World War, over President Wilson's veto. Within a few years, however, it became apparent to the supporters of the literacy test that it was not successful in the way they had expected. And thus, in the search for a more effective instrument of racial and ethnic discrimination, the national origins quota system was born.

The national origins quota system is a formula for the selection of immigrants in proportion to the percentage which that racial or ethnic stock represented in the total white population in the United States in 1920. This system became the cornerstone of American immigration policy by an act of Congress in 1924 (the Johnson Act) which set an annual limit of 154,000 immigrants. Nearly 80% of the annual quotas were assigned to the countries of Northern and Western Europe, on the frank assumption that persons of British or Irish or German ancestry would make better Americans than persons of Italian, Russian, or Greek origin. Despite the fact that only about one-sixth of the quotas from Great Britain and Ireland were used each year, and the waiting lists for the small-quota countries were heart-breakingly long, the unused quotas could not be allotted to countries that would use them.

RACISM IN THE LAW

The national origins quota system undoubtedly reflected the nervous and inflamed state of public opinion in the years immediately following the First World War. Anti-foreign sentiment ran high, reinforced by the prevailing isolationist mood and the fever of "Red" hunting which swept the country after the war. The Ku Klux Klan, with five-million members, was a powerful force in many Southern and Mid-Western states, and many members of Congress were members of the hate-ridden organization. In this unhealthy atmosphere, racism rationalized as a national origins quota system was accepted as the yardstick for American immigration policy.

That the framers of the national origins quota conceived it as a device of racial discrimination is clearly revealed in the report submitted by Dr. Harry Laughlin, appointed in 1922 by the House Committee on Immigration to study the biological basis of immigration—a report frequently cited in defense of the national origins system:

> "Our outstanding conclusion is that making all logical allowances for environmental conditions which may be favorable to the immigrant, the recent immigrants (southern and eastern Europe) as a whole present a higher percentage of *inborn* socially inadequate qualities than do the older stocks . . ."

Between 1920 and 1952, a few voices were raised in criticism of our basic immigration policies. The Union of American Hebrew Congregations and the Central Conference of American Rabbis were among the few American organizations which consistently condemned the quota system as an abandonment of the American policy of "keeping America a haven of refuge for the persecuted and downtrodden of the world." For the most part, Americans were either too preoccupied with a series of national and international crises, or were reluctant to agitate this inflammable question lest they revive the ugly Klan-like reactions of the post-war years.

The tragic plight of Displaced Persons at the end of World War II led to the enactment in 1948 of the Displaced Persons Act and the admission to the U. S. of over 300,000 persons. It must be pointed out, however, that this humanitarian legislation was achieved only after a bitter Congressional controversy and as a result of one of the best organized citizens' campaigns in American history spearheaded by the Citizens Committee for Displaced Persons. The D.P. Act, while it briefly revived the American spirit of hospitality toward the immigrant, was an emergency, temporary measure. Like the Refugee Relief Act of 1953, it was carefully kept outside the framework of basic U. S. immigration policy. If anything, these laws underscored the need to go beyond palliative measures and to correct our basic immigration policies.

In the late 40's, however, the entire question of American immigration policy was reopened as Congress addressed itself to a codification of all immigration laws adopted over a thirty-year period. Here, many thought, was a rare opportunity to give American immigration policy a fresh look, free of the prejudices of the past which had been repudiated by modern social science. Here was an opportunity to create a policy geared to the needs of an America which stands as the leader of the free world, a policy which would be consistent with the American traditions of humanity and fair play.

But the opportunity was lost. Or, rather, it was seized by those who wanted to make our immigration policy even more restrictive than it already was. The result was the McCarran-Walter Act of 1952, called by *Newsweek* magazine the most controversial law of the land, by others the most un-American act in our legislative history.

Essentially, the Immigration and Nationality Act of 1952 (Public Law 414, 82nd Congress) re-affirms the Immigration Act of 1924 and specifically maintains the national origins quota system.

It fails even to change the base year of computation of quotas from 1920 to 1950. In addition, the act substantially affects the rights of aliens and naturalized Americans; impairs our relations with the rest of the world; and creates an immigration system which reeks of suspicion and regards every potential immigrant as a liability and commodity rather than a valuable asset and a human being. To make matters worse, the act failed to revise the mortgaging provisions of the Displaced Persons Act of 1948. The D.P. Act had charged persons admitted to the U. S. against future quotas of the countries of their origin. Thus, half the quotas of countries with small quotas will be unavailable well into the next century (Latvia until 2274, Poland 1999, etc.). In fairness, it should be pointed out that the law has the following positive benefits: (1) it does codify what was a chaotic mass of separate immigration laws; (2) it does give every nation in the world a quota—for the first time—even though they are tiny; (3) it does eliminate sex discrimination; (4) it made aliens of Japanese origin eligible for naturalization.

Nonetheless, the law is grounded in discrimination and hostility. That the purpose of the national origins quota system, as adopted in 1924 and re-affirmed in 1952, was discriminatory was readily acknowledged by chief sponsors of the McCarran-Walter Act. Any other plans of selection, the late Senator McCarran insisted, "would in the course of a generation or so change the ethnic or cultural composition of the nation." The venerable reactionary added: "We have a good mixture now." Senator Walter George, who was in the Senate when the original 1924 law was adopted, assured the Senate that the original intention was "to preserve something of the homogeneity of the American people, something of the character of the men who loved self-government, who understood it and had some concept of it."

The Senate Judiciary Committee which submitted the bill that became the Immigration and Nationality Act of 1952 (the Mc-Carran-Walter Act) said:

"Without giving credence to any theory of Nordic superiority, the sub-committee believes that the adoption of the national origins formula was a rational and logical method of numerically restricting immigration in such a manner as to *best preserve the sociological and cultural balance in the population of the United States.* There is no doubt that it favored the peoples of the countries of northern and western Europe over those of southern and eastern Europe, but the sub-committee holds that the peoples who had made the greatest contribution to the development of this country were fully justified in determining that the country was no longer a field for further colonization, and henceforth, *further immigration would not only be restricted but directed to admit immigrants considered to be more readily assimilated because of the similarity of their cultural background* to those of the principal components of our population." [Underscoring ours]

The Act is strongly defended, primarily on the following grounds: (1) It was the result of a long and arduous legislative process; (2) It achieves a necessary codification of the welter of immigration statutes never before pulled together; (3) It was passed by Congress even over President Truman's veto; (4) It protects our national security by setting up elaborate tests of immigrants, resident aliens, and naturalized citizens; (5) It keeps immigration down to a minimum; (6) The act "is complimented by the nature of those who seek to have it repealed or destroyed by amendment," in the words of Senator McCarran. McCarran's compatriot, Congressman Walter, had been even more frank, indicating in the Congress that he felt that "professional Jews" were foremost among those forces opposing the act.

Actually, the American people at large seem to have become aware since the adoption of the McCarran-Walter Act of the extent to which outdated prejudices have been allowed to determine our immigration policies, and the extent to which this law is woefully inadequate to meet the needs of the United States today. A Gallup poll in 1955 showed that most Americans desire a more liberal policy of immigration. Extreme right-wing "patriotic" societies are the chief defenders of the principles of the act, while Dwight Eisenhower, Adlai Stevenson, Harry Truman, the AFL-CIO, the League of Women Voters, the American Civil Liberties Union, and virtually every other responsible organization in American life have found reason for deep concern. The President's Commission on Immigration and Naturalization, after study based on months of public hearings and on the basis of 638 oral and written statements from specialists in every field of American life, concluded that the act must be completely "rewritten . . . because it flouts fundamental American traditions and ideas . . . displays a lack of faith in America's future . . . damages American prestige and position among other nations . . . ignores the lessons of the American way of life." Experience with the law has confirmed the validity of these charges.

A TEST OF OUR PRINCIPLES

Though immigration law is to some extent a technical and complex matter, it is an issue of vital concern to every American. It affects our economy; the United States needs more manpower and more immigration to fill this need. It affects our foreign policy. We are losing friends because we are the only nation in the world which has written discrimination into its immigration law. It bears on our traditional civil liberties. Moreover, a nation's immigration policy is one measure of its well-being and its dedication to the principles which underlie both Christianity and Judaism: the sanctity of every individual, the brotherhood of man, the dictates of justice and mercy. For this reason, every major religious group in the United States has spoken out for a better, more humane, spiritual approach to U. S. immigration policy. In November, 1955, at hearings on U. S. immigration policy, spokesmen for the National Catholic Welfare Conference, National Council of Churches of Christ in U.S.A., and the Synagogue Council of America called for drastic revision of the McCarran-Walter Immigration Law and especially of its national origins quota system.

A better immigration policy will not be won easily and quickly. Fundamental revision of existing legislation will require intensive and steady effort of a long-range nature. Only when the American people are fully aware of the noxious implications and effects of our current immigration policies, of the damage they are doing to our international prestige and to our democratic ideals, then—and only then—will thoroughgoing corrective action take place. Few greater challenges confront synagogues and churches which take seriously the application of their religious ideals to contemporary affairs.

THE ROLE OF THE SYNAGOGUE

The synagogue has an important part to play both in the educational process and in vital grass-roots action. The congregation-at-large should be made aware of the traditional Jewish attitude toward immigration, and the implications of a restrictive and discriminatory immigration policy in a democratic society. The Social Action Committee should keep the congregation informed of important national developments, such as the status of legislation designed to achieve revisions of current immigration law, so that individual members of the congregation who so desire may communicate their views to their congressmen and senators and other public officials, write letters to the editor of the local newspaper, or take other appropriate action.

The synagogue should join with other forward-looking groups in the community in spearheading community interest and action. Many communities throughout the country have inter-sectarian committees on immigration to coordinate local activities on this issue. Such committees are representative of the various groups in the community—religious, nationality, civic, labor, veterans, welfare, etc. Where such committees exist, the synagogue should be part of the effort. Should no such committee be in existence, synagogue social action committees should consider the possibility of priming the pump to create such a needed instrumentality. In addition, contact should be established with the National Committee on Immigration and Citizenship, an organization of distinguished citizens striving for increased public understanding of the need for an enlightened U. S. immigration policy.

In view of the substantial measure of agreement among Protestant, Catholic, and Jewish religious bodies on the need to revise basic U. S. immigration policy, this is an ideal issue in which to develop effective interfaith activity. Representatives of the Synagogue Social Action Committee should meet with church leaders to explore the possibility of joint activities, such as a three-faith conference, open to the public, on immigration policy; joint statement; special religious service; or an interfaith effort to convene a community-wide Committee on Immigration.

Many resources are available to individual synagogues seeking guidance and assistance in working on U. S. immigration policy. The NCRAC Immigration Committee, which formulates policy for NCRAC agencies in connection with immigration matters, is available to every Jewish community or synagogue group for consultation and information. Technical assistance in handling individual immigration cases can be secured from United-HIAS, and in special cases from the American Jewish Congress.

Educational materials are available also from the American Jewish Congress, American Jewish Committee, Friends Service Committee, National Catholic Welfare Conference, National Council of Churches, Anti-Defamation League of B'nai B'rith, and the American Immigration Conference.

BIBLIOGRAPHY

BACHRACH, PETER. *Problems in Freedom*. Harrisburg, Pa.: Stack-pole Co., 1954.

BARKWAY, MICHAEL. "Turning Point for Immigration." Toronto: Canadian Institute of International Affairs, 1958. Pamphlet.

BERNARD, WILLIAM S. *American Immigration Policy*. New York: Harper and Bros., 1950.

BRUCE, J. CAMPBELL. *The Golden Door*. New York: Random House, 1954.

DAVIE, MAURICE R. *Refugees in America*. New York: Harper and Bros., 1947.

HANDLIN, OSCAR. *Boston's Immigrants:* A Study in Acculturation. Cambridge, Mass.: Harvard University Press, 1959.

HANDLIN, OSCAR. "Immigration as a Factor in American History." N. J.: Prentice-Hall, 1959. Paperback.

HANDLIN, OSCAR. *The Uprooted: The Epic Story of the Great Migrations that Made the American People*. Boston: Little, Brown and Co., 1951.

HANSEN, MARCUS L. *The Immigrant in American History*. Cambridge, Mass.: Harvard University Press, 1940.

HIGHAM, JOHN. *Strangers in the Land. Patterns of American Nativism, 1860–1925*. New Brunswick: Rutgers University Press, 1955.

HUMPHREY, SENATOR HUBERT. "The Stranger at Our Gate, America's Immigration Policy." A Public Affairs Committee pamphlet published in cooperation with the American Jewish Congress.

KENNEDY, JOHN F. "A Nation of Immigrants." New York: Anti-Defamation League, 1959. Pamphlet.

KONVITZ, MILTON. *Civil Rights in Immigration*. Ithaca, N. Y.: Cornell University Press, 1953.

National Conference of Catholic Charities. "Immigration—Truths and Prejudices." A pamphlet.

REES, ELFAN. "We Strangers and Afraid: The Refugee Story Today." New York: Carnegie Endowment for International Peace, 1959. Pamphlet.

TYLER, POYNTZ, ed. *Immigration and the United States*. N. Y.: H. W. Wilson Co., 1956.

PEACE AND INTERNATIONAL RELATIONS

"And He shall judge between many peoples,
And shall decide concerning mighty nations
    afar off;
And they shall beat their swords into plow-
    shares,
And their spears into pruning-hooks;
Nation shall not lift up sword against nation,
Neither shall they learn war any more."
    (Micah 4:3–4)

THE LOFTY PEACE-INTOXICATED passage from Micah notwithstanding, the ancient Hebrews were not pacifists or lovers of peace at any price. Not unlike other nations of the time,

Israel was swept by strife and war throughout the centuries. The idealistic prophet proclaimed "Not by might nor by power, but by My spirit, saith the Lord" (Zech. 4:6), but the people of Israel, like people in all other lands, not only fought wars but said they fought them in God's name and for His glory. It was not until the destruction of Israel's statehood in 70 C.E. that the prophetic vision of peace became the dream of the people. From that time on, the ideal of universal peace as the mission of Israel became inseparable from Jewish thought.

George Holley Gilbert, in *The Bible and Universal Peace,* describes the emergence of this national ideal:

> "The ancient Hebrews had a warlike career. They fought the battles of Yahweh from century to century. But when at last their national existence was no more, when they sat and sighed by the ruins of their holy city or far away among the nations, some among them dreamed of a new and wondrous age that was yet to come. They thought of their past, glorified, indeed, in the far retrospect, but they did not long to have those ages return unchanged. They dreamed of a future that should be far better than the best that their fathers had ever known, and one constant element of that great future— one on which they dwelt with satisfaction—was peace. Out of the soul of centuries of strife and bloodshed blossomed, as a fair flower, the vision of a time when peace should flow as a river. By this vision the Hebrew prophets became leaders of the race toward a future kingdom whose realization is still among the treasures of hope."

The word *shalom* (peace) was the greeting of Israel. But the Hebrew *shalom* has a far broader meaning than the English word, "peace." When Jacob dispatched Joseph to find out how his brothers and their flock were doing, he directed him to "Go now and see the peace of thy brethren and the peace of the flock." (*Gen. 37:14*) Personal well-being and group welfare are comprehended in the word. "How beautiful upon the mountains are the feet of the messengers of good tidings, that announceth peace, the harbinger of good tidings, that announceth salvation." (*Isa. 52:8*)

The Apocrypha, the Midrash, and the Talmud place the same high valuation on the ideal of peace. Commenting on the rabbinic teachings in this regard, Professor Moritz Lazarus in *The Ethics of Judaism,* says: "No chapter of the doctrines of morality is developed with such exuberance of thought and depth of feeling as that on the value of peace among men."

The great contribution which Israel made to civilization was not merely its elevation of the ideal of peace at a time when war was the normal, accepted state of affairs nor its dynamic and broad concept of peace; it was also the remarkable vision of a *universal* peace—not for Israel alone, but for all nations. Spoken at a time when nations were separated from each other by a gulf seldom bridged except by war, Micah's prophecy cast a shadow forward across the centuries to such peace covenants of modern times as the United Nations.

Not only were the prophets the first to enunciate the dreams of universal peace, they were also the first to proclaim that such a peace must be based upon justice. Angus Dun and Reinhold Niebuhr declared in an article entitled, "God Wills Both Justice and Peace":

> "The struggle for justice and the struggle for peace have the same sanction in the commandment of love. Both present a moral imperative. But justice has the prior claim, for while order may be conducive to justice, there can be no lasting peace without justice. The Biblical concept is expressed by Isaiah: 'And the effect of righteousness will be peace' (*Isa. 32:17*). The just war position gains strength from the consideration that the triumph of an unjust cause would defeat both the ends of justice and the future hope of peace."

The yearning for peace is expressed in our most solemn prayers:

> "Grant us peace, Thy most precious gift, O Thou eternal source of peace, and enable Israel to be its messenger unto the peoples of the earth. Bless our country that it may ever be a stronghold of peace, and its advocate in the council of nations. May contentment reign within its borders, health and happiness within its homes. Strengthen the bonds of friendship and fellowship among the inhabitants of all lands. Plant virtue in every soul, and may the love of Thy name hallow every home and every heart. Praised be Thou, O Lord, Giver of peace." (*Union Prayerbook, Vol. I, p. 22*)

The resolutions and statements of position of Jewish religious bodies in modern times reflect a continuing dedication to the goal of a universal and just peace. In general, Jewish religious groups, while recognizing the necessity of self-defense and resistance to aggression, have thrown their moral support behind every effort which seemed to lead to genuine international cooperation for the achievement of disarmament and peace. A glimpse at some of the resolutions adopted by Jewish religious organizations over the past four decades probably mirrors with reasonable accuracy the prevailing Jewish attitude toward major problems of peace and war:

"We give assurance to President Wilson of our fullest support in the establishment of the League of Nations and in his strivings to bring forth a just peace for mankind." (*CCAR, 1919*)

* * *

"Apprehending that competitive and naval preparations presage war among civilized nations in opposition to the spirit of the Kellogg Peace Pact, signed and ratified by our government and other nations; therefore be it

Resolved that this 32nd Council of the Union of American Hebrew Congregations, in convention here assembled, endorses the outlawry of war and the pacific settlement of all international disputes." (*UAHC, 1931*)

* * *

". . . The world has risked so much for war. Let it risk as much for peace." (*Closing words of resolution on international relations, May, 1933, Rabbinical Assembly of America.*)

* * *

"We hail preliminary plans announced for a democratic world organization to include small nations. We favor the establishment of an international assembly of nations which would create a body of international laws and which would have the power to enforce them. We urge such international cooperation on the highest religious grounds." (*CCAR, 1944*)

* * *

". . . We believe that the United Nations should be expanded and its powers increased, so that in time it will become the nucleus of a world government." (*UAHC, 1948*)

* * *

". . . We urge that the United Nations be made in deed as well as in word the cornerstone of U. S. foreign policy. There is little doubt that the prestige and influence of the United Nations have been weakened by a tendency to by-pass it, or to fail to make full use of its machinery in crucial matters. Our task must be to strengthen the United Nations. We believe that such strengthening requires the United Nations to become truly a world organization which it cannot be until it becomes a council of all nations. We darken the hope of world peace when we neglect the United Nations, disparage its values, and especially when we give vent to irresponsible threats to withdraw from this assembly of nations." (*UAHC, 1955*)

Religious groups in American life, as evidenced by the above resolutions, which are substantially parallelled by Protestant and Catholic statements, have recognized their stake in the United Nations. Indeed, religious bodies are at least partly responsible for the participation of the United States in the United Nations. The immense moral influence of the church and the synagogue helped to create a climate of opinion which was receptive to world organization. The unanimity of the three major faiths in American life on the basic principles of peace for the post-war world was reflected in a joint statement prepared by the Synagogue Council of America, Federal Council of the Churches of Christ, and the National Catholic Welfare Conference signed by representative individuals of all faiths and issued in 1943. It was entitled, "The Pattern for Peace," and is published in full in the Appendix. (See page 268)

The United Nations Today

Now, after more than a decade of experience with the United Nations, despite the many defects and inadequacies which have become apparent over the years, religious bodies in America maintain their faith in the United Nations. Typical is a statement of the trustees of the Church Peace Union which, in June, 1952, characterized the UN as "the best political agency now available for the expression on the international scene of . . . faith in a universal righteous God and in a universal moral law."

Does the United Nations merit this characterization? What has it achieved? Where has it failed? And, finally, what can religious forces, and specifically the synagogues in America, do to make the United Nations an even more effective instrumentality for the maintenance of genuine peace based on righteousness?

PURPOSES AND STRUCTURE

"To save succeeding generations from the scourge of war . . . to take effective collective measures for the prevention and removal of threats to the peace and for the suppression of acts of aggression . . . to achieve international cooperation in solving international problems of an economic, social, cultural or humanitarian character and in . . . encouraging respect for human rights"—

these are the high purposes of the United Nations as outlined in the eloquent words of the Charter. The Security Council, comprising five permanent, and six non-permanent members, is vested by the Charter with "primary responsibility for the maintenance of international peace and security." The General Assembly, which is made up of representatives from all member nations, is authorized to "discuss any questions" relating to the preservation of peace. These two, together with the Trusteeship Council, the International Court of Justice, and the Secretariat, make up the six regular organs of the United Nations. Augmenting their work are the many specialized agencies and commissions which have been created to provide machinery through which the peoples of the world can cooperate in coming to grips with such common problems as ignorance, poverty, and sickness.

UN as Peacemaker

The UN was set up on the assumption that the major victorious powers of World War II would be able to agree on the basic terms of peace in the post-war world. It was not intended that the new international organization would be responsible for framing the post-war peace. Rather, it was expected that the major powers would quickly agree on peace treaties with the defeated nations, and that the UN would work largely to bind up the wounds of conflict and bring the nations into "one world."

Instead, however, the UN has had two strikes against it from the outset. Since 1945, the world has been split into two armed camps, polarized by a cold war of fluctuating intensity. Treaties with Japan, without Russia's ratification, were signed in 1951, and with Austria in 1955, with Russian participation. The Soviet Union, also unilaterally, has signed peace treaties with Bulgaria, Hungary and Rumania. And treaties with Germany were still the subject of embittered debate at the end of 1955. Thus the United Nations, designed to function in a world of peace, has had to operate in a world in which, though World War II was over, real peace had not followed. Thoughtless persons have called the UN a failure because it has not created genuine peace. But, as President Dwight D. Eisenhower said, the UN is nothing more than a mirror in which the world can see its true self. The amazing thing is that, under the terrible strain imposed upon it from the beginning, the UN has done as well as it has in preventing armed conflict and aggression between member nations.

The UN helped to achieve a withdrawal of Russian troops from Iran in 1946. It secured a cease-fire in the dispute between Kashmir and India. Through the UN, an armistice was reached ending the armed aggression against Israel. In Greece, UN representatives investigated the assistance Greek Communists were getting from Communist satellite countries, their report producing a needed determination in the democratic world to keep Greece free.

Through its powers of mediation, the UN eased the dispute between the Netherlands Government and Indonesia, serving as midwife to the new independent nation of Indonesia. The channels and contacts of the UN contributed indirectly also to the conversations that ended the Berlin blockade in 1948–49 and the French-Indochina armed conflict in 1954.

Alongside these successes of the UN must be placed its monumental achievement of collective resistance to armed aggression in Korea. In this unprecedented action, the UN succeeded in repelling aggression and safeguarding the independence of South Korea. It should be noted that the action of the UN authorizing the defense of South Korea was taken by the Security Council through the fortuitous circumstance that the Soviet delegate was absent from the council at the time.

In addition to the important precedent for collective resistance of aggression, the Korean conflict had another incidental but far-reaching result. The power of the veto in the Security Council to stymie the UN in reacting to acts of aggression was limited in 1950 by action of the General Assembly. In a series of actions called the "Uniting for Peace" resolution, the General Assembly assumed the responsibility, in the event of failure by the Security Council to act against aggression, to recommend to its members "collective measures, including . . . the use of armed force when necessary, to maintain or restore international peace and security." A Peace Observation Commission was set up to report on situations "in any area where . . . international tension . . . is likely to endanger . . . international peace." Member nations were also asked to maintain units within their armed forces which could be used by the UN to maintain peace.

Building World Understanding

"Since wars begin in the minds of men, it is in the minds of men that the defenses of peace must be constructed." This sentence from the preamble of the constitution of the United Nations Educational, Scientific and Cultural Organization indicates the essential purpose of UNESCO. Through UNESCO, the minds of men have been better equipped with the knowledge which helps them to achieve a more cooperative life with their fellow men throughout the world. Through UNESCO, the peoples of the world have worked together to attack the basic causes of war by promoting higher standards of living, a greater measure of freedom, and by creating necessary conditions of well-being.

UNESCO has helped to reconstruct educational systems in war-devastated countries. It publishes international journals to give teachers and others in less developed areas materials not available to them in their countries, and publishes teachers' guides dealing with human rights. It helps governments to organize public library systems. It sets up centers for scientific material and information in various parts of the world. It provides fellowships which help students to study abroad. Through films and radio, student exchanges, international seminars, and in many other ways, UNESCO carries on the long-range objective of educating for international understanding.

One activity of UNESCO which is of particular significance is its program of "fundamental education" against illiteracy. Since more than half of the people of the world can neither read nor write any language, this is a vast undertaking. Fundamental education, as UNESCO conceives it, involves not only teaching how to read and write but also imparting a minimum of knowledge on such matters as elementary health and work requirements. In Haiti, thanks to UNESCO, reading material has been prepared in the Creole language and a local newspaper is published. In Brazil and India, UNESCO has arranged institutes on adult education. In other regions of the world, centers have been developed where teachers can be trained.

Man's Humanity to Man

The UN International Children's Fund (UNICEF) was set up as a temporary agency to save the lives of children who, in the wake of World War II, were threatened by disease and starvation. For close to sixty million children in seventy-five countries, it has provided extra meals, milk, vitamins. It has built penicillin plants. Mothers have been educated in child care, and nurses given special training. UNICEF has spearheaded campaigns against child-crippling and killing diseases, such as whooping cough, diphtheria, and tuberculosis. In these and many other such humanitarian activities, UNICEF has achieved so remarkable a record that the UN Economic and Social Council voted to make it a permanent agency.

WORLD HEALTH ORGANIZATION

WHO is a continuation of the international health agency of the League of Nations. It helps governments to counteract epidemics, frequently sending teams of experts to fight communicable diseases. Its work is, by its very nature, frequently more dramatic and demonstrably effective than some of the other specialized agencies. For example, through WHO assistance, malaria, a disease which affects three-hundred million persons a year and exacts a toll of three-million deaths, has been virtually eliminated in Italy, Ceylon, Brazil and Greece, by spraying with DDT the breeding-places of germ-bearing mosquitoes. The annual death rate in Ceylon, as a result of WHO campaigns, has been cut in half. Armed with new miracle drugs and the best medical knowledge and techniques, WHO is an invaluable ally in humanity's continuing world war against disease.

TECHNICAL ASSISTANCE

Through its TAA (Technical Assistance Agency), the UN has a shining opportunity to harness constructively the social revolution now burgeoning in underdeveloped areas of the earth. One-billion people living in underdeveloped areas have an average annual income of $80 per person. They are constant victims of poverty, disease, illiteracy, and general conditions of misery. Today, they are no longer willing to resign themselves to this miserable lot. They feel they are entitled to a better life and that, with a minimum of help, they can achieve it.

The UN technical assistance program is designed to help these persons break through the road-blocks that have restrained economic and social progress. TAA provides the services of technical experts to meet the needs of countries that request them. By the beginning of 1953, more than 1600 experts—educators, scientists, engineers, public health specialists, agriculturists—from sixty-four different nations were given technical assistance in sixty-two different countries.

The TAA does not itself solve the economic or social problem of a given country. It helps the interested country to help itself by demonstrating new methods and new approaches. One example: In Afghanistan, TAA experts advised the substitution of scythes for sickles in cutting grain, with the result that the Afghan farmer was able to cut five times as much grain in an hour.

The vast promise in the technical assistance program lies in the fact that it is not based on a spirit of philanthropy. It develops a sense of genuine partnership of nations. In order to get TAA assistance, a country must ask for it, have its project approved by the TAA Board, and put up a considerable part of the cost. Furthermore, a country which receives experts for particular services frequently is able to provide its own experts to other nations for other services. In India, for example, one hundred and thirty-six foreign experts came in in 1952, while eighty-four Indian experts went to other countries.

Achieving Human Rights

Immediately after stating the UN's first objective—"to save succeeding generations from the scourge of war"—the Charter pledges the international organization "to reaffirm faith in fundamental human rights, in the dignity and worth of the human person, in the equal rights of men and women and of nations large and small." So deep was their concern that the framers actually wrote into the Charter a Commission on Human Rights.

Under the dedicated leadership of Mrs. Franklin D. Roosevelt, the commission labored for three years and produced a twenty-eight-article Declaration of Human Rights, a bill of rights for the world. The document, product of arduous debate and negotiation, was finally approved by the Third General Assembly on December 10, 1948 by a vote of 48 to 0, with 8 abstentions. The Declaration is not legally binding on anyone. It is a statement of objectives in human rights, with only the weight of public opinion behind it. The commission has continued its work, drawing up draft covenants embodying the approved rights in forms that can ultimately be adopted by the nations of the world as treaties. The possibility of successful completion of this project appears clouded by Communist double-talk on human rights and by the announcement of the U. S. in 1953 that it will not ratify a Human Rights treaty, contending that international treaties are not proper ways to advance human rights.

While it would appear that the somewhat extravagant hopes which some people put into the UN Human Rights program will never be realized, the UN Declaration has already resulted in many positive benefits. Three years after its adoption, the Declaration was circulating in thirty-six languages, and had influenced various resolutions of the General Assembly. It had also been utilized in drawing up the new constitutions of Indonesia, Costa Rica, Syria, El Salvador and Haiti. It had been cited in legislation of Canada and Western Germany, and in various American court decisions. More important, however, is the fact that the Declaration has been distributed to opinion-makers in nations throughout the world, and has served as an international challenge and standard against which nations can measure their own progress or shortcomings.

Genocide Convention

The wanton destruction of entire groups of human beings—including the six million Jews who perished at Hitler's hand—gave rise to a new term, genocide, and to a strenuous international effort to prevent by treaty any such recurrence of mass extermination of human beings. Dr. Raphael Lemkin evolved the idea of a convention on "Prevention and Punishment of the Crime of Genocide," won its adoption by the United Nations in 1948, and stirred public opinion throughout the world to the need for machinery to prevent this blackest of evils.

The convention took effect as an international treaty in 1951 upon the ratification of the required number (twenty) of countries. Since then the number of states ratifying has grown to almost fifty, including the Soviet Union and West Germany. The continued absence of the United States from this list is a national disgrace.

The U. S. voted for the Genocide Convention in the 1948 UN Assembly and the U. S. representative signed it on instructions from President Truman. As a treaty, it had to be submitted to the Senate for ratification. A Senate sub-committee held hearings and reported to the Senate Foreign Relations Committee. The committee has never acted, despite strong public sympathy and the support of fifty major American organizations, including those representing the three religious faiths, labor, education, and women. Why has the U. S. failed to act?

There seem to be at least four general reasons. The most charitable explanation is ignorance, a distorted idea of what the Genocide Convention really is. Some feared that it might be applied to lynching, and thus interfere with our right to handle the problem in our way. This misconception, of course, is absurd, since the convention clearly applies to mass murder, or attempts to destroy an entire racial or religious group. Lynching is murder of an individual, terrible indeed, but not mass murder. Second, at that time, about 1950, a new isolationism was emerging, one form of which was anti-United Nations feeling. The United Nations' honeymoon was ending, and people who had never really favored it, or who lost faith when the going got hard, pulled back from anything which seemed to involve this country any further in the United Nations program. Third, the old doctrine of states rights played a part, on the ground that in a federal system approval of such a treaty by the federal government might overrule a state law. This, too, is an error. No state has ever passed or would pass a law dealing with crime of such enormous proportions. It is clearly a matter for federal action, a matter of foreign policy.

Fourth, it was alleged that it might lead to American citizens being tried in foreign countries for crimes committed in the United States. This is another misconception. Article V of the convention declares that ratifying nations will enact "in accordance with their respective constitutions" necessary legislation and "effective penalties."

Not only is genocide a matter of tragic concern to the Jewish people, but its prevention is a terrifying humanitarian and moral challenge to the civilized world. Some 20,000,000 people have perished through genocide in the first half of the twentieth century. We have not yet put savagery behind us. That it should not be United States' policy, after over four years of delay, to support the Genocide Convention is shameful.

A TASK OF LEADERSHIP

Whether or not we like it, the United States has, since the end of World War II, been thrust into a position of world leadership. The manner in which we bear this burden of leadership will determine, in large measure, the future of the world: whether the cold war will be frozen into permanence, erupt into an atomic holocaust, or give way gradually to an honorable and enduring peace.

America's record during the past ten years has been mixed. At the close of the Second World War, over-eager to return our soldiers to civilian life, we allowed ourselves to believe that the end of hostilities automatically ushered in a lasting era of world peace. Later, when the aggressive tendencies of the Soviet Union and her satellites became starkly clear, the pendulum of American public opinion swung to fear and anxiety. In addition to the necessary task of rebuilding our defenses and the strength of the free world, in our developing crusade against communism, we frequently tended to become rigid and doctrinaire. Sometimes we became contemptuous of the very processes of negotiation and compromise, and some Americans regarded co-existence with the Communist world as an immoral and unthinkable arrangement.

At other times during this period, the U.S. acted with dignity and with courage. Notable was the Marshall Plan which restored Western Europe and U.S. leadership, under President Truman, in repelling the Communist aggression against South Korea. Promising for the future was the bold initiative of President Eisenhower in 1959-1960 in his conferences with Nikita Khrushchev and other world leaders designed to "melt the ice" of the cold war. Despite mixed assessments of the results of these actions, many believe that there developed a stronger recognition on both sides that thermonuclear weapons and ballistic missiles have made a world war unthinkable. If this is so, the East-West struggle may become essentially political and economic, one which may continue for generations.

Religious bodies must stir in the hearts of the American people a new faith in peace, a new faith in man and in God. Religion, and certainly Judaism, must proclaim that loss of faith in peace is an affront against God, that to cease pursuing every path which may lead to peace, including the path of honorable negotiation, is a negation of our history, and that to trade our lofty visions for the slogans of a negative anti-communism is a betrayal of the dynamic religious principles which underlie our heritage.

Second, we must make the United Nations in deed as well as in word the cornerstone of American foreign policy. This must not be taken to mean that we have a right to regard the United Nations as an agency of the United States of America. Too often in recent years, the United States, along with other great powers, has chosen to act outside the United Nations when to have acted within the UN would have contributed immeasurably to the vitality and effectiveness of the international body and, in addition, would have bolstered confidence and trust in our purposes throughout the world. The Point Four Program is but one example of an opportunity missed by the U. S. to strengthen the UN by channeling our aid through the UN's Technical Assistance Division instead of proceeding unilaterally. There is justifiable fear in many quarters that, despite our repeated avowals of fidelity to the United Nations, we may gradually develop, through independent action, a system of coalitions which will by-pass and ultimately undermine the UN itself.

Religious groups, which can lift men above the clangor of narrow political considerations, must summon the American people to a deeper understanding of the indispensability of the UN, to an attitude less proprietary, less self-righteous and more mature. Americans would do well to ponder the words of Sir Anthony Eden about the UN: "There is no other organization in the world today which offers the same facilities for building world peace." And of Dag Hammerskjold, Secretary General: "It creates a reasonable guarantee that all this change in the world, these tremendous political and economic developments, this ferment, can be channelized, kept orderly. The UN is a mold that keeps the hot metal from spilling over." The task of the United States, however difficult and exasperating, is not to break the mold but to exert every sinew of mind and body to make it work even better.

The fundamental contest between democracy and tyranny is a struggle for the loyalties and minds of men. Armaments alone, however necessary and however awesome, cannot win this contest. Democracy can win, ultimately, only by demonstrating conclusively that it is dynamic, that it spurns colonialism and racism, that it can and will address itself to the basic problems of world poverty, that it offers a way for people to solve their crushing problems and still be free. To accomplish this, we must be generous. We must not lose the effect of our economic aid by tying it to essentially military programs. A nation which owns 40% of the world's wealth, which doubled its productive capacity and fought a world war with practically no reduction in its standard of living, can use at least a fraction of that wealth and capacity for peace. The U. S. is now spending about $50 billion a year on armaments. If only one-billion dollars were used annually in a bold economic and technical assistance program to lift the burden of economic and social despair which oppresses a third of the people of the world, we would do more to win the global struggle against communism and to improve the prospects of peace than we can possibly achieve through a thousand atomic weapons.

We cannot afford to be afraid of change. Our forefathers came to this land seeking change, and much of the world seeks change now. Both our traditions and our self-interest demand that we accept the revolutionary changes shaking the world, and seek to guide them into democratic and peaceful channels.

Specifically, what can the synagogue do to support the UN and to foster peace?

Many churches and synagogues have long been active in support of the UN and in the study of international relations. This is especially true of the women's organizations. Such groups as the Methodist Women, the National Federation of Temple Sisterhoods, the Women's League of the United Synagogue of America, and others have stimulated local study groups, distributed materials, and urged appropriate action on their constituents. Within the Reform Jewish movement, more than two hundred and fifty sisterhoods have established committees on Peace and World Relations. Affiliated with the National Federation of Temple Sisterhoods, such committees receive material and guidance from their parent body to aid them in continuing study of the United Nations to the end that individual congregants may effectively discharge their duties as citizens. Some of these committees, recognizing the interrelatedness of national and international issues, have broadened their scope of interest to include other areas of social action.

Whether planned and conducted by the Sisterhood Committee on Peace and World Relations or as a part of the overall function of the Social Action Committee, a continuing educational program on the United Nations and problems of peace should be developed for the congregation. Members of the congregation should be made particularly aware of the traditional Jewish attitude toward peace and its contemporary implications.

Through the Social Action Committee, the moral prestige of the synagogue should be placed behind the United Nations. The congregation should join with other forward-looking groups in the community in resisting organized attacks on the UN such as have occurred in several American cities in recent years. The right and duty of the public schools to teach about the United Nations must not be denied as a result of pressure from vigilante forces. But the forces of repression can only be combatted when the decent folk in the community are as vigilant, alert, and vigorous as their opponents are. In recent years, UNESCO has been the favorite target of many know-nothing groups, such as those which forced a partial ban on UN materials in Los Angeles public schools. The usual charge is that UNESCO literature is "un-American" and that the organization seeks in the name of "world citizenship" to destroy "loyalty to the United States." The charges are preposterous, but they reflect an anti-foreign prejudice operating beneath the surface of American life. Unless quickly spiked by the leaders of the community, including those of the synagogue and church, such campaigns can often do a great deal of mischief locally. Vigilance should be maintained regarding national legislation and other developments involving UN and U. S. foreign policy.

Synagogue Social Action Committees should press for U. S. ratification of the Genocide Convention. Through joint efforts with church groups and other bodies in the community which favor the Genocide Convention, the synagogue should help keep the issue of the Genocide Convention alive before the general public.

Special occasions such as United Nations Week should be fully exploited by synagogues as an opportunity to dramatize the importance of the UN today. Several Reform synagogues have used the occasion of United Nations Week to dedicate a United Nations flag in their temple buildings. Others have utilized United Nations films, conducted special services, distributed literature, conducted forums, and engaged in similar activities to focus the attention of their congregants and the community-at-large on the United Nations.

The chief resource for information and material in the area of international relations is the United Nations itself. Important citizens' organizations in this area are the American Association for the United Nations; Foreign Policy Association; Carnegie Endowment for International Peace; Woodrow Wilson Foundation. Of particular interest to synagogues and churches is the Church Peace Union, an agency which seeks to interpret, in the light of fundamental religious principles, ways to achieve world order and peace with justice. The Church Peace Union makes material on the UN available upon request. Within the Jewish community, the National Federation of Temple Sisterhoods, is particularly active in UN affairs and publishes materials specifically suited to Jewish congregations.

BIBLIOGRAPHY

BOWLES, CHESTER. *The New Dimensions of Peace.* New York: Harper and Bros., 1955.
BRICKNER, BALFOUR. *As Driven Sands: The Arab Refugees.* UAHC Commission on Social Action, 1958.

GREEN, JAMES FREDERICK. *The United Nations and Human Rights.* Washington, D. C.: Brookings Institute, 1956.

HEILBRONER, ROBERT L. "Mankind's Children: The Story of UNICEF." N. Y.: Public Affairs Committee, 1959. Pamphlet.

KISSINGER, HENRY A. *Nuclear Weapons and Foreign Policy.* N. Y.: Harper and Brothers, 1957.

MORGENTHAU, HANS J. *Politics Among the Nations.* New York: Alfred A. Knopf, 1948.

NIXON, JUSTINE WROE. *Man's New Hope:* A Religious Approach to Foreign Aid. N. Y.: Church Peace Union, 1957. Pamphlet.

NIXON, JUSTINE WROE. "The United Nations and Our Religious Heritage." A pamphlet published by Church Peace Union.

PEARSON, LESTER B. *Democracy in World Politics.* Princeton University Press, 1955.

THOMAS, FRANCES A. *To Unite Our Strength.* A study course on the United Nations published by the National Federation of Temple Sisterhoods, 1949.

THOMAS, FRANCES A. *United States Foreign Policy—A Brief Study with Reference to the Principles of Judaism.* Published by National Federation of Temple Sisterhoods for the Commission on Social Action of Reform Judaism, 1955.

United Nations Department of Public Information. *Everyman's United Nations.* Introduction by Trygve Lie. New York: Funk and Wagnalls Co. in association with United Nations World, 1948.

VAN KIRK, WALTER. *The Churches and the United Nations.* National Council of Churches of Christ.

For everyone that disavows religion because some ancient doctrine outrages his intelligence, hundreds become irreligious because the social impotence of religion outrages their conscience.

—REINHOLD NIEBUHR.

The day is short, the work is much, the laborers are slothful, the reward is much and the Master is urgent. It is not incumbent upon thee to complete the work, but neither art thou free to desist from it.

—RABBI TARPHON, SAYINGS OF THE FATHERS.

Directory of Organizations

Mentioned in This Volume as Possible Resources

AMERICAN ASSOCIATION FOR THE UNITED NATIONS,
345 East 46 Street, New York, N. Y.

AMERICAN CIVIL LIBERTIES UNION,
170 Fifth Avenue, New York, N. Y.

ACTION, AMERICAN COUNCIL TO IMPROVE OUR
NEIGHBORHOODS,
P.O. Box 500 Radio City, New York 20, N. Y.

AMERICAN FRIENDS SERVICE COMMITTEE,
144 East 20 Street, New York, N. Y.

AMERICAN IMMIGRATION CONFERENCE,
509 Madison Avenue, New York, N. Y.

AMERICAN JEWISH COMMITTEE,
386 Fourth Avenue, New York, N. Y.

AMERICAN JEWISH CONGRESS,
15 East 84 Street, New York, N. Y.

ANTI-DEFAMATION LEAGUE OF B'NAI B'RITH,
515 Madison Avenue, New York, N. Y.

CARNEGIE ENDOWMENT FOR INTERNATIONAL PEACE,
345 East 46 Street, New York, N. Y.

CENTRAL CONFERENCE OF AMERICAN RABBIS,
40 West 68 Street, New York, N. Y.

CHURCH PEACE UNION,
170 East 64 Street, New York, N. Y.

CONFERENCE ON ECONOMIC PROGRESS,
1001 Connecticut Ave., N.W., Washington, D. C.

FOREIGN POLICY ASSOCIATION,
345 East 46 Street, New York, N. Y.

JEWISH AGRICULTURAL SOCIETY,
386 Fourth Avenue, New York, N. Y.

JEWISH LABOR COMMITTEE,
25 East 78 Street, New York, N. Y.

NATIONAL ASSOCIATION FOR THE ADVANCEMENT OF
COLORED PEOPLE,
20 West 40 Street, New York, N. Y.

NATIONAL CIVIL LIBERTIES CLEARING HOUSE,
1637 Massachusetts Avenue, N.W., Washington, D. C.

NATIONAL COMMITTEE AGAINST DISCRIMINATION IN
HOUSING,
35 West 32 Street, New York, N. Y.

NATIONAL COMMITTEE ON IMMIGRATION AND
CITIZENSHIP,
40 East 40 Street, New York, N. Y.

NATIONAL CATHOLIC WELFARE CONFERENCE,
1312 Massachusetts Avenue, N.W., Washington, D. C.

NATIONAL COMMUNITY RELATIONS ADVISORY COUNCIL,
9 East 38 Street, New York, N. Y.

NATIONAL CONFERENCE OF CHRISTIANS AND JEWS,
43 West 57 Street, New York, N. Y.

NATIONAL COUNCIL OF CHURCHES OF CHRIST IN THE
U.S.A.,
297 Fourth Avenue, New York, N. Y.

NATIONAL COUNCIL OF JEWISH WOMEN,
1 West 47 Street, New York, N. Y.

NATIONAL EDUCATION ASSOCIATION,
1201–16 Street, N.W., Washington, D. C.

NATIONAL FEDERATION OF TEMPLE BROTHERHOODS,
838 5th Ave., New York, N. Y.

NATIONAL FEDERATION OF TEMPLE SISTERHOODS,
838 5th Ave., New York, N. Y.

NATIONAL PROBATION AND PAROLE ASSOCIATION,
1790 Broadway, New York, N. Y.

NATIONAL RELIGION AND LABOR FOUNDATION,
3494½ N. High Street, Columbus, Ohio

NATIONAL URBAN LEAGUE,
1133 Broadway, New York, N. Y.

RABBINICAL ASSEMBLY OF AMERICA,
3080 Broadway, New York, N. Y.

SOUTHERN REGIONAL COUNCIL,
63 Auburn Avenue, N.E., Atlanta, Ga.

SYNAGOGUE COUNCIL OF AMERICA,
110 West 42 Street, New York, N. Y.

UNION OF ORTHODOX JEWISH CONGREGATIONS,
305 Broadway, New York, N. Y.

UNITED HIAS,
425 Lafayette Street, New York, N. Y.

UNITED SYNAGOGUE OF AMERICA,
3080 Broadway, New York, N. Y.

WOODROW WILSON FOUNDATION,
45 East 65 Street, New York, N. Y.

APPENDIX DOCUMENTS

A.

Twenty Questions on
The Synagogue and Social Action

(1) **WHAT IS SYNAGOGUE SOCIAL ACTION?**

Synagogue social action is the process of translating the principles of Judaism into action in our communities, the nation, and the world, through the synagogue. It is the contemporary expression of the passion for social justice which characterized the prophets of Israel and which is intrinsic in Judaism.

(2) **WHY SHOULD THE SYNAGOGUE BE CONCERNED WITH SOCIAL ISSUES?**

Judaism is not merely a set of beliefs; it is a way of life. Judaism is not an other-worldly religion. In our tradition, man is called the co-worker of God in the creation of a better world here and now. In Judaism, social justice is a religious duty. What does God expect of us? Judaism answers: "To do justly, to love mercy, and to walk humbly with thy God."

(3) **WHAT NATIONAL GROUP IS CONCERNED WITH SOCIAL ACTION IN REFORM JUDAISM?**

The Commission on Social Action of Reform Judaism. It comprises the Union of American Hebrew Congregations, the Central Conference of American Rabbis, the National Federation of Temple Sisterhoods, National Federation of Temple Youth, and National Federation of Temple Brotherhoods—the entire family of Reform Judaism.

(4) **HOW DOES THE NATIONAL COMMISSION RELATE TO INDIVIDUAL REFORM SYNAGOGUES?**

The primary objective of the Commission on Social Action is the stimulation in Reform synagogues of a program of study and action on those contemporary issues about which Judaism has something to say. It is our hope that every Reform synagogue will conduct a program of social justice, the first aim of which will be to sensitize its congregants to the relationship between Jewish ethical principles and modern problems. The Commission sends study materials on these subjects to every congregation. The Commission has no authority to direct a congregation to study any specific problem or to take any particular action. It offers guidance and counsel.

(5) WHAT ELSE DOES THE COMMISSION DO?

It cooperates with other groups in American life, Jewish and non-Jewish, in seeking to implement the positions on social issues taken by the Union at its biennial conventions. Examples of such issues are civil rights, civil liberties, U. S. immigration policy, separation of church and state, and strengthening the United Nations.

(6) HOW DOES A SYNAGOGUE START SUCH A PROGRAM?

By creating a standing committee to carry on the social action program within the synagogue. Such a committee gives to this area of synagogue work the same ongoing attention that the Ritual Committee, Education Committee, Building Committee, and all other committees give to their areas of endeavor. The committee should include representatives of the sisterhood, brotherhood, youth group, as well as the congregation itself.

(7) WHAT ARE SOME EXAMPLES OF SYNAGOGUE SOCIAL ACTION PROGRAMS?

Some of the local groups have developed study programs on such topics as the United Nations, immigration, separation of church and state, segregation. A few have undertaken to stimulate the organization of Jewish Community Councils in their communities. One initiated a community-wide effort to improve housing in a Negro section of town. Another developed an inter-faith program to achieve de-segregation in a segregated city. Another looked into the need for a community mental health clinic.

(8) WHO DECIDES WHAT ISSUES A SYNAGOGUE COMMITTEE WILL DEAL WITH?

The individual group itself. The national Commission offers materials and program suggestions but each individual synagogue decides for itself what local, national, or world problems it wishes to work on.

(9) DOES THE SOCIAL ACTION GROUP SPEAK FOR THE TEMPLE?

Each synagogue evolves its own pattern of operation. In some congregations, the committee is limited to carrying out a program of study within the congregation, with each individual taking such action as he feels impelled to take. Often, the Social Action group is created by the Board, reports to the Board, and is free to conduct its program except that it must receive authorization from the Board in order to make a public statement.

(10) DOESN'T SOCIAL ACTION INVOLVE A SYNAGOGUE IN POLITICS?

Some people talk about politics as if it were a dirty word. But what is it? Webster's Universal Unabridged Dictionary defines politics as: "The science of government; that part of ethics (underline ours) which consists in the regulation and government of a nation or state, for the preservation of its safety, peace and prosperity . . . and the protection of its citizens in their rights, with the preservation and improvement of their morals." (underline ours)

Obviously, Judaism, a religion grounded in ethics, must be concerned with politics in this sense. The ethical insights of prophetic Judaism must be applied to the specific social and political problems of our time. Such questions as civil rights, genocide, Point Four, immigration, have political aspects, but they involve ethical concepts on which Judaism must have something to say.

It is partisan politics that the synagogue must and does avoid. It is not our task to further Republicans over Democrats or vice versa, but it is our task to apply the principles we profess in the world in which we live.

(11) DOES THE SYNAGOGUE HAVE A RIGHT TO SPEAK FOR THE ENTIRE JEWISH COMMUNITY?

No. Reform Judaism believes in cooperation, both on the national and on the local level. Thus, nationally, the Union is a member of the National Community Relations Advisory Council, which comprises major national and local Jewish agencies and which develops coordination and cooperation among them; and of the Synagogue Council of America. On the local level, we support the development of Jewish Community Councils which embrace all Jewish organizations, including all synagogues, so that joint thinking and action can be secured on matters affecting the entire Jewish community.

(12) DO CONSERVATIVE AND ORTHODOX JUDAISM HAVE PROGRAMS OF SOCIAL ACTION?

Yes. The United Synagogue of America (Conservative) and the Union of Orthodox Jewish Congregations (Orthodox) are also members of the NCRAC. Both groups are likewise developing social action programs nationally and within their congregations. The three Jewish religious bodies work together closely in this area.

(13) DO CHRISTIAN GROUPS HAVE SUCH PROGRAMS?

Yes. In fact, they have set the pace in this direction. The Roman Catholic Church and virtually every Protestant denomination have social action programs functioning nationally and in many local churches.

(14) ISN'T SOCIAL ACTION CONTROVERSIAL?

Yes. Some people challenge the idea that the synagogue should go beyond prayer and ritual and the religious school. The Reform movement has overwhelmingly registered its disagreement with that viewpoint. Successive biennial assemblies of the UAHC have stated categorically that the synagogue must be concerned with the moral issues of society, even though controversy may result. Judaism divorced from life is an empty shell which must repel many intelligent, deeply-committed, religious Jews.

(15) WHY SHOULD THE SYNAGOGUE HAVE A PROGRAM OF SOCIAL ACTION WHEN THERE ARE SO MANY OTHER ORGANIZATIONS IN THE COMMUNITY WORKING ON SUCH MATTERS? ISN'T THIS DUPLICATION?

There is a significant difference between the approach of the synagogue and that of lay organizations such as, for example, the League of Women Voters or the American Jewish Committee. The approach of the synagogue is not based on defense or community relations; it is based on the ethical and religious demands of Judaism. Thus, even when concerned with the same issues, the rationale and approach of the synagogue are different. In addition, there are many issues—such as inter-religious activities in the community—where the synagogue plays a unique role.

Duplication can and should be reduced through cooperation among all interested groups in the community. Thus, locally the synagogue participates in the Jewish Community Council and in similar over-all coordinating bodies for the general community.

(16) MUST A SYNAGOGUE COMMITTEE OF THIS TYPE CALL ITSELF SOCIAL ACTION?

No. Some synagogues call their committees Social Study, Social Justice, Community Affairs, Community Relations, or something similar. The name is of little consequence.

(17) MUST A SYNAGOGUE PROGRAM INVOLVE ACTION OR CAN IT BE LIMITED TO STUDY?

This question is partly answered under Question 9. The task of study and of informing the congregation on the relevancy of Judaism to contemporary social problems is an indispensable aspect of any effective program. The rabbis of old asked: which is more important—study or action? And they responded: the most important thing is study which leads to action. Inasmuch as the function and purpose of belief in Judaism has always been to motivate action, the Commission believes that a full synagogue social action program should flow from principle to practice.

(18) DOES IT VIOLATE THE PRINCIPLE OF SEPARATION OF CHURCH AND STATE FOR A SYNAGOGUE TO ENGAGE IN SOCIAL ACTION?

No. The only circumstance in which the principle of separation of religion and the state might be violated would involve an attempt by a religious group to impose its will upon the community by coercion. Because of our deep commitment to the principle of separation and to democracy generally, Jewish religious bodies guard zealously against such practices and protest against incidents of this type, regardless of their source.

We maintain that religious institutions have not only the right, but the solemn duty to articulate their ethical principles and to project them into the larger community so that action will result for the betterment of society.

(19) WHY SHOULD WE APPROACH SUCH CIVIC PROBLEMS AS AMERICAN IMMIGRATION POLICY OR CIVIL LIBERTIES, AS JEWS? WHY NOT AS AMERICAN CITIZENS?

We are American citizens and enjoy the same democratic rights as do all other Americans. The greatness of American democracy is not only the political freedoms it vests in each individual; it is equally important that American democracy encourages all religious, racial, and cultural groups to maintain their identity and vitality and to contribute their group values to the American scene. The vitality of such groups helps to enrich American culture.

Jewish religious groups contribute significantly to the strengthening of American democracy to the extent that they are aware of and can apply in practice those fundamental moral principles which underlie both democracy and Judaism alike. This is both good citizenship and good Jewish living.

(20) HOW CAN A SOCIAL ACTION PROGRAM STRENGTHEN THE SYNAGOGUE?

Social action is Judaism in practice. By giving dynamic vitality to the synagogue, it helps to bridge the gap between prayer and practice, creed and conduct, thus bringing a sense of greater reality to our faith. A Reform synagogue with a well-established social action program described the effects as follows: ". . . given sensitive and social-minded

Jews a sense of rootage in the congregation . . . inspired youth groups with the conviction that the synagogue is as much interested in bettering the future as in preserving its link with the past . . . given real meaning to the beautiful prayers for democracy, peace and justice in our prayerbooks . . . helped our membership to a healthier degree of personal integrity."

B.

A Statement of Basic Principles on the Synagogue and Social Action

A statement of principles adopted by 43rd General Assembly of the Union of American Hebrew Congregations in Los Angeles, California, February 15, 1955 upon recommendation of the Commission on Social Action

WE ARE THE heirs of the great Jewish religious tradition which conceives of its ultimate goal as the establishment of the Kingdom of God on earth. The God whom we serve is a God of righteousness who would have us be holy as He is holy. The Torah which we cherish is a guide for spiritual living concerned with every aspect of human experience. The prophets of Israel, dedicated to God and the welfare of their fellow men, bade us pursue justice, seek peace, and establish brotherhood among all of God's creatures.

Judaism offers no easy escape from the problems of life. It rejects the device of passing all responsibility for social problems to God. In our tradition, man is called the co-worker or partner of God in the creation of a better world. Judaism insists that we must apply constantly the sharp ethical insights of the prophets to the specific social problems of our generation, as well as to the personal and individual problems of our lives.

It is in loyalty to this heritage, and in the furtherance of our ideal of righteousness, that Reform Judaism has developed a program of social action which relates the ethical and spiritual teachings of our faith to the problems of our communities, of our country, and of the world, and which strives for a society guided by the principles of divine justice and mercy. This program is conducted through the Commission on Social Action, a joint instrumentality of the Union of American Hebrew Congregations, the Central Conference of American Rabbis, the National Federation of Temple Sisterhoods, National Federation of Temple Brotherhoods, and the National Federation of Temple Youth. The primary objective of this Commission is, through programs of social study and social action in each Reform synagogue, to activate the ideals of Judaism in the lives of our congregants. Such programs must be integral and essential aspects of synagogue activity. A synagogue which isolates itself from the fundamental issues of social justice confronting the community and the nation is false to the deepest traditions and values of the Jewish heritage.

What are these traditions? What are these values? And what are some of their implications for us today?

Judaism gave to the world the concept of the sanctity and dignity of the individual. All men are equal in that they are created in the image of God. "One law and one ordinance shall be both for you, and for the stranger that sojourneth with you" (*Numbers 15:16*). Respect for the civil rights of all men is each man's duty to God. We Jews are challenged by our religion to support the basic human rights of every one: "What is hateful unto thee, do not do unto thy neighbor" (*Talmud Shabbos 8*). As Jews and as Americans, dedicated to the democratic tradition, we are impelled to join with our fellows in overcoming bigotry and prejudice, in seeking through education and legislation the elimination of discrimination and segregation because of race, religion, or national origin, in demanding for ourselves and for all other Americans equality of opportunity in work, home, health and education.

Judaism teaches that each man has a right to express or keep private the dictates of his soul, for the soul is the divine element in man and cannot be interfered with by other men or governments of men. "The spirit of man is the light of the Lord" (*Proverbs 20:27*). The Talmud teaches that where honest differences prevail and agreements are difficult: "These *and* those are the words of the living God." It was that "flaming fire within" (*Jeremiah 25:9*) that impelled the prophet to speak out even at grave personal risk. These rights of conscience were enshrined in the Bill of Rights, the cornerstone of the American constitutional system.

We view with deep concern the growing attack upon these principles in American life today. Judaism is fundamentally antagonistic to tyranny—whether it be totalitarian tyranny manipulated from abroad, or a domestic tyranny foisted on the American people in the name of anti-communism. We believe that subversion and espionage can and must be effectively opposed without destroying the tradition of individual freedom on which democracy is based. We have faith in freedom and in democracy. We believe that the religious ideals of justice and security for all men can be fulfilled only in an atmosphere of freedom and security, not in an atmosphere of fearful conformity and suspicion. We pledge ourselves to join with all freedom-loving forces in our community and nation to reverse the alarming trend toward suspicion, recrimination, fear, and the equation of dissent with disloyalty. We pledge our unremitting vigilance to the end that neither Communist intrigue nor reckless demagoguery shall be allowed to corrode the fundamental liberties which have their origin in religious ideals.

Judaism has always emphasized that our ethical ideals must also be applied to the economic processes of society. Our society must be judged by the extent to which men are enabled to achieve, through their work, a decent standard of living, and to provide for themselves and their families the fullest possible protection of their mental and physical health. We pledge ourselves to the achievement of this ideal not only on the national and world scenes, but most particularly in the conduct of our individual business and professional lives.

Another of the most sacred of our Jewish religious teachings is the vision given us by the prophets of a Messianic Age of peace, the time when nations shall beat their swords into plowshares and their spears into pruning hooks. Motivated by our belief in world brotherhood, the Jewish community has supported enthusiastically the United Nations as the best available instrumentality for the gradual accomplishment of world peace. We have rejoiced in its constructive achievements in the improvement of health standards in many parts of the world, in the control of narcotics traffic, in child welfare, in technical assistance to underdeveloped nations, in the UN's prophetic declarations on Human Rights, Genocide, and similar world problems. We have been deeply concerned about the lack of progress recorded within the councils of the United Nations in easing international tensions. Yet we have remained hopeful that our country, committed firmly to international cooperative action and backed strongly by our citizenry, could continue to exercise leadership in the UN in the direction of world peace.

But we see powerful, organized forces in America striving to weaken the UN and its agencies, pressing even to force the withdrawal of our country from the United Nations. We see a movement to prohibit teaching in our schools about the UN and its activities. We see isolationist groups attempting to sabotage the Covenant on Human Rights and the ratification of the Genocide Convention. We see these tendencies and we are deeply disturbed. We pledge ourselves to the task of strengthening international cooperation for peace.

We must be constantly aware that the fundamental contest between democracy and tyranny is a struggle for the loyalties and minds of men. Armaments, however necessary and however awesome, cannot win this all-important contest. We can win ultimately only by demonstrating constantly and conclusively that democracy is dynamic, that it spurns colonialism and racism, that it can and will address itself to the continuing problem of world poverty, that it offers a way for people to solve their crushing problems and still be free.

We can win this contest only by affirmative deeds. A Marshall Plan, a Point Four program of technical assistance, President Eisenhower's plan for an international atomic pool for peaceful pursuits, achievements of a more humane U. S. immigration policy than the one we now have, can be mightier weapons in this contest than a thousand H-Bombs. A decision by the U. S. Supreme Court, outlawing segregation in American public schools, speaks more loudly than a thousand propaganda broadcasts over a thousand Voices of America. In the same way, resolute action by the American people to cleanse our nations of the poison of fear and suspicion would immeasurably strengthen us in the continuing ideological struggle against communism. We must constantly prove that democracy works. Thus, the propaganda bombardments of world communism will be revealed as a collection of false and cynical slogans, and democracy will be welcomed in places where its blessings will lift hearts and hopes and point the way to a more promising future. We pledge ourselves to this momentous task.

Jewish religious bodies—and certainly Reform synagogues—have a deep responsibility to seek to strengthen democracy and the ideals of justice by translating our faith into concrete social action. Such Jewish ideals as reverence for individual freedom, love of peace, concern for the weak, equitable relationships between employer and employee, regard for the stranger, and many others are strikingly relevant to the current world scene. We urge establishment of a standing committee charged with the responsibility of educating the membership on the application of these ideals to contemporary social issues as an indispensable part of the program of every synagogue. Such committees will enable us to orient our individual lives and help shape our society by the ethical imperatives of our faith.

Through an intelligent program of social justice in the synagogue, we help to bridge the gap between confession and commitment, between word and deed and thus bring a sense of greater reality to our faith. We as Jews fulfill ourselves by working for the establishment of justice and peace which are fundamental to Judaism as they are to democracy. In the words of our prayer book: "O may all created in Thine image recognize that they are brethren, so that, one in spirit and one in fellowship, they may be forever united before Thee. Then shall Thy kingdom be established on earth and the word of Thine ancient seer be fulfilled. The Lord will reign forever and ever."

C.

Revised Charter of the Joint Commission for Social Action of the UAHC and CCAR

Preamble

We are the heirs of the great Jewish tradition which conceives of its ultimate goal as the establishment of the Kingdom of Heaven on earth. The God whom we serve is a God of righteousness who would have us be holy as He is holy. The Torah which we cherish is a guide for spiritual living concerned with every aspect of human experience. The prophets of Israel, dedicated to God and the welfare of their fellow men, bid us pursue justice, seek peace, and attain brotherhood with everyone of God's creatures, whatever their race, creed, or class. In loyalty to our priceless heritage, in the furtherance of our historic ideal of righteousness. we, the Union of American Hebrew Congregations and the Central Conference of American Rabbis, jointly create a Commission for Social Action and dedicate it to the following goals:

I.

The Social Action Commission shall relate the ethical and spiritual principles of Judaism as expressed in the teachings of the Torah, of the prophets, of the sages and rabbis of Israel to the problems of the world we know today, in order that our society may be established on the principles of divine justice and love and of human brotherhood.

II.

The Commission shall prepare studies with the aid of authorities and specialists on challenging social issues and suggest specific solutions wherever possible, taking appropriate action when deemed advisable.

    A. It shall uphold the inalienable divine rights of men as interpreted in our Torah and in the American Bill of Rights and Constitution. It shall seek to extend these rights and secure them whenever and wherever denied.

B. It shall work to eliminate discrimination based on race, religion, or national origin to the end that all men may enjoy equality of opportunity.

C. It shall study the causes of war and advocate measures which will advance the establishment of a lasting peace based on the principles of justice and world unity.

D. It shall examine the relations between management and labor where ethical issues are involved. It shall suggest solutions in keeping with Judaism's teachings of righteousness.

E. It may urge other policies and practices that will enable society to develop and utilize God's abundant earth for the welfare of all mankind.

III.

It may communicate its findings to the Union of American Hebrew Congregations and to its constituent congregations, to the Central Conference of American Rabbis and its individual members, and to such other organizations and individuals as it may deem proper for its purposes. It shall urge acceptance of these principles and appropriate action thereon. It shall encourage the promotion of social action committees within the congregations.

It shall likewise disseminate as widely as possible the results of its studies.

IV.

It may cooperate with like-minded groups in any phase of its work and may join with them in issuing statements.

D.

Report to 1955 Biennial Convention of United Synagogue of America

by Joint Commission on Social Action of United Synagogue and Rabbinical Assembly of America

Formally organized the winter of 1954, the Joint Commission on Social Action has the financial support and active participation of The Rabbinical Assembly of America, The United Synagogue of America and The National Women's League of the United Synagogue. The National Federation of Jewish Men's Clubs and the Young People's League are represented on the Commission.

The Commission's objectives are:

(1) To study and evaluate those areas in American life which might affect the welfare of the Jewish community; and to study and evaluate the contribution which the Jewish community can make to the strengthening of American democracy.

(2) To make articulate the particular approach of the Conservative Movement in Judaism on questions affecting community relations and social action.

(3) To make our congregations and congregants aware of our responsibility to make our approach to Judaism a force in American and Jewish life, both on the local and national levels.

The United Synagogue has been a full-fledged member of the National Community Relations Advisory Council since June 1953. However, with the organization of the Joint Commission and the hiring of a part-time Executive Secretary, our viewpoint as a religious organization has been more effectively represented on the national scene through the NCRAC.

"Justice, Justice Shalt Thou Pursue," a compilation of resolutions on social action passed by the constituent bodies of the Conservative Movement, has received a wide distribution already and many favorable comments.

The goal of the Commission is the creation of social action committees in each congregation. To aid and guide this process, the Joint Commission has under preparation a brochure on how to organize a local social action committee.

E.

1918 Report of Committee on Synagogue and Industrial Relations

TO THE CENTRAL CONFERENCE OF AMERICAN RABBIS,

Gentlemen: The next few decades will have as their chief concern the rectification of social and economic evils. The world will busy itself not only with the establishment of political, but also with the achievement of industrial democracy through social justice. The ideal of social justice has always been an integral part of Judaism. It is in accordance with tradition, therefore, that the Central Conference of American Rabbis submits the following declaration of principles as a program for the attainment of which the followers of our faith should strive:

(1) A more equitable distribution of the profits of industry.

(2) A minimum wage which will insure for all workers a fair standard of living.

(3) The legal enactment of an eight hour day as a maximum for all industrial workers.

(4) A compulsory one day of rest in seven for all workers.

(5) Regulation of industrial conditions to give all workers a safe and sanitary working environment, with particular reference to the special needs of women.

(6) Abolition of child labor and raising the standard of age wherever the legal age limit is lower than is consistent with moral and physical health.

(7) Adequate workmen's compensation for industrial accidents and occupational diseases.

(8) Legislative provision for universal workmen's health insurance and careful study of social insurance methods for meeting the contingencies of unemployment and old age.

(9) An adequate, permanent national system of public employment bureaus to make possible the proper distribution of the labor forces of America.

(10) Recognition of the right of labor to organize and to bargain collectively.

(11) The application of the principles of mediation, conciliation and arbitration to industrial disputes.

(12) Proper housing for working people, secured through government regulation when necessary.

(13) The preservation and integrity of the home by a system of mothers' pensions.

(14) Constructive care of dependents, defectives and criminals, with the aim of restoring them to normal life wherever possible.

Respectfully submitted,

HORACE J. WOLF, *Chairman*
MOSES J. S. ABELS
LOUIS BERNSTEIN
A. BLUM
SEYMOUR G. BOTTIGHEIMER
ABRAM BRILL
RUDOLPH I. COFFEE
HENRY COHEN
JACOB FEUERLICHT

ABRAM HIRSCHBERG
CHARLES B. LATZ
EMIL W. LEIPZIGER
HARRY S. LEWIS
SOLOMON C. LOWENSTEIN
HARRY H. MAYER
MAURICE M. MAZURE
ALFRED G. MOSES
SIMON PEISER

F.

1928 Report of Commission on Social Justice

Deriving our inspiration for social justice from the great teachings of the prophets of Israel and the other great traditions of our faith, and applying these teachings concretely to the economic and social problems of today, we, the Central Conference of American Rabbis, make this declaration of social principles:

I. The Duty of Social Mindedness

It is the tragic record of human-kind that many of those who find comfort in the existing order often fail to apply themselves seriously to the ills that plague society. It is part of the great social message of the prophets of our faith that salvation can be achieved only through the salvation of society as a whole. It is therefore incumbent upon all men to study the ills of the existing social order and to form intelligent opinions on the subject of social reconstruction. Instead of questioning God's goodness because of the evils in individual and communal life, we should address our God-given intelligence to the extermination of those circumstances which allow slums, vice, feeble-mindedness, poverty, degeneracy and the like to continue, with only palliative efforts for their improvement. We call this situation to the attention of all elements in industry, employers, employees and investors. Too often are investors content to accept profits from industries administered out of harmony with principles of social justice. The investor has the moral duty to know the ethics of the business from which he derives his dividends and to take a definite stand regarding its moral administration.

II. The Distribution and Responsibilities of Wealth

We regard those tendencies to be unjust which would make the fundamental goal of industry the exploitation of the material world on the basis of unbridled competition and the unlimited and unrestricted accretion of goods in the hands of a few while millions are in want. Inequalities of wealth can find no moral justification in a society where poverty and want, due to exploitation, exist. We sympathize with measures designed to prevent private monopoly. We regard all ownership as a social trust implying the responsibility of administration for the good of all mankind. We maintain that the unrestrained and unlimited exercise of the right of private ownership without regard for social results is morally untenable.

III. Industrial Democracy
In the production and distribution of the material goods of life, the dictatorship of any class, capital or labor, employer or employee, is alike autocracy. The solution of the ills which beset our social order are to be found not in any class conscious struggle but in the triumph of sound humanitarian principles which regard mankind as ONE. No materialistic philosophy, whether it be exploitation for the many or the few, can solve these problems. It is in a finer industrial democracy that we place our hopes. The worker who invests his life's energies and stakes the welfare of his family in the industry in which he works has inviolable rights along with him who stakes his family's welfare in that industry through the investment of capital.

IV. The Sacredness of the Individual Personality
The mechanization of our present age and the building of large industries employing hundreds and thousands of workers have led to the custom of regarding labor as a mass in which the personality of the individual is lost or is not considered. We who uphold a religious philosophy of life cannot sanction this practice which tends more and more to treat labor as only an instrument. The dignity of the individual soul before God cannot be lost sight of before men. Machinery and industry exist for man and not man for them.

V. The Right of Organization
The same rights of organization which rest with employers rest also with those whom he employs. Modern life has permitted wealth to consolidate itself through organization into corporations. Workers have the same inalienable right to organize according to their own plan for their common good and to bargain collectively with their employers through such honorable means as they may choose.

VI. The Fundamental Rights of Society
Contribution to the common good and not the selfish service of a class is the touchstone of all moral endeavor. A moral order in in-

dustry must achieve the betterment of society as a whole above all else. Those who labor, those who lead labor, as well as those who employ labor or invest capital in industry must alike recognize this principle in the exercise of any and all functions, rights and privileges.

VII. Arbitration of Industrial Disputes

In conformity with the principle of the welfare of society as fundamental, we regard our adherence to the principle of arbitration of industrial disputes rather than resort to open conflict. In any break in industrial relations, the moral responsibility for the evils that ensue rests with that group which refuses to enter into the orderly processes of arbitration and mediation.

VIII. The Moral Right to a Living Wage

In the moral stewardship of the earth, society must guarantee each of its members the chance to labor and to earn a living wage. Such a wage must be considered the first charge upon any industry. Those industries which do not pay their workers a living wage or which try to establish themselves economically by beating down the standards of living of their employees cannot be tolerated by any just social order. The definition of a living wage includes more than the immediate needs of the worker and his family on a generally accepted standard. It implies also sufficient to enable him to make full provision against sickness and old age.

IX. Unemployment

The right to work is a spiritual necessity. Unemployment not only breeds poverty; it is the source of moral disintegration from which every man and his family must be protected. The increase of labor saving machinery, the processes of efficiency in industry and the intensification of mass production are making the problem of unemployment of ever-increasing social importance. We advocate the adoption by business, state and nation of some form of unemployment insurance, as well as some system of nationally interlocking employment agencies and vocational guidance agencies which will intelligently direct labor and aid in averting crises of unemployment. We urge the adoption of such plans as provide for the formation of municipal, state and national sinking funds in times of employment and prosperity, which can be administered in times of depression for the speeding up of necessary public works. We feel, moreover, that there should be an effort at some more permanent stabilization of employment than exists today. We urge that employers, without unduly jeopardizing their rights, but if necessary, at some inconvenience and cost to themselves, adopt the system in times of depression of working all, or at least a greater number of their employees, part time rather than only some few of them at full time; thus avoiding shifting the entire burden of unemployment on any one particular group.

X. Social Insurance
We record our endorsement of pensions for old age which give the worker and his wife dignity in age and rid him of the fear of ultimate pauperism and the poorhouse after a life of labor; of sickness and disability insurance which will protect the worker from poverty in event of accident or illness, of mothers' pensions which will prevent the separation of children of poor widows from their natural guardian and protect the integrity of the home, of special protection of the worker from industrial dangers and diseases, and of the rehabilitation of industrial cripples under the direction of the state.

XI. Hours of Labor and Days of Rest
Particularly under the nervous strain of our present mechanical age are the tensions of fatigues of factory life extremely exhausting to the worker. With a complete physical and nervous exhaustion comes an inability to appreciate and enjoy those finer interpretations of life which religion holds to be the noblest achievement of the human soul. We therefore stand for the reduction of the hours of labor to the lowest possible point consistent with physical, mental and moral good, with a maximum of eight hours per day, and for the reduction of the working week to five instead of six days where, after a thorough and just examination, this is at all possible.

XII. Women in Industry
Women, in particular, must be protected from the nerve-wracking and debilitating effects of industrial excesses. Especially where women are employed must safe and sanitary conditions prevail. There must be for women in industry an absolute maximum of an eight-hour day. There must be no exploitation of women in industry by giving them less than equal pay with men for equal work.

XIII. Child Labor
It is our moral responsibility to children to see that they are well born, properly nourished and educated and given the fullest op-

portunity to develop their physical, mental and moral powers. Chief among the factors which interfere with these developments is child labor in its various forms. We therefore oppose child labor unqualifiedly and call upon society to enact proper legislation to bring it to an end. If such legislation is not possible from a Federal point of view, the individual states must handle the problem without equivocation or delay.

XIV. Prisons and Penal Laws

Society has the right to protect itself against those who constitute social menaces. This right, however, implies the solemn obligation to do everything possible to remove the causes which tend to make men criminals and to make punishment corrective in its spirit rather than retributional.

XV. Lynching

In the spirit of justice to all men, regardless of race, color or creed, we decry the mob violence of lynching and heartily condemn both the deed itself and the moral attitude which actuates or condones it.

XVI. Civil Liberties

Society's means of protecting the individual's claims to social justice are exemplified in government by constitutional rights. We urge the unqualified adherence to these rights, especially with regard to freedom of speech, press and peaceable assemblage. We maintain not only the just right but the just duty of a free pulpit. Among the encroachments on constitutional liberty, we view with dismay the uses to which the Federal injunction has, on many occasions, been put, particularly in inhibiting freedom in the expression of economic, political and social points of view. We condemn this use of the injunction as contrary to the spirit of our governmental freedom and of all social justice.

XVII. Social Justice in International Relations

We believe in the outlawry of war by the nations of the earth. We support all movements which conscientiously and honestly strive to that end. We denounce all types of economic imperialism which lead to greater armaments to protect national greed. We deplore and denounce the policy of State Department to support the claims of investors in foreign countries by force of arms and equally denounce the attitude of investors in foreign countries who refuse to abide by the laws of the country in which their investment is made.

We re-emphasize the stand of the conference that a popular referendum precede any declaration of war by Congress and that there
be no restrictions on freedom of speech or press during this referendum. We also re-emphasize our support of an international conference to prevent the manufacture of arms by private citizens. We
reaffirm our opposition to the militarization of our schools and colleges by compulsory military training. We advocate in all educational systems an increasing emphasis on the comity and partnership of nations and, rather than the extolment of military prowess,
the glorification of the heroes who have made for peace and
progress.

Respectfully submitted,
EDWARD L. ISRAEL, *Chairman*
HENRY J. BERKOWITZ,
RUDOLPH I. COFFEE,
ABRAHAM CRONBACH,
HARRY W. ETTELSON,
G. GEORGE FOX,
EPHRAIM FRISCH,
SAMUEL H. GOLDENSON,
FERDINAND M. ISSERMAN,
SAMUEL KOCH,
EMIL W. LEIPZIGER,
SAMUEL S. MAYERBERG,
LOUIS A. MISCHKIND,
VICTOR E. REICHERT,
LOUIS WOLSEY.

G.

Statements of NCRAC

1. Statement of principles on released
   time practices in the public schools
   adopted in 1947 by the National
   Community Relations Advisory
   Council and the Synagogue Council
   of America

The utilization in any manner of time, facilities, personnel, or funds of the public school system for purposes of religious instruction should not be permitted.

We therefore believe that Jewish communities are justified in objecting to released time or dismissal time programs.

Where such programs cannot be avoided the following statement is presented for community guidance:

a. Religious instruction of children is the responsibility of the synagogue, the church and the home; and not of the public schools.

b. Jewish communities are urged to maintain as a major community responsibility a program of religious education wholly independent of the public schools.

c. Inherent in dismissal time are many, though not all, of the faults of released time. Nevertheless when confronted with the necessity of a choice, we regard dismissal time as less objectionable.

d. Where a program of released time or dismissal time is in effect, or may be adopted, the Jewish community shall insist upon the following safeguards against possible abuses:

(1) No religious instruction shall be given on public school premises;

(2) The administrative machinery of the public school system shall not be employed to record or encourage attendance at religious instruction centers of students who avail themselves of either program;

(3) There shall be no proselytizing on school premises;

(4) All children participating in such programs shall be

dismissed together, and all grouping, separation, or identification by religion or by participation or non-participation
in such programs shall be avoided;

(5) Children shall not be assembled on public school premises for the purpose of being led to religious instruction
centers nor shall any representative of such religious instruction center meet the children on such premises to facilitate the operation of either program.

e. A Joint Advisory Committee on Religious Instruction and
the Public Schools shall be established by the Synagogue Council
of America and the NCRAC in order to make available to local
Jewish communities such guidance and direction as they may request and local Jewish communities are urged to consult with the
Joint Advisory Committee about such problems. Until the establishment of the Joint Advisory Committee, the Joint Conference
Committee of the Synagogue Council and the NCRAC is en-
powered to act temporarily as such advisory committee. The Joint
Advisory Committee shall continuously study this problem in the
light of research now or hereafter being conducted and from time
to time shall keep the communities advised of its findings. It is
realized that the methods of coping with this problem in a local
community must take into consideration the local situation.

2. **Statement of principles on sectarian practices in the public schools
adopted in 1948 by the National
Community Relations Advisory
Council and the Synagogue Council of America**

(1) The American democratic system is founded in large
part upon ethical and moral concepts derived from the great
religions of mankind. The preservation and fostering of these concepts are essential to the fullest realization of the American ideal;
and their growth and development as major forces in American
life should be the deep concern of every citizen.

(2) Religion has always been and continues to be the central core of Jewish life. The Jewish community of America is deeply concerned with secularistic tendencies in contemporary American life, which, if permitted to grow unchecked, may work great harm to the moral and spiritual basis of American democracy. We urge all religious groups to unite in an intensified national program, designed to enroll all the children of our country in religious educational institutions of their respective faiths. We urge the religious bodies to avail themselves of all media of mass communication for this program, such as the press, radio, motion pictures, speakers' platforms, and special dramatic projects.

(3) We reaffirm the position enunciated in the Joint Resolution of the Synagogue Council of America and the NCRAC on Religious Instruction and the Public School that the maintenance and furtherance of all religion are the responsibility of the synagogue, the church and the home, and not of the public school system, the time, facilities, funds or personnel of which should not be utilized for religious purposes.

(4) Therefore, and mindful of the dangers inherent in any violation of the traditional American principle of separation of church and state, we are opposed to religious practices or observances in the public elementary and high schools.

(5) We are opposed to the use of public school premises during school hours for religious education, meetings, or worship. Where public school premises are made available after school hours to civic groups outside the school system, they should be made available on the same basis to religious groups.

(6) We are opposed to governmental aid to schools under the supervision or control of any religious denomination or sect, whether Jewish, Protestant, or Catholic, including outright subsidies, transportation, text-books and other supplies. We are not opposed to the use of any school for the provision of lunches, medical and dental services to children.

(7) We are opposed to sectarian observances and festivals in the public schools. We recommend that further consideration and study be given to the presentation of the religious practices of various groups as part of the program of intercultural education.

(8) We look with concern upon proposals for the integration of religion into the public school program. The Joint Advisory Committee of the Synagogue Council of America and the NCRAC is directed to continue the study of all programs and proposals in this regard.

(9) All matters dealt with in this statement shall come within the purview of the Joint Advisory Committee. The Committee shall make available to local Jewish communities such guidance and

direction as they may request, and local Jewish communities are urged to consult with the Joint Advisory Committee about such problems. It is realized that the methods of coping with such problems in a local community must take into consideration the local situation.

(10) The Joint Advisory Committee shall include in its program a continuing examination into the problems of religion in publicly supported institutions of higher education.

3. Statement of principles on religious holiday observances in public schools adopted at twelfth plenary session of the NCRAC, June, 1954

In keeping with the principles underlying the relationship of religion and public education set forth in the joint resolutions of the Synagogue Council of America and for the National Community Relations Advisory Council regarding released time, and regarding other sectarian practices in the public schools, and reaffirming those principles and applying them to the specific question of religious holiday observances in the public school, we state:

(1) We are opposed to the observance of religious holidays in the public elementary and high schools because in our view such observance constitutes a violation of the traditional American principle of the separation of church and state.

(2) Joint religious observances such as Christmas-Chanukah and Easter-Passover, are in our opinion no less a breach of the principle of separation of church and state and violate the conscience of many religious persons, Jews and Christians alike.

(3) Where religious holiday observances are nevertheless held in public schools, Jewish children have a right to refrain from participation. We recommend that the local Jewish communities take such action as may be appropriate to safeguard this right of nonparticipation.

(4) We urge that local Jewish communities consult with the Joint Advisory Committee of the Synagogue Council of America

and the National Community Relations Advisory Council before taking formal or public action on all these matters.

(5) Before experimentation in intercultural education aimed at developing a better understanding among adherents of the various religions takes place, it should be ascertained by the Joint Advisory Committee of the Synagogue Council of America and the National Community Relations Advisory Council as to whether the proposed material is violative of the foregoing principles.

4. STATEMENT OF POSITION of the Synagogue Council of America and the National Community Relations Advisory Council on Three Approaches to the Issue of The Role of the Public Schools in Dealing with Religion

1. The Teaching of "Moral and Spiritual" Values
2. The "Factual" or "Objective" Teaching of Religion
3. The Teaching of a "Common Core" of Religion

(ADOPTED 1955)

This statement of position represents the concerted views of the rabbinic and congregational bodies comprising the Synagogue Council of America and the national Jewish organizations and Jewish community agencies comprising the National Community Relations Advisory Council. It is offered to all Jewish organizations and individuals for their guidance. All programs and proposals involving the subject matter of this statement should receive continuing attention and study by the Joint Advisory Committee of the Synagogue Council of America and the National Community Relations Advisory Council. Local Jewish communities are urged to consult with the Joint Advisory Committee regarding all such programs and proposals.

Affirmation of Principle

We have several times affirmed and now reiterate that:

We are deeply concerned with religious education and are making every effort to bring religious training to our children, in consonance with the principle that the maintenance and furtherance of religion are the responsibility of home, synagogue and church, and not of the public school.

The growth of democracy in the United States is in large measure a product of that unique principle in our basic law that puts religion outside the jurisdiction of the state. Any impairment of that principle threatens religious liberty and brings other basic freedoms into jeopardy.

The public schools must recognize the realities of religious differences in the community and among their pupils. They should continue as they have done throughout their history to teach pupils that acceptance of and respect for such differences are basic to American democracy and contribute toward harmonious living in a free society. This implies no need, however, on the part of the public schools to teach religious doctrines or to teach about religious doctrines.

Statement

We have therefore joined in declarations of policy, derived from these affirmations, in opposition to released time and to other sectarian practices in the public schools.

On the basis of these affirmations, we have considered current proposals for the teaching of "moral and spiritual values," for the "factual study of religion" and for the teaching of a "common core" of religious belief in the public schools, and we declare as follows:

1. *Regarding the teaching of "moral and spiritual values"*

Insofar as the teaching of "spiritual values" may be understood to signify religious teaching, this must remain as it has been the responsibility of the home, the synagogue and the church. Insofar as it is understood to signify the teaching of morality, ethics and good citizenship, a deep commitment to such values has been successfully inculcated by our public schools in successive generations of Americans. The public schools must continue to share responsibility for fostering a commitment to these moral values, without presenting or teaching any sectarian or theological sources or sanctions for such values.

2. *Regarding "objective" or "factual" teaching about religion*

The public schools must and should teach with full objectivity the role that religion has played in the life of mankind and in the

266   JUSTICE AND JUDAISM

development of society, when such teaching is intrinsic to the regular subject matter being studied. We are opposed to attempts by the public elementary and secondary schools to go beyond this, and teach about the *doctrines* of religion. Without passing upon the question of whether or not such teaching is inconsistent with the principle of separation of church and state, we believe that factual, objective and impartial teaching about the doctrines of religion is an unattainable objective. Any attempt to introduce such teaching into the public schools poses the grave threat of pressures upon school personnel from sectarian groups and compromises the impartiality of teaching and the integrity of the public educational system. Our opposition to such teaching rests on these grounds.

3. *Regarding the teaching of a "common core"*

We are opposed to any public school program that seeks to inculcate as doctrine any body of principles, beliefs or concepts that is represented as the "common core" of several or all religious faiths. The effort to extract from the religions current among us such a common denominator or "common core" can lead only to a watering down, a vitiation, of all that is spiritually meaningful in every religious faith. We submit, moreover, that attempts at religious inculcation in the public schools, even of articles of faith drawn from all religions and endorsed by representatives of all, violate the traditional American principle of separation of church and state.

H.

Patterns for Peace

An interfaith statement adopted in 1943 by Protestant, Catholic and Jewish leaders and issued through the National Council of Churches of Christ in U.S.A., National Catholic Welfare Conference and the Synagogue Council of America

(1) The moral law must govern world order. The organization of a just peace depends upon practical recognition of the fact that not only individuals but nations, states and international society are subject to the sovereignty of God and to the moral law which comes from God.

(2) The rights of the individual must be assured. The dignity of the human person as the image of God must be set forth in all its essential implications in an international declaration of rights, and be vindicated by the positive action of national governments and international organizations. States as well as individuals must repudiate racial, religious or other discrimination in violation of those rights.

(3) The rights of oppressed, weak or colonial peoples must be protected. The rights of all peoples, large and small, subject to the good of the organized world community, must be safeguarded within the framework of collective security. The progress of undeveloped, colonial or oppressed peoples toward political responsibility must be the object of international concern.

(4) The rights of minorities must be secured. National governments and international organizations must respect and guarantee the rights of ethnic, religious and cultural minorities to economic livelihood, to equal opportunity for educational and cultural development, and to political equality.

(5) International institutions to maintain peace with justice must be organized. An enduring peace requires the organization of international law; guarantee the faithful fulfillment of international

obligations, and revise them when necessary; assure collective security by drastic limitation and continuing control of armaments, compulsory arbitration and adjudication of controversies, and the use when necessary of adequate sanctions to enforce the law.

(6) International economic cooperation must be developed. International economic collaboration to assist all states to provide an adequate standard of living for their citizens must replace the present economic monopoly and exploitation of natural resources by privileged groups and states.

(7) A just social order within each state must be achieved. Since the harmony and well-being of the world community are intimately bound up with the internal equilibrium and social order of the individual states, steps must be taken to provide for the security of the family, the collaboration of all groups and classes in the interest of the common good, a standard of living adequate for self-development and family life, decent conditions of work, and participation by labor in decisions affecting its welfare.

Commission on Social Action
of Reform Judaism

AFFILIATES

UNION OF AMERICAN HEBREW CONGREGATIONS
CENTRAL CONFERENCE OF AMERICAN RABBIS
NATIONAL FEDERATION OF TEMPLE SISTERHOODS
NATIONAL FEDERATION OF TEMPLE BROTHERHOODS
NATIONAL FEDERATION OF TEMPLE YOUTH
   838 Fifth Avenue, N. Y. 21, N. Y.

I. CYRUS GORDON, Rockville Centre, N. Y., *Chairman*

RABBI EUGENE J. LIPMAN, *Director*

ALBERT VORSPAN, *Director*

MEMBERS

RABBI SIDNEY BALLON, West Hempstead, N. Y.

RABBI HERBERT I. BLOOM, Kingston, N. Y.

MARVIN BRAITERMAN, Baltimore

GEORGE BRUSSEL, JR., New York

RABBI MAURICE N. EISENDRATH, New York

MISS JANE EVANS, New York

IRVING JAY FAIN, Pawtucket, R. I.

RABBI LEON I. FEUER, Toledo, Ohio

RABBI ALFRED FRIEDMAN, Brooklyn

LEONARD FUCHS, Chicago

RABBI ROLAND B. GITTELSOHN, Boston

RABBI ROBERT E. GOLDBURG, New Haven, Conn.

DAVID GRUTMAN, Los Angeles

PHILIP B. HELLER, Roslyn Heights, N. Y.

IRVING KANE, Cleveland

KIVIE KAPLAN, Boston

RABBI EDWARD E. KLEIN, New York

RABBI DAVID LEFKOWITZ, JR., Shreveport, La.

MRS. LEO A. LEVI, Chicago

ROBERT LEVI, Newton, Mass.

JULIAN LYONS, Lincoln, Neb.

RABBI CHARLES MANTINBAND, Hattiesburg, Miss.

RABBI CARL I. MILLER, Gary, Ind.

MRS. HENRY MONSKY, Los Angeles

HON. ABRAHAM MULTER, New York

CHARLES NATHANSON, Detroit

JOSEPH L. RAUH, JR., Washington, D. C.

RABBI SIDNEY L. REGNER, New York

RABBI JACOB M. ROTHSCHILD, Atlanta

RABBI JACOB P. RUDIN, Great Neck, L.I., N. Y.

RABBI SELWYN D. RUSLANDER, Dayton, Ohio

MYER O. SIGAL, Macon, Ga.

RABBI WILLIAM B. SILVERMAN, Nashville

RABBI EDGAR E. SISKIN, Glencoe, Ill.

DR. ERNEST SOLOMON, Highland Park, Ill.

RABBI SAMUEL D. SOSKIN, Brooklyn

LOUIS STERNHEIMER, Richmond, Va.

SOLBERT WASSERSTROM, Kansas City

RABBI MELVIN WEINMAN, Waterbury, Conn.

RABBI JACOB WEINSTEIN, Chicago

STANLEY J. WINKELMAN, Detroit

ROGER WOLF, Cambridge, Mass.